AGREEMENT

BETWEEN

HOUSE OF MASTERS

AN̶

BOBBY

BEN 567006

NINNA

Where as the above named parties agrees as follows.

For the consideration of the sum, fifty thousand dollars ($50,000.00), paid by the House of Masters to Mr. Hull, Mr. Hull agrees to the following:

1) to be available to the House of Masters as a model for their commercials of which content has to be agreeable to both parties.

2) Mr. Hull must avail Himself, on reasonable notice, four times per year for commercial productions as a model.

3) Mr. Hull is to avail Himself, on reasonable notice, four times per year for special personal appearances, at the place of business of the House of Masters, or any such place they choose.

ANY
_____

d Hockey Association (hereafter the "League").

icipate in exhibitions, regularly scheduled and

with other players in the League.

erein the following salary:

led season, a salary of Twenty-Six sand Dollars ($7,000) on or before in consecutive semi monthly in-

PLAYERS
_____

te 22 avil 1952
EAU
_____
St CROIX
LE
BEC
ince or State Qué
ut Year 1931
Height 6 3"
CENTRE
t? LEFT.
an All-Star Team? YES
49-50-50-51-51-52
Q.S.H.L

(Girls)
P.R. LAVAL DAIRY

---

scc:
Mr. C.S. Campbell

attach to Richard Contra

CLUB DE HOCKEY CANADIEN INC.

2313 St. Catherine St. West · Tel. WEllington 2-6134 Montreal 25, P.Q.

Le 16 octobre 1968.

NATIONAL HOCKEY LEAGUE
REC'D SEEN
Nov 14 9 28 AM '68
ACTION

PERSONNELLE & CONFIDENTIELLE

Monsieur Henri Richard,
2,000, boulevard de la Concorde,
Duvernay,
Cité Laval, Québec.

Cher Henri,

La présente fait suite à notre conversation d'hier matin relativement à l'ajustement apporté à votre salaire, soit de $37,500.00 pour la saison 1968-69 au lieu de ce qui était stipulé sur votre contrat.

Aussi, tel que je vous ai mentionné, après avoir vérifié vos records, établis au cours des treize (13) dernières années, votre moyenne de points durant une saison régulière se chiffrerait à 57, et ce tout en incluant la saison dernière. Ainsi, si vous atteigniez 57 points au cours de la présente saison, nous vous remettrions un boni additionnel de $2,500.00.

De plus, l'an dernier, d'après les statistiques de la Ligue, au cours de la saison régulière, vous vous classiez en tant que joueur d'ordre 'plus quatre', ce qui est inférieur à votre potentiel habituel. Nous vous accorderons un boni additionnel de $1,000.00 si vous vous classez en tant que joueur d'ordre 'plus dix' ou mieux encore, au cours de la saison régulière cette année et, un second boni de $1,000.00 vous sera remis si vous at-

BLUE LINES,
GOAL LINES &
BOTTOM LINES

PLAYERS GAME RATING

NAME ....

TEAM ....

AMATEUR ☑   PRO ☐

vs. .... OPPONENT

POS. .... SCORE ....

DATE ....

HEIGHT .... AT ....

WEIGHT .... LEAGUE ....

CHECK "√" RATING

ORIGINAL FORWARD / Desire Toughness / Skating / Puck Ch. Playmaking / Shot Scoring / Checking

GOAL TENDER / Concentration / Angles / Stand Up / Relieves Recovery / Shot Blocking

Exceptional / Very Good / Good / Average / Fair / Poor

POTENTIAL

NOW — I
FUTURE —

☐ N.H.L.   ☐ MINOR   ☐ I.H.L.   ☐ NO PROSPECT

COMMENTS:

CANADIAN AMATEUR HOCKEY ASSOCIATION
Professional Try-out Application For
SEASON 1938-1939

The undersigned player hereby applies to the Canadian Amateur Hockey Association for p
with the Toronto Maple Leaf Hockey Club of the National
League under the conditions set out below.

The undersigned player may try-out and practice providing no contract has been signed a
outside of legitimate travelling and living expenses.

The player granted this privilege may not, under any circumstances, take part in a professio

Upon the issue of this sanction the player shall be debarred from participation in amateur
being again permitted to participate in amateur competition, such player must return to the Bra
set out unless he has already given notice of his intention to transfer to another Branch, in whi
tion shall be subject to the regular transfer rules.

If a player does not conform with these regulations in trying out with a professional team,
suspended.

Date of signing   Sept 19   1938   Ernie Dickens

Countersigned,   1488 Elgin Ave.

Registrar-Treasurer
CANADIAN AMATEUR HOCKEY ASSOCIATION

---

476 ....
Winnipeg
July

Dear Hap,

I am very sorry for not writing soon
my wife and I only recently returned to th
both wish to thank you for the kind inv
to stay at the Royal York, unfortunately we
were.

The marks arrived and surprisingly
I had only two failures. I intend to write
and carry the other. In this way I will
year and therefore wish to continue at s
have written to St. Michael's College requested
calendar and date of commencement.

I would prefer to play for M Marlboro
attend St. Mikes. This way I will endeavo
have more time for school which is of
importance to me. Hoping this is satisfacto

Sincerely,
Frank M.....

RULES FOR ELECTION TO
THE INTERNATIONAL HOCKEY HALL OF FAME

1. Elections to The International Hockey Hall of Fame shall be made
   by the Board of Governors in accordance with the powers conferred
   by Article VIII of the Constitution as follows:-
   "Board of Governors

   (a) The Board of Governors by its own methods rules and
   regulations shall select for enshrinement the members of The International Hockey Hall of Fame. Any resident or former resident
   of the Dominion of Canada or of the United States of America,
   who is or has been distinguished in hockey as a player or as a
   hockey executive, and including any member of the Board of
   Governors, shall be eligible as worthy to be honored by being
   selected as a member of The International Hockey Hall of Fame.
   When and if a member for The International Hockey Hall of Fame
   is selected the name of such person shall be certified to the
   President of the Executive Committee, who will thereupon enroll
   such name in The International Hockey Hall of Fame in the manner
   as provided for.

TIME OF ELECTION

2. Elections shall be held at least once in each calendar year and
   additional elections may be held with the approval of the majority
   of the Board. The time of holding the election shall be fixed
   by the Board.

ELIGIBILITY FOR ELECTION

3. Any resident or former resident of the Dominion of Canada or of
   the United States of America who is or has been distinguished in
   hockey as a player or as a hockey executive shall be eligible
   for election provided however that candidates shall have completed

HOCKEY CONTRACTS & HISTORICAL DOCUMENTS

BLUE LINES,

GOAL LINES &

BOTTOM LINES

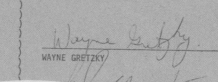

FROM THE COLLECTION OF ALLAN STITT

GREG OLIVER

ECW Press

Published by ECW Press
665 Gerrard Street East
Toronto, ON M4M 1Y2
416-694-3348 / info@ecwpress.com

Library and Archives Canada Cataloguing in Publication

Oliver, Greg, author
Blue lines, goal lines & bottom lines : hockey contracts and historical documents from the collection of Allan Stitt / Greg Oliver.

Issued in print and electronic formats.
ISBN 978-1-77041-251-4 (hardback)
ISBN 978-1-77090-775-1 (pdf)
ISBN 978-1-77090-776-8 (epub)

1. National Hockey League—History—Sources. 2. Hockey players—History—Sources. 3. Hockey teams—History—Sources. 4. Hockey—History—Sources. 5. Professional sports contracts—History—Sources. 6. Stitt, Allan J. I. Title.

GV846.5.O45 2016   796.962'6409   C2016-902362-1
C2016-902363-X

Editor for the press: Michael Holmes
Cover and text design: Tania Craan
Cover photo is of Dick Duff's Los Angeles Kings jersey, 1969–70, part of the Allan Stitt Collection. Photo taken by Tania Craan.
Author photo: Meredith Renwick (Greg Oliver); Radek Cecha (Allan Stitt)

Printed and bound in Canada
by Friesens   5   4   3   2   1

The publication of *Blue Lines, Goal Lines & Bottom Lines* has been generously supported by the Government of Canada through the Canada Book Fund. *Ce livre est financé en partie par le gouvernement du Canada.* We also acknowledge the contribution of the Government of Ontario through the Ontario Book Publishing Tax Credit and the Ontario Media Development Corporation.

Get the eBook free!

Purchase the print edition and receive the eBook free! For details, go to ecwpress.com/eBook

Here's to the players that take the time to write back to their fans, aided no doubt by secretaries, public relations representatives, agents, and family members. It doesn't take much to make someone's day.

Bobby Hull signs autographs on the fly.

CONTENTS

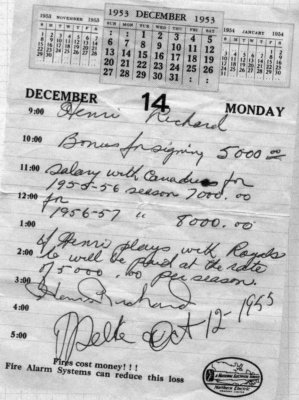

EXPANSION · 126

WORLD HOCKEY ASSOCIATION · 180

Pierre Pilote dons an old jersey and is reunited with the Norris Trophy in 2010, which he won three times as a player.

FOREWORD

Over the past few years, I've gotten to know Allan Stitt through the Hockey Hall of Fame, and I was intrigued when I got a copy of *Written in Blue & White: The Toronto Maple Leafs Contracts and Historical Documents from the Collection of Allan Stitt.*

My time with the Leafs was brief, just a season, but reading Allan's book brought back many memories. Every page seemed to reveal another gem. Getting to see the personal correspondence between Toronto management and George Armstrong's parents, for example, was fascinating. It was also surprising.

See, back when I was playing in the National Hockey League, we didn't know what other players made—not even our best friends. I always thought that knowing what the guy sitting next to you in the dressing room was worth could create dissent.

But there I was, flipping through *Written in Blue & White*, thinking "I wish I had known." Not that we would have gotten the millions of dollars hockey players get today—but maybe we would have gotten a little more.

During most of my career with the Chicago Black Hawks, the general manager was Tommy Ivan. We didn't have agents and we had to fight for every raise. At training camp, you'd come off the ice and read "Pilote, see Mr. Ivan at 1:30" on the chalkboard, and that would be when you'd get your contract. He had it all set up. "This is what you made last year," and then he made you an offer. You were lucky to get a few hundred dollars more; if you got a $500 raise, you felt like you had won the lottery. Through the years, I got better at presenting my case, though it rarely improved my bottom line. One season, I systematically mentioned a couple of my strong points to him every day. "I'll think about it," was his reply.

It's great that we all get a chance to see these vintage documents, and it's been great to get to know Allan. When we met, he knew more about me than I knew about him, so I had to find out, "What's this guy about?" That's the way I operate. Since then, I've met his family, and I've tried to help him add to his ever-growing collection of hockey memorabilia. We've been golfing, too, but let's just say that Allan should stick to the mediation game. He's far better at selecting teams for the Hockey Hall of Fame playoff pool; I think he's won the last three years.

My personal favourite in this collection of vintage documents is the back-and-forth between Minnesota North Stars GM Wren Blair and General Mills, offering to help Moose Vasko lose weight. Besides being my defensive partner in Chicago for years, Moose was one of my very best friends. And boy did he have weight issues. The Hawks management was always on his case, making him stand on a scale in front of the whole team. It still makes me laugh, thinking about our times together. I was a pretty easy-going guy, and that was the way I played hockey, while Moose was ultra-competitive and tense. We'd come off the ice, and he'd look at me, thin and in shape, barely sweating, while he'd be soaking wet under his uniform.

There are many similar tales in *Blue Lines, Goal Lines & Bottom Lines.* Enjoy!

By Pierre Pilote, Hockey Hall of Fame, Class of 1975

Allan Stitt in his "Team Canada Room" wearing Gary Bergman's
1972 Summit Series jersey.

INTRODUCTION

In Allan Stitt's current collection, you see a whole lot of that 11-year-old kid who waited behind Maple Leaf Gardens after games in the early 1970s, seeking autographs from his favourite hockey players.

While Allan's compilation of vintage hockey contracts, personal letters, memos, and other paperwork is interesting and historically important in its own right, it is in many ways a grown-up version of those fan autographs—just on more expensive and rarer pieces of paper.

And, as intriguing as Henri Richard's rookie contract might be, signed as it is by the Pocket Rocket and Canadiens' general manager Frank Selke on a page from a calendar, in the long run, it doesn't mean as much to Allan as a letter he got in 1972. One is a valuable artifact from the past and a part of hockey history, but the other is a part of his childhood.

It was his cousin who introduced Allan to the thrill of the chase, hanging out on Wood Street, the north side of Maple Leaf Gardens, waiting for the players from both teams to leave and head out to their cars or hotel.

"It was an era when the players were approachable. Most of them were happy to sign autographs after every game. My cousin, Adam Kronick, got me hooked on that," recalled Stitt. "Then he told me, 'By the way, for guys that you can't get, if you write them letters, some of them will send you back autographs. All you have to do is make sure you send them a piece of cardboard or a sheet of paper to sign, or something in a self-addressed stamped envelope so it's really easy for them to just sign it and send it back.'"

A binder full of 40-year-old autographs is a treasure for any fan, and Stitt regularly goes through his to bring back memories.

"One of the guys who I wrote to, of course, was Bobby Orr, because I thought Bobby Orr was the greatest player I had ever seen," said Stitt.

What Stitt got back in 1972 was a black-and-white picture with a stamped signature and, remarkably, a "Dear Allan" letter from his hero, signed personally by Bobby Orr.

"I realize today that Bobby didn't personalize letters to everybody," said Stitt. "But at the time, it felt like Bobby Orr took the time to answer my letter and send a personal message to me. I got a letter from Bobby Orr!"

Of all the letters that he got back, Orr was the only one to personalize it by signing, "Dear Allan." (He did also get letters back from Lanny McDonald and Darryl Sittler.)

Bobby Orr signs autographs during the 1972 Summit Series, where he practised and accompanied the team for the eight-game series against Russia, but did not play.

Those 1972 Bruins, coming off a second Stanley Cup victory in three years, were at their apex of popularity, said centreman Fred Stanfield.

"The whole team got a lot of fan mail then, but Bobby, he'd get bags full of fan mail," he said, adding that he answered his own fan mail at the time, just as he still does today with the occasional autograph hound that has tracked him down. "I did it all myself, but Bobby, he had to hire somebody because it just became too much. He would sign every one personally."

Today, the Allan Stitt Collection continues to grow, and it's with great pleasure that we share with you some of the treasures that exist. *Blue Lines, Goal Lines & Bottom Lines: Hockey Contracts and Historical Documents from the Collection of Allan Stitt* is meant to complement the earlier release, *Written in Blue & White: The Toronto Maple Leafs Contracts and Historical Documents from the Collection of Allan Stitt*. While the first book focused on some of Allan Stitt's Toronto Maple Leaf documents, this book focuses on documents that he's collected that relate to teams other than the Leafs.

It is our hope that you, as well as the 11-year-old fan buried deep within you, enjoys this fascinating trip down memory lane.

BOSTON Ⓑ BRUINS

BOBBY ORR

November 8, 1972

Dear Allan:

Received your letter and just wanted to thank you for taking time to write to me. It was great to hear from you.

I am looking forward to another great season with the Boston Bruins. Naturally, my team mates and I were very happy to win the Stanley Cup and we hope to bring it to Boston again in 1973.

Best wishes to you and keep cheering for me and the Boston Bruins.

Sincerely,

BOBBY ORR

Edmonton Journal-Ken Orr/The Canadian Press

Wayne Gretzky signs a 21-year contract with the WHA's Edmonton Oilers on his 18th birthday, January 26, 1979. Oilers general manager Larry Gordon holds the contract in place, and his father, Walter Gretzky, looks on.

THE GREAT ONES

Every collection has a centrepiece, the one treasure that is prized above all others. For Allan Stitt, it's the Wayne Gretzky contract, which Gretzky signed on his 18th birthday at centre ice at the Northlands Coliseum in Edmonton. Allan recalled how he obtained the document: "It came up for sale at an auction, and I was dying to get it, but it was just too expensive. I couldn't afford it, so I didn't get it. Then about five years later, it came up again at another auction, and I said, 'No way am I letting this one go this time.' But I was afraid to spend so much money."

Surprisingly, it was famed Rush vocalist and bassist Geddy Lee who pushed him into committing. The two are friends through the Toronto tennis courts, and Lee is an avid collector himself, with historic baseball as his passion. "I went over to Geddy's house to talk about it. He said, 'There are a few things to keep in mind. First, it's Wayne Gretzky. And it's his most important contract. When you get the best of the best of something, it's rarely a bad decision. Second, this isn't an expense, it's an investment. It will always be worth something and, more than likely, it will go up in value because it is the best of the best. You won't regret it if you get it, but you will if you don't try.'

"He talked me into it and I took a big gulp, put in my bid, and got it. And of course, he was right. I definitely haven't regretted buying it. And I would for sure have been kicking myself if I didn't get it."

Actually, this was Stitt's *second* Gretzky contract. The first one, obtained years before when Stitt was first bitten by the collecting bug, was Gretzky's deal with the Sault Ste. Marie Greyhounds of the Ontario Major Junior Hockey League. "I was already a Gretzky fan when he was a junior, and I loved the idea of having his OHA [now OHL] contract," said Stitt. And the Gretzky documents didn't even stop there. Stitt recently purchased Gretzky's Player Certificate from when he was 12 years old and played in the PeeWee Tournament in Quebec, as well as his Indianapolis high school admission form from his days as a member of the WHA's Indianapolis Racers.

Wayne Gretzky in September 1979.

Gretzky Knew His Junior Days Would Be Short

In January 1978, there was a Junior World Cup of Hockey in Montreal. It was there that a young centre, playing for Team Canada, predicted that his days as a junior in the northern Ontario outpost of Sault Ste. Marie were almost finished. "At the moment, I would consider it very unlikely that I will play four more years of junior hockey before turning pro," said a 16-year-old Wayne Gretzky. "The NHL rules now say I can't be drafted before [1981], but if and when I'm ready for the pros, I want to be sure I can go." In the same story, he mused about heading to Sweden to play. The next day, he called the tale "part fact, part fiction" and stressed that he was musing about taking power skating lessons in Sweden, not suiting up. Regardless of whether he was misquoted, Gretzky was on the money as far as anticipating the future. With 70 goals and 111 assists in the 1978–79 season, Gretzky finished second in Ontario Major Junior Hockey League scoring, behind Bobby Smith of Ottawa, who had 192 points and was three years older. The young phenomenon also was named Rookie of the Year and took the William Hanley Trophy as the most gentlemanly player. The World Hockey Association, on its last legs in its battle with the National Hockey League, offered Gretzky a pro option. But he had turned down suitors from the WHA twice

Wayne Gretzky suited up with the OMJHL's Sault Ste. Marie Greyhounds for a single season.

IMPORTANT NOTICE TO PLAYER

(1)   Before signing the contract you should
  (A)   consult a barrister, solicitor or lawyer of your choice as to the advisability of signing this contract and to obtain his explanation and opinion as to the obligations imposed upon you and the benefits to which you are entitled hereunder and
  (B)   to be sure that all terms and conditions agreed upon have been incorporated herein.

(2)   The only contract recognized by the Commissioner of the League is the Standard Player's Contract which has been duly executed by you and the Club and filed in the League's Office and approved by him. Therefore, this contract should contain the entire agreement between you and the Club and there should be no oral or written inducements or agreements except as provided therein.

(3)   The Standard Player's Contract shall be executed in triplicate by the Club and the Player and all signed copies shall be delivered in person or by mail to the League Office for approval and registration by the Commissioner, after which the League Office shall forward one copy to the Club, one copy to the Player and one copy shall be retained by the League Office.

(4)   This contract, if not inconsistent with the Constitution and By-Laws shall be valid and binding upon the League Club and the Player immediately upon its execution. The Club agrees to file this contract with the League Commissioner within ten (10) days after its execution.

If, pursuant to the Constitution or By-Laws, the Commissioner disapproves this contract within ten (10) days after its filing in his office, this contract shall thereupon terminate and be of no further force or effect and the Club and the Player shall thereupon be relieved of their respective rights and liabilities hereunder.

Canadian Major Junior Hockey League

Standard Player's Contract

CMJHL   **CMJHL**

THIS AGREEMENT
BETWEEN: Soo Greyhounds Hockey Club
   hereinafter called the "Club" a member of the   Ontario Major Jr.   Hockey League hereinafter called the "League"

— AND —   Wayne   Gretzky
   Brantford   ....   in the Province of .... Ontario ....
hereinafter called the "Player" of ....

WITNESSETH:
   That in consideration of the respective obligations herein and hereby assumed, the parties to this contract severally agree as follows:—

TERM

Section 1
   The Club agrees, subject to the terms and conditions hereof, to employ the Player as an Hockey Player for a term of 4 years commencing on September 1, 19 77 , and expiring on August 31, 19 81 .

COMPENSATION

Section 2
2.1   The Club agrees to pay to the Player for rendering the services and granting the rights described herein to the Club the following salary —

Season	Salary	Accommodation	Bonus
1977-78	$25.00	$40.00	
1978-79	$25.00	$40.00	
1979-80	$30.00	$40.00	
1980-81	$30.00	$40.00	

2.2   Payment of such salary shall be in consecutive **weekly** instalments following the commencement of the regular League Championship Schedule of Games or following the date of reporting, whichever is later; provided however, that if the Player is not in the employ of the Club for the whole period of the Club's games in the Ontario Major Jr. Hockey League Championship Schedule, then he shall receive only part of the salary in the ratio of the number of days of actual employment to the number of days of the League Championship Schedule of Games.

2.3   In addition to the foregoing payment the Club shall pay:
  (a)   travelling expenses and meals reasonably incurred by the Player in his travel from his home to the Club's Training Camp. At the conclusion of the season, the Club shall provide transportation direct to the Player's home.
  (b)   reasonable travelling, lodging and meal expenses for the Player while "on the road" for the Club in other than the Club's home city.
  (c)   tuition fees (or school taxes in the case of a Player who is attending a Public or Separate School in a municipality other than the municipality in which his parents reside) and for the cost of books for a Player in a recognized educational institution on receiving an authentic statement of account from such educational institution, municipality or Player.

2.4   If the Club qualifies for play in the League Play-Offs and Memorial Cup Series at the conclusion of the Championship Schedule of Games, the Club agrees to pay to the Player for rendering his services as a hockey player during such Play-Offs and Memorial Cup Series a salary of $ .... per week for each week or any part thereof for so long as the Club continues playing in such Play-Offs and Series.

EMPLOYMENT AND DUTIES

Section 3
3.1   The Player agrees to give his services and to play hockey in all League Championship, All-Star, Exhibition, Play-Off and Memorial Cup Games to the best of his ability under the direction and control of the Club for the period for which this Agreement is expressed to continue in force including any period for which the Agreement remains in force as a result of the Club's exercise of the option or options conferred on it by Section 16 and in accordance with the provisions hereof.

3.2   The Player further agrees,
  (a)   to report to the Club Training Camp at the time and place fixed by the Club, in good physical condition.
  (b)   to keep himself in good physical condition at all times during the season.
  (c)   to give his best services and loyalty to the Club and to play hockey only for the Club unless his contract is released, assigned, exchanged or loaned by the Club.
  (d)   to cooperate with the Club and participate in any and all promotional activities of the Club and the League which will, in the opinion of the Club, promote the welfare of the Club or hockey generally.
  (e)   to conduct himself on and off the rink according to the highest standard of honesty, morality, fair play and sportsmanship, and to refrain from conduct detrimental to the best interests of the Club, the League or hockey generally.

RIGHT OF RENEWAL (OPTION)

.... day of August, 19 .... , the Club may, upon notice in writing to the Player by prepaid registered
.... , renew this contract for a further term
.... (Player's address)
...., on the same terms and conditions as contained in this contract except that after such renewal
.... further right (option) to renew the contract.

LEAGUE CONSTITUTION, BY-LAW

.... severally and mutually promise and agree to be legally bound by the Constitution, By-law and
.... all the terms and provisions thereof, a copy of which shall be open and available for inspection
.... and the Player, at the main office of the League and at the main office of the Club.
.... further agree that in case of dispute between them, the dispute shall be referred within one year
.... missioner of the League as an arbitrator and his decision shall be accepted as final by both parties.
.... further agree that all fines imposed upon the Player under the Playing Rules, and
.... or Regulations shall be deducted from the salary of the Player and be remitted by the Club to

ACKNOWLEDGMENT OF CONSIDERATION

.... acknowledge that:
.... yer to play hockey only with the Club or such other Club as provided in Sections 3 and 11;
.... nted by the Player to the Club as provided in Section 16;
.... the Player to the Club to take pictures of him and to televise him as provided in Section 10;
.... tion in determining the monies payable to the Player under Section 2.

APPROVAL BY LEAGUE COMMISSIONER

.... ent with the Constitution and By-laws shall be valid and binding upon the Club and the Player
.... he Club agrees to file this contract with the League Commissioner within ten (10) days after its

.... on or By-laws, the Commissioner disapproves this contract within ten (10) days after its filing
.... ereupon terminate and be of no further force or effect and the Club and the Player shall
.... ctive rights and liabilities hereunder.

NO REPRESENTATIONS ETC.

.... greed that the only contracts recognized by the Commissioner of the League are the Standard
.... duly executed and filed in the League's office and approved by him, and that this Agreement
.... n the Parties and there are no oral or written inducements, promises or agreements except as

.... YER ACKNOWLEDGMENT OF LEGAL ADVICE

.... the Club requested that he consult a barrister and/or solicitor as to the advisability of his
....

.... ELLANEOUS AND PROCEDURAL PROVISIONS

.... to be given under this agreement shall be sufficient if in writing, sent by prepaid registered
.... Player's residence or to the Club's Office.

.... ed and construed according to the laws of the Province of ....
.... tion of this agreement should be held or become invalid, then all remaining parts, paragraphs
.... lly effective.

.... ERTIFICATE OF INDEPENDENT ADVICE
.... SARLO
(Name of Solicitor) .... a member of the Bar of the
.... tario .... hereby acknowledges that

WAYNE GRETZKY .... as to
(name of player)
.... Standard Player's Contract.

.... behalf of the Club or the League and am consulted by the player and have advised him
.... age, its officers and employees. I have placed his position and the consequences of his
.... tract fully and plainly before him and he declared that he fully understood the nature and
.... contract and acknowledged that he is executing it freely and voluntarily and as his own
.... threat, influence or compulsion of, from or by the Club, the League, its officers and

.... rio   **Ontario**
   in the Province (State) of

this   December 14th   , 197 7   CAPUTO, SARLO, AIELLO, VAILLANCOURT &
   (Municipality)   WHALEN
(Signature of Solicitor)   116 Spring Street   (Firm Name)
(Address)   ....   (Municipality)   Sault Ste. Marie
Ontario   9524901
(Province)   (Telephone No.)

EXECUTION BY PARTIES

IN WITNESS WHEREOF, the Parties hereto have signed and set their seals hereunto this ...... day of ......
A.D. 19 ....

SIGNED, SEALED AND DELIVERED
IN THE PRESENCE OF

.... By: ....   Name of Club
.... President   (Seal)
.... Address of Club
Witness   ....   Player   (Seal)
.... 42 Vardi Home Address Brantford, Ont.
.... N3R 3N3
Witness   26   01   Birth Date of Player
.... Social Insurance Number

EXECUTION BY COMMISSIONER

I hereby certify that I have, on this date, received, examined and noted on record the within contract, and that it is in regular form.
DATED at   Walkerton   , this   6th   day of   January   , 19 78 .
....
   Commissioner   , of the
   Ontario Major Junior Hockey League

Wayne Gretzky of the Greyhounds winds
up for a shot against the Ottawa 67's.

before accepting his famed deal with Nelson Skalbania,
owner of the Indianapolis Racers, in June 1978. The earlier
offers? When he was 15, Jack Kelley of the New England
Whalers promised him $50,000 for three years, followed by
$150,000 a year for four years, along with a $25,000 signing
bonus. Next up was John F. Bassett, the Toronto media mag-
nate who was moving the Toronto Toros to Birmingham,
Alabama; he offered a two-year deal at $80,000 a season. "I
would have signed right then and there," Gretzky said in
Al Strachan's *99: Gretzky: His Game, His Story*, "but my old
man said, 'You're going back to school.'" Interestingly, one
of Stitt's good friends growing up was John C. Bassett, son
of John F. Bassett.

INDIANAPOLIS PUBLIC SCHOOLS
PUPIL'S CUMULATIVE RECORD
BROAD RIPPLE HIGH SCHOOL *Evening Division*

Date of Birth 1-26-1961

School Last Attended Canada

Name Wayne Gretzky M

Address 12512 Windsor Dr.
Carmel, Ind. 46032

Subject		Cr	Mark	Date	Date Failed
ENGLISH	I	1	C	1/76	
	II	1	C	6/76	
	III	1	D	1/77	
	IV	1	D	6/77	
	V	1	D	1/78	
	VI	1	D	6/78	
	VII	1			
	VIII	1			
	IX	1			
	X	1			
SPEECH		1			
DRAMATICS	I	1			
	II	1			
LIB. EXP.	I	½			
	II	½			
DEVELOP. READ.		1			
MATH.	I	1	C	1/76	
PRE ALG	II	1	C	6/76	
ALGEBRA	I	1	C	1/77	
	II	1	C	6/77	
GEOMETRY	I	1			
	II	1			
ALGEBRA	III	1			
	IV	1			
COL. ALG.		1			
SOL. GEOM.		1			
TRIG.		1			
MATH. X		1			
A.G. CALCULUS	I	1			
	II	1			

Subject		Cr	Mark	Date	Date Failed
LANGUAGE					
FRENCH	I	1	B	1/76	
	II	1	B	6/76	
	III	1			
	IV	1			
	V	1			
	VI	1			
	VII	1			
	VIII	1			
	I	1			
	II	1			
	III	1			
	IV	1			
DERIVATIVES		1			
CANADA HIST I		1	C	1/76	
" " II		1	C	6/76	
SOCIOLOGY		1			
WORLD HIST.	I	1	C	1/77	
	II	1	C	6/77	
U.S. HIST.	I	1			W 1/78
	II	1			
U.S. GOVT.		1			
ECONOMICS		1			
METRO. PROB.		1			W 1/78
INTL. REL.		1			
PSYCHOLOGY		1			
WORLD GEO.	I	1	C	1/77	
	I	1	C	6/77	
ASTRONOMY	I	1			
	I	1			

Subject		Cr	Mark	Date	Date Failed
BIOLOGY	I	1	C	1/77	
	II	1	C	6/77	
PHYSICS	I	1			
	II	1			
PHYS. SCI.	I	1	C	1/76	
	II	1	C	6/76	
CHEMISTRY	I	1			
	II	1			
		1			
DATA PROC.		1			
BUS. ARITH.	I	1			
	II	1			
GEN. BUS.	I	1			
	II	1			
BOOKKEEP'G	I	1	C	1/77	
	II	1	C	6/77	
BUS. LAW		1			
SHORTHAND	I	1			
	II	1			
	III	1			
	IV	1			
WK. EXP.		2			
TYPING	I	1			
	II	1			
	III	1			
	IV	1			
SALESM'SHIP	I	1			
MDSE.	I	1	C	1/78	
OFF. PRACT.		1	C	6/78	
CRAFT ART	I	½			
	II	½			

Subject		Cr	Mark	Date	Date Failed
ART	I	1			
	II	1			
	III	1			
	IV	1			
	V	1			
	VI	1			
CERAMICS	I	1			
	II	1			
	III	1			
	IV	1			
ELECTRONICS	I	1			
	II	1			
	III	1			
	IV	1			
WOOD WORK	I	1			
	II	1			
	III	1			
	IV	1			
GEN. METALS	I	1			
	II	1			
	III	1			
	IV	1			
MECH. DR.	I	1			
	II	1			
	III	1			
	IV	1			
ARCH. DR.	I	1			
	II	1			
	III	1			
	IV	1			

signature attached

Subject		Cr	Mark	Date	Date Failed
POWER MECH.	I	1			
	II	1			
	III	1			
	IV	1			
FOODS	I	1			
	II	1			
	III	1			
	IV	1			
CLOTHING	I	1			
	II	1			
	III	1			
	IV	1			
FAM. LIVING		1			
HLTH. & SFTY.		1	B	1/77	
DR. EDUC.		½			
ALC. EDUC.		1			
CHORUS	I	½			
	II	½			
	III	½			
	IV	½			
	V	½			
	VI	½			
	VII	½			
	VIII	½			
MUSIC THER.	I	1			
	II	1			
MUSIC APP.	I	½			
	II	½			
ORCH.	I	½			
	II	½			
	III	½			
	IV	½			

Subject		Cr	Mark	Date	Date Failed
BAND	I	½			
	II	½			
	III	½			
	IV	½			
	V	½			
	VI	½			
	VII	½			
	VIII	½			
PHYS. ED	I	1	B	1/76	
	II	1	B	6/76	
	III	1	B	6/77	
	IV	½			
	V	½			
	VI	½			
	VII	½			
	VIII	½			
R.O.T.C.	I	½			
	II	½			
	III	½			
	IV	½			
	V	½			
	VI	½			
	VII	½			
	VIII	½			

Name Wayne Gretzky

Date of Entry 9-11-1978 WD RE Date Graduated

Diploma Earned: ☐ Academic; ☐ Fine & Prac. Arts; ☐ Vocational; ☐ Gene

Senior Average Rank in Class No. in Class

Major 1. ENGLISH Minor 1.

2. 2.

Transcripts Sent to
30 credits from West [illegible] Coll, Inst, Canad

Mark: A. Honor Standing B. High C. Average D. Low F. Failure

Code: S. Satisfactory I. Incomplete W. Withdrawal WF. Withdrawal & Fail

Date of Certification

Principal

Wayne Gretzky of the Edmonton Oilers with the Art Ross and Hart Memorial trophies at the 1981 NHL Awards Show.

Great Deal for The Great One

At the time it was inked on January 26, 1979, Wayne Gretzky's birthday deal was the longest contract ever signed by a professional athlete in North America, beating out right fielder Hank Aaron's 20-year deal with the Atlanta Braves by a season. Actually, to clarify, it was a contract extension, taking Gretzky's seven-year personal services deal that he'd agreed to on June 12, 1978, with the WHA's Indianapolis Racers, and adding a ton of option clauses that would prolong the deal to a total of 21 years. "Wayne Gretzky is the greatest young player in the world right now," said Oilers owner Peter Pocklington at the time. "One day he'll likely be the oldest. Edmonton fans deserve the best, and in Wayne Gretzky I feel that's what they're getting." Part of Pocklington's intention with the big deal was to deter any NHL clubs from trying to snap him up should the proposed WHA-NHL merger go through in the upcoming season. Witnessing the deal at centre ice were Gretzky's parents, his three younger brothers, and his agent, Gus Badali, though it was Oilers vice-president and general manager Larry Gordon in most of the photos that moved along the media wires. "Scouts obviously felt he could be a tremendous player. I don't know if anyone in their right mind at that time thought he could be the dominating force he has been to the game of hockey. In the long run, especially [when] Wayne ended up in Los Angeles, it was good for the game of hockey," said Gordon later. Of course, hockey fans know it didn't turn into a 21-year deal. Gretzky signed a new five-year deal in 1987 with the Oilers, and then again when he was dealt to Los Angeles in the summer of 1988 and Kings owner Bruce McNall ripped up the old contract and signed The Great One to an even more lucrative deal. The Hockey Hall of Fame inducted The Great One as an Honoured Member in 1999, immediately after he retired.

THIS MEMORANDUM OF AGREEMENT, made the 26th day of January, A.D. 1979

BETWEEN:

WAYNE GRETZKY, of the City of Brantford, in the Province of Ontario

(OF THE FIRST PART, hereinafter referred to as "Gretzky")

- and -

PETER POCKLINGTON, of the City of Edmonton, in the Province of Alberta

(OF THE SECOND PART, hereinafter referred to as "Pocklington")

WHEREAS Gretzky is a hockey player of unique skill and ability;

AND WHEREAS Pocklington desires to retain the exclusive service of Gretzky as a professional hockey player:

IN CONSIDERATION OF the mutual convenants and conditions herein contained, the parties agree as follows:

1.   Pocklington agrees to retain the services of Gretzky as a professional hockey player, and Gretzky agrees to exclusively provide Pocklington with his services as a professional hockey player during the term of this agreement, ending June 30, 1987.

2.   Pocklington agrees to pay Gretzky, in consideration for rendering his services as a professional hockey player the following sums:
(i) Salary -

(a) A salary in the amount of One Hundred Thousand Dollars ($100,000.00) shall be paid for the 1978-79 hockey season. Gretzky acknowledges that Pocklington's obligation for the 1978-79 hockey season is reduced by the sum of Fifteen Thousand Four Hundred Ninety-Two Dollars Fifty Cents ($15,492.50) for salary payments received under agreement made with Nelson M. Skalbania, dated the 10th day of June, 1978;

ADDENDUM

THE PARTIES DO HEREBY ADOPT THIS ADDENDUM AND INCORPORATE SAME AS PART OF THE
ATTACHED WORLD HOCKEY ASSOCIATION STANDARD PLAYER'S CONTRACT.

WHEREAS Wayne Gretzky is party to an agreement with Peter Pocklington,
dated January 26, 1979;

AND WHEREAS Peter Pocklington has, under the terms of the said
agreement of January 26, 1979 directed Wayne Gretzky to render services to
Edmonton World Hockey Enterprises Ltd. in accordance with the terms of the
World Hockey Association Player's Contract attached;

NOW THEREFORE, the CLUB and the PLAYER agree to the following:

A. COMPENSATION

The CLUB and the PLAYER hereby agree that subparagraph 1.1 and 1.2 of paragraph
1, entitled "Compensation", are hereby deleted and shall be replaced by the
following:

1.1 This Agreement shall be for nine (9) consecutive hockey seasons, beginning
with the 1978-79 season, and the CLUB hereby agrees to pay the PLAYER for
rendering services described herein:

   a) A Salary in the amount of One Hundred Thousand Dollars ($100,000.00)
   shall be paid for the 1978-79 season. The PLAYER acknowledges that
   the CLUB's obligation for this season only is reduced by Fifteen
   Thousand Four Hundred Ninety-Two and 50/100 Dollars ($15,492.50) for
   salary payments received from the PLAYER's former team.

   b) A Salary in the amount of One Hundred and Fifty Thousand Dollars
   ($150,000.00) shall be paid for the 1979-80 season.

   c) A Salary in the amount of One Hundred and Fifty Thousand Dollars
   ($150,000.00) shall be paid for the 1980-81 season.

   d) A Salary in the amount of One Hundred and Seventy-Five Thousand Dollars
   ($175,000.00) shall be paid for the 1981-82 season.

   e) A Salary in the amount of Two Hundred and Eighty Thousand Dollars
   ($280,000.00) shall be paid for the 1982-83 season.

   f) A Salary in the amount of Two Hundred and Eighty Thousand Dollars
   ($280,000.00) shall be paid for the 1983-84 season.

   g) A Salary in the amount of Two Hundred and Eighty Thousand Dollars
   ($280,000.00) shall be paid for the 1984-85 season.

   h) A Salary in the amount of Two Hundred and Eighty Thousand Dollars
   ($280,000.00) shall be paid for the 1985-86 season.

   i) A Salary in the amount of Two Hundred and Eighty Thousand Dollars
   ($280,000.00) shall be paid for the 1986-87 season.

1.2 Both the CLUB and the PLAYER agree that the Salary listed for each hockey
season shall be payable in sixteen (16) equal semi-monthly installments,
the first installment to be paid on October 15th of each hockey season.

1.3 In addition to the salaries listed in 1.1 above, the CLUB agrees to pay
the PLAYER a pre-performance bonus or lump sum of Three Hundred and Fifty
Thousand Dollars ($350,000.00) as follows:

   a) Two Hundred Fifty Thousand Dollars ($250,000.00) on or before January
   26, 1979. The PLAYER acknowledges that the CLUB's obligation on
   January 26, 1979 is reduced by One Hundred Twenty Thousand Dollars
   ($120,000.00) for the following reasons:

      i) A credit of One Hundred Thousand Dollars ($100,000.00) is acknow-
      ledged for pre-performance bonuses received by the PLAYER from the
      PLAYER's former team.

the PLAYER releases the CLUB from any and every additional obligation, liability, claim or demand.

F. TRANSFERABILITY OF CONTRACT

9.4 The CLUB agrees that, pursuant to subparagraph 9.0 of the Standard Players
Contract, any sale, assignment, exchange, transfer or other conveyance of
This Contract, shall be restricted to professional hockey within the World
Hockey Association or the National Hockey League.

20,000.00) is acknowledged
of the CLUB making payment
ments owing to Algoma
nds) and for obtaining for
other obligations of the
Hockey Promotions Limited,

shall be paid to the PLAYER

w this Contract on terms
first option shall be for
the 1987-88 season. The
exercised, shall be for
the 1993-94 season.

Thousand Dollars
ould the CLUB inform
(6) year option, and
Contract.

Thousand Dollars
ould the CLUB inform
(6) year option,
the Contract.

B that, if an option to
mutually agreeable
arising over contractual
fore a neutral arbitrator
ion Act.

w automobile equivalent
e PLAYER may, at his
ning with the 1982-83
automobile insurance

be in full force and
ockey league the CLUB

played for the
t of the CLUB's
of this Contract
so unfit, but in
shall pay the PLAYER
compensation benefits

accordance with subparagraph 10.2
's default has been served upon the
reasonable time, to cure such default.

the provisions of this Contract and
ws of the League, the provisions of

THEIR SIGNATURES BELOW, DESIRE TO MAKE IT PART OF THE ATTACHED WHA STANDARD
PLAYER'S CONTRACT EFFECTIVE THIS 26th DAY OF JANUARY, 1979.

EDMONTON WORLD HOCKEY ENTERPRISES LTD.

_____   BY: _____
WITNESS OF SIGNATURE   LARRY GORDON - GENERAL MANAGER

_____   BY: _____
WITNESS OF SIGNATURE   WAYNE GRETZKY - PLAYER

World Hockey Association
PLAYER'S CONTRACT
MARCH, 1974

This is a contract between

a World Hockey Association Club, and _____ a Player

in the World Hockey Association.

I hereby certify that I have received
and examined this Contract, and
approved it _____ to form
as of this date.

_____ World Hockey Association
Executive Director

Dated _____ 19___

CLUB'S COPY

World Hockey Association

Player's Contract

By this contract,

EDMONTON WORLD HOCKEY ENTERPRISES LTD.
(hereafter "Club") employs

WAYNE GRETZKY

(hereafter "Player"), to perform in or on behalf of the Club's participation in the World Hockey Association (hereafter the "League").

This Contract is based on the following facts: SEE ADDENDUM

1. The Club is a member and holds a franchise in the League and will participate in exhibitions, regularly scheduled and championship games sponsored by the League.

2. Player has the skill, or potential skill, and training to enable him to compete with other players in the League.

Agreement

1. Compensation.
   1.1 The Club agrees to pay the Player for rendering the services described herein the following salary:

SEE ADDENDUM

THE PARTIES ACKNOWLEDGE THAT THEY HAVE EACH READ THIS AGREEMENT AND THAT, BY ADDING THEIR SIGNATURES BELOW, DESIRE TO MAKE IT EFFECTIVE THIS 26th DAY OF January 19 79.

_____
Witness to Signature

_____
Witness to Signature

_____
Witness to Signature

EDMONTON WORLD HOCKEY ENTERPRISES LTD.
(CLUB)

BY: L.D. Gordon
L.D. GORDON - GENERAL MANAGER

BY:

Wayne Gretzky
WAYNE GRETZKY (PLAYER)

(PLAYER'S ADDRESS)

EDMONTON OILERS HOCKEY CLUB

OPERATED BY
EDMONTON WORLD HOCKEY ENTERPRISES LTD.

EDMONTON COLISEUM
EDMONTON, ALBERTA
CANADA T5B 4M9

TELEPHONE (403) 474-8561
TELEX 037-3595

January 29, 1979

Mr. Ron Ryan
Executive Director
World Hockey Association
17th floor
One Financial Plaza
Hartford, Conn. 06103
U.S.A.

Dear Ron:

Please find enclosed three copies of the new contracts recently signed
between the Edmonton Oilers and Wayne Gretzky and Ron Chipperfield.

Please approve the contracts as to form and return two copies to our
attention.

Thanks for your help.

Best regards,

EDMONTON OILERS HOCKEY CLUB

L. D. Gordon -
General Manager

LDG/mn
Encls.

Getting to Know Jean Béliveau

It's interesting that Jean Béliveau filled out this player questionnaire on April 22, 1952. It's not like he was an unknown to the Canadiens organization. He had played two games in 1950–51 while still a junior, and he was closely watched by the entire province while starring with senior hockey's Quebec Aces. If anything, he was modest on the form, unusual for most young men who had received that level of notoriety. On the personal side, Béliveau listed himself as single (with his interests being "golf and women"), though he had most definitely already met his future bride, Élise Couture, in Quebec City. They got engaged at Christmas in 1952, just after another three-game NHL trial, and they married June 27, 1953. In his autobiography, Béliveau describes how Élise was his confidante and able ally through ever-growing media scrutiny. "Élise and I had been prepared for the glare of the celebrity spotlight by our time in Quebec City," wrote Béliveau. "We had learned to cope with media demands, although these intensified when we moved to Montreal. Every week, or so it seemed, a newspaper or magazine was knocking on the door, seeking fresh insight into the lives of the Béliveaus. We were posed in pictures of domestic bliss—cooking, eating, reading, enjoying music. Our fans expected this sort of coverage, and we were usually happy to oblige." The Hockey Hall of Fame inducted him as an Honoured Member in 1972.

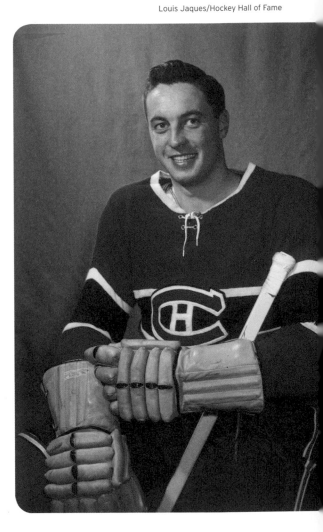

A young Jean Béliveau poses for a photo before the 1954–55 season.

QUESTIONNAIRE FOR PLAYERS

PLEASE "BLOCK" LETTERS IN ANSWERS   Date 22 Avril 1952

NAME IN FULL ... JEAN BELIVEAU

Nick Name ... Bill

HOME ADDRESS — Number and Street ... 5 Blv. St Croix

City ... VICTORIAVILLE

Province or State ... QUEBEC

BIRTHPLACE — City ... TROIS-RIVIERES ... Province or State ... QUE

Day 31 ... Month AOÛT ... Year 1931

Weight ... 205 ... Height ... 6 3"

What Position do you Play? ... CENTRE

Do you Handle Stick Right or Left? ... LEFT.

Have you Ever Been Selected for an All-Star Team? ... YES

What Year or Years? ... 48-49 - 49-50 - 50-51 - 51-52

By Whom? ... T.A.H.A. & Q.S.H.L.

Are you Married or Single? ... S-

Children? .... (Boys) .... (Girls) ....

What is your Summer Occupation? ... P.R. LAVAL DAIRY

What are Your Hobbies? ... GOLF & WOMEN

GENERAL REMARKS

Rocket Richard Went Out a Champion

While the 1956–57 season was towards the end of Maurice "Rocket" Richard's storied career—he played only three more seasons—he was not going quietly into the night. The Montreal Canadiens won their eighth Stanley Cup, the second of five straight, and Richard was second in the NHL in goals with 33 (to Gordie Howe's 44) for a .52 goals per game average. In Dick Irvin's book, *The Habs*, Frank Selke Jr., general manager in Montreal, talked about The Rocket: "He wasn't the best hockey player, but he was the most unpredictable and certainly the most exciting player I ever remember." It's not an assessment that Richard himself disputed: "I was never the best player in the league. I knew that. I was a bad skater, but I worked hard," he told Irvin. "I had more drive from the blue line in. That's what gave me the chance to score more goals." Richard, of course, ended up with 544 career goals, a league record at the time, and another 82 in 133 playoff games. Did the team lose something besides a right winger when he called it quits? Selke Jr. thought so: "[W]hen Rocket retired in 1960, he not only took his talent and skills away with him, he took his heart too. I think maybe that had more to do with the team not being able to win the next year, win a sixth straight, than anything else. It wasn't the same team without his fire." The Hockey Hall of Fame inducted him as an Honoured Member in 1961.

Maurice Richard went out a winner, receiving the 1960 Stanley Cup from NHL president Clarence Campbell. Above, he poses with two unknown women and the Lou Marsh Trophy as Canada's athlete of the year for 1957 at Toronto's Exhibition Grounds.

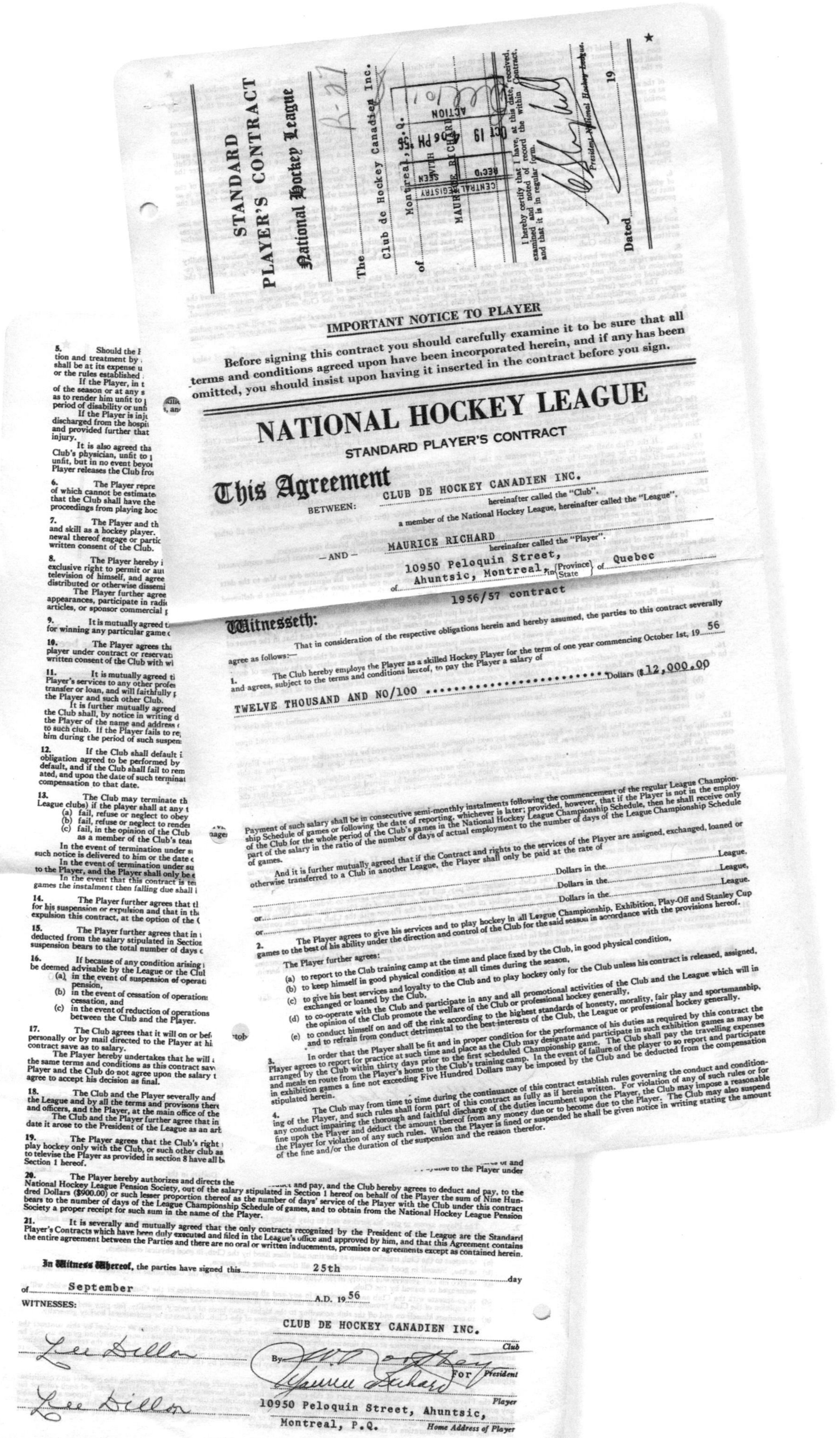

IMPORTANT NOTICE TO PLAYER

Before signing this contract you should carefully examine it to be sure that all terms and conditions agreed upon have been incorporated herein, and if any has been omitted, you should insist upon having it inserted in the contract before you sign.

NATIONAL HOCKEY LEAGUE
STANDARD PLAYER'S CONTRACT

This Agreement

BETWEEN: CLUB DE HOCKEY CANADIEN INC.

hereinafter called the "Club".

a member of the National Hockey League, hereinafter called the "League".

— AND —   MAURICE RICHARD

hereinafter called the "Player".

10950 Peloquin Street,
of Ahuntsic, Montreal, in (Province) of Quebec
(State)

1956/57 contract

Witnesseth:

That in consideration of the respective obligations herein and hereby assumed, the parties to this contract severally agree as follows:—

1.   The Club hereby employs the Player as a skilled Hockey Player for the term of one year commencing October 1st, 19 56 and agrees, subject to the terms and conditions hereof, to pay the Player a salary of

TWELVE THOUSAND AND NO/100 .... Dollars ($12,000.00

Payment of such salary shall be in consecutive semi-monthly instalments following the commencement of the regular League Championship Schedule of games or following the date of reporting, whichever is later; provided, however, that if the Player is not in the employ of the Club for the whole period of days of the Club's games in the National Hockey League Championship Schedule, then he shall receive only part of the salary in the ratio of the number of days of actual employment to the number of days of the League Championship Schedule of games.

And it is further mutually agreed that if the Contract and rights to the services of the Player are assigned, exchanged, loaned or otherwise transferred to a Club in another League, the Player shall only be paid at the rate of

    Dollars in the .... League.

    Dollars in the .... League.

    Dollars in the .... League.

or

games to give his services and to play hockey in all League Championship, Exhibition, Play-Off and Stanley Cup games to the best of his ability under the direction and control of the Club for the said season in accordance with the provisions hereof.

2.   The Player agrees to give his services and to play hockey in all League Championship, Exhibition, Play-Off and Stanley Cup games to the best of his ability under the direction and control of the Club for the said season in accordance with the provisions hereof.

The Player further agrees:

  (a) to report to the Club training camp at the time and place fixed by the Club, in good physical condition,

  (b) to keep himself in good physical condition at all times during the season.

  (c) to give his best services and loyalty to the Club and to play hockey only for the Club unless his contract is released, assigned, exchanged or loaned by the Club.

  (d) to co-operate with the Club and participate in any and all promotional activities of the Club and the League which will in the opinion of the Club promote the welfare of the Club or professional hockey generally, and to conduct himself on and off the rink according to the highest standards of honesty, morality, fair play and sportsmanship,

  (e) to refrain himself from conduct detrimental to the best interests of the Club, the League or professional hockey generally.

3.   In order that the Player shall be fit and in proper condition for the performance of his duties as required by this contract the Player agrees to report for practice at such time and place as the Club may designate and participate in such exhibition games as may be arranged by the Club within thirty days prior to the first scheduled Championship game. The Club shall pay the Player's travelling expenses and meals en route from the Player's home to the Club's training camp. In the event of failure of the player to so report and participate in exhibition games a fine not exceeding Five Hundred Dollars may be imposed by the Club and be deducted from the compensation stipulated herein.

4.   The Club may from time to time during the continuance of this contract establish rules governing the conduct and condition-ing of the Player, and such rules shall form part of this contract as fully as if herein written. For violation of any of such rules or for any conduct impairing the thorough and faithful discharge of the duties incumbent upon the Player, the Club may impose a reasonable fine upon the Player and deduct the amount thereof from any money due or to become due to the Player. The Club may also suspend the Player for violation of any such rules. When the Player is fined or suspended he shall be given notice in writing stating the amount of the fine and/or the duration of the suspension and the reason therefor.

.... to the Player under

and pay, and the Club hereby agrees to deduct and pay, to the National Hockey League Pension Society, out of the salary stipulated in Section 1 hereof on behalf of the Player the sum of Nine Hun-dred Dollars ($900.00) or such lesser proportion thereof as the number of days' service of the Player with the Club under this contract bears to the number of days of the League Championship Schedule of games, and to obtain from the National Hockey League Pension Society a proper receipt for such sum in the name of the Player.

21.   It is severally and mutually agreed that the only contracts recognized by the President of the League are the Standard Player's Contracts which have been duly executed and filed in the League's office and approved by him, and that this Agreement contains the entire agreement between the Parties and there are no oral or written inducements, promises or agreements except as contained herein.

In Witness Whereof, the parties have signed this .... 25th .... day

of .... September .... A.D. 19 56

WITNESSES:

CLUB DE HOCKEY CANADIEN INC.

Lee Dillon

Lee Dillon

By: *[signature]* For President

Maurice Richard Player

10950 Peloquin Street, Ahuntsic,
Montreal, P.Q.   Home Address of Player

[Left partial column, faintly visible:]

5. Should the P...
6. The Player repre...
7. The Player and th...
8. The Player hereby...
9. It is mutually agreed...
10. The Player agrees th...
11. It is mutually agreed...
12. If the Club shall default...
13. The Club may terminate...
14. The Player further agrees...
15. The Player further agrees...
16. If because of any condition...
17. The Club agrees that it will...
18. The Club and the Player severally...
19. The Player agrees that the Club's right...
20. The Player hereby authorizes and directs the...

Lord Stanley Donates a Cup

Some of the back story of this letter from Frederick Arthur Stanley—better known as Lord Stanley of Preston—is lost to time, but the key dates in his life, and for hockey, are well known. As the youngest son of the 14th Earl of Derby, the former British Prime Minister Edward Smith-Stanley, Frederick studied at Eton College before following his father into politics. After serving in a number of capacities, including Lord of the Admiralty and Secretary of State for the Colonies, Queen Victoria selected him to serve as Governor General of Canada. He was 47 years old when he assumed office on June 11, 1888, bringing with him his wife and four of their eight children to the new country, just three months after writing the letter found in Allan Stitt's Collection and reproduced here. The Stanleys were soon introduced to a new game too, witnessing hockey for the first time on February 4, 1889, at the Montreal Winter Carnival. Politically, Lord Stanley played a major role as the Dominion began to stand on its own, a country more and more independent of England. Biographer Kevin Shea called Lord Stanley "a man of the people" who "was a much more important historical figure than he's been given credit for." Their children truly fell in love with hockey and began playing and organizing games around Ottawa, and Arthur was a major proponent of the growth of the sport in Great Britain. To celebrate the game, Lord Stanley bought a silver rose bowl for 10 guineas and donated it as the Dominion Hockey Challenge Cup, which became known almost immediately as the Stanley Cup. In 1893, the year his Cup was first presented, Lord Stanley returned to England following his brother's death and became the 16th Earl of Derby. Lord Stanley died in 1908, never having returned to Canada to see the prize his Cup had become. The Hockey Hall of Fame inducted him as an Honoured Member in the Builder category in 1945.

Lord Frederick Stanley, 16th Earl of Derby.

The Aide-de-Camp in waiting is commanded by

Their Excellencies

The Governor-General and The Lady Stanley of Preston.

to invite

Dr and Mrs Stewart

to Dinner on Saturday the 13

of September at 8 o'clock

An answer is requested to the A.D.C. in waiting.

5 Portland Place

March 9th 1888.

Dear Mr Macnamara,

I was sorry to have to send you a telegram to ask you not to come & see my son today, but his illness has turned to typhoid fever, although at present of a very mild type, & of course we are obliged to keep him very quiet.

Do not trouble to answer this, but my telegram seemed to require explanation.

Yours faithfully

Stanley of Preston

MANAGEMENT AND MINOR LEAGUES

All Honours for Frank Calder

When Frank Calder passed away in February 1943, two weeks after having a heart attack during an NHL Board of Governors meeting in Toronto, a who's who of hockey turned out for his funeral in Montreal. Not only were owners and executives from all levels of hockey present, but also all of the players from two teams—the Canadiens and Bruins—turned out for the ceremony. Such was the importance of Calder, who up until that point, had been the only president the National Hockey League had ever known. Born in Bristol, England, in 1877, Calder arrived in Canada as a young man and taught at a private school in Montreal. Switching careers, Calder became a sportswriter with the *Montreal Witness*, and then he was the editor for sports and business at the *Montreal Herald*. His love of sports got him involved as a secretary for the National Hockey Association, the forerunner of the NHL. In 1917, with the formation of the NHL, Calder was elected to lead it. Guiding the top hockey league through two World Wars, and plenty of internal fighting, Calder was inducted into the Hockey Hall of Fame as an Honoured Member in the Builder category in 1947. In his memoir, long-time Rangers player and executive Frank Boucher called Calder "a quiet, scholarly man," and Calder was certainly modest when he was honoured during the NHL's 20th anniversary. Surrounded by 150 of the top hockey people at the dinner in New York City, the 60-year-old Calder dismissed the hype: "Excuse me if I have a big head. I suspect you are talking about another person." The Calder Memorial Trophy, given to the NHL's top rookie, and the AHL's Calder Cup, are named in his memory.

Frank Calder was the NHL president from the 1917-18 season through 1941-42.

NATIONAL HOCKEY LEAGUE

PRESIDENT
FRANK CALDER
603 SUN LIFE BUILDING
TEL. MARQUETTE 3438
RESIDENCE. ELWOOD 5917

MONTREAL, June 17th 1937

Connie Smythe Esq.,
Maple Leaf Gardens,
Toronto.

Dear Connie:-

I am enclosing herewith cheque for
$2500 payable by Madison Square Garden
Corporation to the order of Toronto Maple
Leaf Hockey Club in settlement of the drafting
of player Mann from Syracuse.

Please acknowledge.

Sincerely yours,

Frank Calder

Imperial Oil - Turofsky/Hockey Hall of Fame   Imperial Oil - Turofsky/Hockey Hall of Fame

Clarence Campbell's Hall of Fame Dreams

The Hockey Hall of Fame as it is known today has only existed as a physical entity since 1957, based initially in a shared space with the Canadian Sports Hall of Fame on the Canadian National Exhibition grounds in Toronto. So what was NHL president Clarence Campbell ruminating about in July 1948? The first class of inductees was chosen in 1945: Howie Morenz, Tom Phillips, Georges Vezina, Hod Stuart, Frank McGee, Eddie Gerard, Charlie "Chuck" Gardiner, Hobey Baker, and Harvey Pulford. The intention was that the Hockey Hall of Fame would be located in Kingston, Ontario. The second group of honourees wasn't announced until 1958, along with details of the cooperation with the Canadian Sports Hall of Fame for a Toronto location. In the interim 13 years, Campbell assigned Canadiens GM Frank Selke as a committee of one to flesh out his ideas and make it all happen. And in 1948, Campbell drafted what are likely the first set of "rules" for admission to the Hall, reproduced here. "There's been an awful lot of talk about a Hall of Fame," Selke told writer Dick Bacon in 1961, "but no action. The plans for the Kingston Hall of Fame seemed to have died a natural death. It should be in Toronto or Montreal, not because either claims to be the birthplace of hockey but because more people would be able to visit a Hockey Hall of Fame in either city." Canadian Prime Minister John Diefenbaker spoke at the opening of the Hockey Hall of Fame in Toronto on August 26, 1961. "The opening of Hockey's Hall of Fame is a significant event in the history of Canadian athletics. It is also a fine example of the close ties existing between Canada and the United States and the unity we have built in the pursuit of recreation," he said. "We share the heroes of hockey as no other countries on earth do. This building has the fame of solidarity between the two nations. Two-thirds of the money for this building was raised in the land of Canada's neighbour, but here it stands to honour the deeds of hockey players from both sides of the border."

Conn Smythe, J.P. Bickell, Clarence Campbell, Hockey Hall of Fame curator Bobby Hewitson, and Frank Selke check out the space for the facility at Exhibition Place in Toronto circa 1960; Canadian Prime Minister John Diefenbaker officially opened it August 26, 1961.

NATIONAL HOCKEY LEAGUE

603 Sun Life Building
Montreal

PRESIDENT'S OFFICE

July 27th 1948.

re
Hockey Hall
of Fame

Mr. Conn Smythe
Maple Leaf Gardens Ltd.,
TORONTO 2, Ont.

Dear Mr. Smythe,

Last winter, after I had been included in the list of additional Governors of the International Hockey Hall of Fame, I made inquiries from several persons as to the nature of the duties of the Governors and also how the elections to membership in the Hall of Fame were conducted. In the course of those inquiries it appeared clear that there was no definite procedure laid down. Frankly, I felt some rather grave misgivings about the standard of selections if some steps were not taken to ensure for the future that all candidates elected to the Hall of Fame would have such a high proportion of support from the selectors that their selections could never be called in question in future years.

It was, and is, my opinion that ill-considered or unwarranted elections to the Hall of Fame will do much harm to this institution whereas if the elections are carefully and thoughtfully conducted, the Hall of Fame can become a very useful and worthy organization for the advancement of the game of hockey.

With this object in mind I have in the past few months discussed the matter with several Governors of the Hall of Fame and I have also made a study of the methods of election to the Baseball Hall of Fame. Out of those discussions and investigations the enclosed draft of "Rules of Election" have been evolved and I send them to you for your consideration and comment. They are entirely unofficial and criticisms or suggestions for amendment will be welcome.

- 2 -   July 27th 1948.

You will note from the Constitution that the Governors have the right and duty to establish their own "rules and regulations" for the election of candidates and I am strongly of the opinion that no further selections should be made until some "Rules and Regulations" have been established.

What I have said above is not intended as a reflection upon any selections made thus far, but I believe that there are others worthy of selection who have so far been omitted and there is the danger that with each passing year we are risking the loss of the first hand opinion and advice of old timers who knew the records and qualities of the former "greats" of the game.

If you will be good enough to consider the enclosed draft and write your comments to me as soon as possible, I will accept the responsibility of circulating the results of this canvass and I hope that it will produce a sound basis upon which we can proceed to discharge our responsibilities as Governors.

Thanking you in anticipation of your earliest possible reply, I am,

Yours very truly,

CSC:W

Encl.

<u>RULES FOR ELECTION TO</u>
<u>THE INTERNATIONAL HOCKEY HALL OF FAME</u>

1. Elections to The International Hockey Hall of Fame shall be made
by the Board of Governors in accordance with the powers conferred
by Article VIII of the Constitution as follows:-
"Board of Governors

    (a) The Board of Governors by its own methods rules and
regulations shall select for enshrinement the members of The International Hockey Hall of Fame. Any resident or former resident
of the Dominion of Canada or of the United States of America,
who is or has been distinguished in hockey as a player or as a
hockey executive, and including any member of the Board of
Governors, shall be eligible as worthy to be honored by being
selected as a member of The International Hockey Hall of Fame.
When and if a member for The International Hockey Hall of Fame
is selected the name of such person shall be certified to the
President of the Executive Committee, who will thereupon enroll
such name in The International Hockey Hall of Fame in the manner
as provided for.

<u>TIME OF ELECTION</u>

2. Elections shall be held at least once in each calendar year and
additional elections may be held with the approval of the majority
of the Board. The time of holding the election shall be fixed
by the Board.

<u>ELIGIBILITY FOR ELECTION</u>

3. Any resident or former resident of the Dominion of Canada or of
the United States of America who is or has been distinguished in
hockey as a player or as a hockey executive shall be eligible
for election provided however that candidates shall have completed

their careers as players prior to the date of election but they
may be otherwise connected with hockey.

<u>BASIS OF SELECTION</u>

4. Candidates for election shall be chosen on the basis of playing
ability, integrity, sportsmanship, character and their contribution to their team and hockey in general.

<u>ORGANIZATION OF THE BOARD</u>

5. (a) The Board shall elect by ballot from among its Members a
Chairman who shall preside at all meetings of the Board and of
its Selection Committee. He shall act as Secretary of the Board
and of the Selection Committee and do all acts necessary to
facilitate the proper functioning of the Board in the discharge
of its duties under the Constitution. His term of office shall
coincide with that of the Board.

(b) The Board shall select from among its members a Selection
Committee of three, with power to add, whose duty it shall be to
receive and consider all nominations, conduct such research as
they deem advisable, and make recommendations to the Board of
Governors respecting each candidate before the election takes
place.

<u>NOMINATION OF CANDIDATES</u>

6. Any member of the Board may make not more than three nominations
on proper nominating ballots giving fullest possible data as to
the record and merits of the candidate nominated. Such ballots
shall be filed with the Chairman not less than sixty days before
the date fixed for the election, who shall then refer such
nominations to the Selection Committee for investigation and
report. A candidate may be nominated any number of times.

3

METHOD OF ELECTION

7. (a) The Chairman shall prepare a summary of the record of all
nominees together with the recommendations, if any, of the
Selection Committee with respect to each. He shall distribute
to each Member of the Board a copy of such summary together with
a ballot on which spaces are provided for the member to fill in
the names of not more than ten eligible candidates that he
believes to be entitled to be elected to the Hall of Fame. The
member shall fill in the names of his candidates, sign the
ballot and return it to the Chairman within fifteen days.

(b) The vote shall be tabulated by the Chairman and any candidates
receiving approval of seventy-five per cent of all the Members
of the Board shall be elected to Membership in The International
Hockey Hall of Fame.

(c) If no candidate received approval of seventy-five per cent of
the Members of the Board then a final ballot will be prepared
by the Chairman containing the names of the ten candidates
receiving the highest number of votes on the first ballot. All
candidates tied for tenth place on the first ballot shall be
included. The final ballot will then be distributed to all
Members of the Board with instructions to vote for the five
candidates appearing on the ballot that he believes should be
elected to the Hall of Fame. The Members shall then sign the
ballot and return it to the Chairman within fifteen days. Any
candidate receiving approval of seventy-five per cent of all
Members of the Board shall be elected to membership in The
International Hockey Hall of Fame.

4

CERTIFICATION OF ELECTION

8. The results of the election shall be certified and transmitted to
the President of The International Hockey Hall of Fame by the
Chairman.

PUBLICATION

9. The President shall release the election results for general
publication. No member shall divulge or disclose the result
or other particulars of the balloting in advance of such general
release nor shall he disclose his own vote or that of any other
member at any time.

The League-Leading Lawyer

There's only one man in the American Hockey League's Hall of Fame (class of 2011) and the Naismith Memorial Basketball Hall of Fame (class of 1974), and he didn't lace up skates or shoot hoops. His name is Maurice Podoloff, and his contributions to both sports are important and unparalleled. For a time, he was commissioner of the newly formed Basketball Association of America and led the merger with the National Basketball League to form the National Basketball Association. He was also president of the AHL at the same time. Podoloff was born in Russia in 1890, and moved to New Haven, Connecticut, when he was six years old. He attended Yale and got a law degree. The Podoloff family built the New Haven Arena in 1926, and they launched the New Haven Eagles hockey team as a charter member of the Canadian-American Hockey League. Maurice started as a governor and moved up the ranks to secretary-treasurer of the league. The CAHL merged with the International Hockey League in 1936, with Podoloff as president, and in 1940, it was officially renamed the AHL. In 1946, the start-up BAA hired Podoloff as leader for the basketball league; he ran both leagues until 1952. "He was the first president at the time when it was unclear whether pro basketball could ever be successful in this country," said NBA commissioner David Stern upon Podoloff's death in 1995. In a 1977 interview, Podoloff admitted he never took to basketball, which has named the regular season MVP trophy in his name: "I don't like the game. I never liked the game." Podoloff is also in the International Jewish Sports Hall of Fame.

AHL president Maurice Podoloff, NHL president Clarence Campbell, and Cleveland Barons general manager Jim Hendy at a meeting during the 1951–52 hockey season.

INTERNATIONAL AMERICAN HOCKEY LEAGUE

EASTERN DIVISION			WESTERN DIVISION
NEW HAVEN	PRESIDENT	VICE PRESIDENT	CLEVELAND
PHILADELPHIA	MAURICE PODOLOFF	JOHN D. CHICK	HERSHEY
PROVIDENCE	42 GROVE STREET	1319 McDOUGALL STREET	PITTSBURGH
SPRINGFIELD	NEW HAVEN, CONN.	WINDSOR, ONTARIO, CANADA	SYRACUSE
	TEL. 8-0177	TEL. 3-1133	

NEW HAVEN, CONNECTICUT

March 11, 1939

RECEIVED

MAR 1 3 1939

Mr. Connie Smythe
Maple Leaf Gardens
Toronto, Ont.

Dear Mr. Smythe:

I have for acknowledgment assignment agreement
covering player Murray Armstrong.

Sincerely,
INTERNATIONAL AMERICAN HOCKEY LEAGUE

By
President

MP:JG

AMERICAN HOCKEY LEAGUE

EASTERN DIVISION			WESTERN DIVISION
NEW HAVEN	PRESIDENT	VICE PRESIDENT	BUFFALO
PHILADELPHIA	MAURICE PODOLOFF	JOHN D. CHICK	CLEVELAND
PROVIDENCE	42 GROVE STREET	1319 McDOUGALL STREET	HERSHEY
SPRINGFIELD	NEW HAVEN, CONN.	WINDSOR, ONTARIO, CANADA	INDIANAPOLIS
	TEL. 8-0177	TEL. 3-1133	PITTSBURGH

NEW HAVEN, CONNECTICUT

November 10, 1941

RECEIVED

NOV 12 1941

Miss J. Sievert
Maple Leaf Garden Ltd.
Toronto, Ontario
Canada

Dear Miss Sievert:

I have for acknowledgment assignments in re Players Mann, Goldham
and Eddolls.

Sincerely,

AMERICAN HOCKEY LEAGUE

By

MP:JG

The Dean of Hall of Fame Writers

There's a reason that the Hockey Hall of Fame gives out the Elmer Ferguson Memorial Award, presented "in recognition of distinguished members of the hockey-writing profession whose words have brought honour to journalism and to hockey." It's because Ferguson was one of the primary chroniclers of the early days of hockey and stayed a respected member of the ink-stained wretch fraternity for years. "Elmer covered the founding meeting of the NHL in November 1917 and the expansion draft of 1967. Quite an accomplishment," said D'Arcy Jenish, author of *The NHL: A Centennial History*. Born in Charlottetown, Prince Edward Island, in 1885, Ferguson started at a newspaper in Moncton, New Brunswick, but really achieved his fame as sports editor of the *Montreal Herald*. After the *Herald* folded in 1957, he continued his influential column—"The Gist and the Jest of It"—in the *Montreal Star* until his death in 1972. He was also a popular guest during *Hockey Night in Canada*'s "Hot Stove Lounge" segments. With the NHL head office based in Montreal, Fergy was a key figure in many ways, and he is believed to have had a hand in standardizing hockey statistics in general. Starting in 1934, he produced a weekly broadsheet of short articles, statistics, and photographs called *Hockey* that went out to newspapers to encourage them to cover the league. The times were different then, said Jenish. "The lines between journalists and subjects were very blurry back in the day. Those guys clearly had to leave certain skeletons in the closet and sweep the dirt under the rug. On the other hand, they had access to the athletes that today's journalists would die for, and it is reflected in the colourful and evocative detail you find in their stories."

Elmer Ferguson at his typewriter.

Form 502D

Montreal Herald

MONTREAL'S OLDEST EVENING NEWSPAPER—ESTABLISHED 1811

THE HERALD PRINTING HOUSE, 265 VITRE ST. W.

MONTREAL - CANADA

THE HERALD PUBLISHING COMPANY LIMITED
EDITORIAL OFFICE
'PHONE LAncaster 5181

ADDRESS ALL COMMUNICATIONS
TO
P. O. Box 4017

Tuesday
2/12/30

Mr. J. Emil Dionn,

　Quebec city.

Dear Mr. Dion --

　　　　Regarding N. H. L. statistics. We furnish a quantity of
forms to every club, and the scorer in each city of the N. H. L. fills
these out and firwards them to Pres. Calder's office immediately after
each game.　We have a double check on this, for not only is there a
straight scoring sheet and a pwnalty sheet, but these and other
statistics are re-compiled in a large general sheet, which includes
stops by goalers, shots on goals by each player, etc.

　　　　These individual statistics are, in turn, entered into a
large book printed for the purpose, and the totals taken off weekly.

　　　　If you wish copies of the forms used, write to Mr. Calder's
office, Castle building, Stanley-St. Catherine, Montreal, and the
stenographer will forward them, if you mention my name.

　　　　With kindest regards,

　　　　　　　　Very truly,

　　　　　　　　Wo Ferguson

Hendy's Cleveland Barons Almost Joined the NHL

James "Jim" C. Hendy grew into the role as boss of the brazen Cleveland Barons, the American Hockey League team that dared to challenge the National Hockey League—and almost joined it. Though born in 1905 on the Caribbean island of Barbados, Hendy grew up in Vancouver, British Columbia. As a young man, he ended up in New York and began as a writer, sending out reports from sporting events at Madison Square Garden. Hendy established many of the statistics that hockey counts on today. He took a job with the New York Rangers as publicity director and then a similar job with the AHL. He was the president of the United States Hockey League for two seasons before taking the role that got him inducted into the Hockey Hall of Fame as an Honoured Member in the Builder category in 1968. In 1949, Hendy was hired to run Cleveland Arena and its main tenant, the Cleveland Barons; later, the job was separated and Hendy ran just the hockey team. The Barons were an independent club, and Hendy was free to deal with any NHL club. One of his first deals was selling Al Rollins to Toronto, knowing that he had Johnny Bower to play net with the Barons. "Quite a dealer that Hendy," said Maple Leafs boss Conn Smythe. "He was going to loan me Rollins, but when I offered to buy him, he put quite a big price on his services." Hendy never lacked confidence, and in February 1951, he boldly said, "Our club, as presently constituted, could make the National Hockey League playoffs." The next year, he applied to be the seventh NHL team, but in May 1952, the application was turned down, as too much of the $425,000 entry fee was borrowed. "I do know that Cleveland is a major-league city and that I have never been more disappointed in all my life over this decision," said Hendy. He ran the Barons until his death from a heart attack in January 1961.

Jim Hendy sits in the stands at Maple Leaf Gardens with Toronto goalie Turk Broda and owner Conn Smythe.

 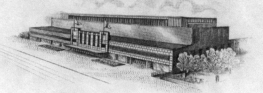

The ARENA

3700 EUCLID AVENUE

CLEVELAND, OHIO

April 18, 1950

RECD APR 19 1950

Mr. Clarence "Hap" Day
Toronto Maple Leafs
Maple Leaf Garden
Toronto 2, Ontario
Canada

Dear Hap:

Al Rollins was right about the matter. There was a balance
of $70.00 due the club and I told Al to forget it.

Lex Cook now knows about this.

Kindest regards.

Sincerely yours,

CLEVELAND ARENA, INC.

James C. Hendy (s.r.)

James C. Hendy
Managing Director

JCH/sr

Mr. Pieri Loved Hockey More than Basketball

To Buster Clegg, Louis A. R. Pieri was always Mr. Pieri. Even as Clegg moved up the ladder, from a player at the University of New Hampshire to the public relations director of Pieri's Providence Reds of the American Hockey League, to general manager of the team, he always kept that respect for his boss. Now the president of the Rhode Island Reds Heritage Society, Clegg treasures his memories of Mr. Pieri. "On the surface, he was gruff, but underneath he had a heart of Jell-O," Clegg said. After graduating from Providence's prestigious Brown University, Pieri took over as manager of the Rhode Island Auditorium and its primary tenant, the Providence Reds, in 1929, and stayed there until his death in 1967. The team won eight AHL division titles and four Calder Cup championships (1938, 1940, 1949, 1956) during Pieri's reign. A member of the AHL's Hall of Fame, Pieri was also a key figure in the history of the National Basketball Association, as a co-owner of the short-lived Providence Steamrollers and later as part of a group that owned the storied Boston Celtics. "He loved basketball, but he loved hockey more," said Clegg. The Reds were independent for the most part, not beholden to the whims of a parent NHL club. "We had no affiliation. We owned all of our players. Now that is a tough, tough grind," said Clegg, listing the challenges of facing Rochester with its Toronto minor leaguers or Springfield with the Rangers prospects. There were times, though, that Pieri came out on top. "He sometimes thought he knew more than the pros did," said Clegg. The Louis A. R. Pieri Memorial Award, which was first handed out in 1967, is awarded each year to the AHL's top coach.

Lou Pieri was a key sporting figure in Rhode Island.

Form C

NATIONAL HOCKEY LEAGUE

Uniform Agreement for Assignment of a Player's Contract to or by Club

———————

This Agreement, made and entered into this ....16th.......... day of

.....November.......... 19 39 ...., by and between ....

TORONTO MAPLE LEAF HOCKEY CLUB LIMITED
(Party of the First Part)

and ....RHODE ISLAND AUDITORIUM, INC. (RHODE ISLAND REDS)..........
(Party of the Second Part)

Witnesseth: The party of the first part hereby assigns to the party of the second part the

contract of Player ....Norman Mann.. upon the following conditions

according to the terms of the agreement as contained in the letter of November 12, 1939,
signed by Mr. Arnold W. Jones, President, and Mr. Louis A. R. Pieri, General Manager,
of R. I. Auditorium, Inc.

In Testimony Whereof we have subscribed hereto, through our respective Presidents or

authorized agents, on the date above written.

TORONTO MAPLE LEAF HOCKEY CLUB LIMITED
CLUB

WITNESS:

Frank Ayerst

By ....
(Party of the First Part)

Marguerite McNamara

R. I. AUDITORIUM, INC.
CLUB

By ....
(Party of the Second Part)

Corporate name of Company, Club or Association of each party should be written in first
paragraph and subscribed hereto.

Hershey Was Always Sweet for Frank Mathers

For three-and-a-half decades, Frank Mathers was associated with the Hershey Bears, first as a player-coach, then as just a coach, then in the front office. He was a part of six Calder Cup teams in Hershey—plus two more as a defenceman with the Pittsburgh Hornets. But in 1948, as he is writing to Leafs boss Hap Day, Mathers is 24 years old, no longer young by hockey standards, his promising youth as a star footballer and hockey player—he was on the 1943 Memorial Cup–winning Winnipeg Rangers nicknamed the "Raggedy Anns" for their well-worn uniforms and had played for the CFL's Ottawa Rough Riders as a halfback—stolen away by three years in the Royal Canadian Air Force as a pilot. He turned pro for the 1948–49 season for the Leafs. "By that time I was 24, and I knew if I didn't make it my first year, I'd never make it as a regular," Mathers told the *Globe and Mail*'s Paul Patton in 1986. He played in only 23 NHL games, in parts of three different seasons, counting only a single goal and three assists. The AHL was something altogether different, and there is little he *didn't* win: he was an All-Star for six straight seasons, won the Louis A.R. Pieri Memorial Award as the AHL's outstanding coach in 1969, received the James C. Hendy Memorial Award as outstanding executive in 1977, and was inducted into the AHL Hall of Fame in 2006. On a grander scale, Mathers was honoured for his contributions to hockey in the United States in 1987 with the Lester Patrick Trophy, and he was inducted into the Hockey Hall of Fame as an Honoured Member in the Builder category in 1992. Mathers told Patton that he was content with his decision to share in the small Pennsylvania town known for its chocolate: "I had my bags packed once, but I decided that the security and the life I wanted was here in Hershey. This is a small town, just 15,000 people, clean and green."

Frank Mathers's name is synonymous with the Hershey Bears.

416 Dominion St.
Winnipeg, Man.
July 29th/48

Dear Hap,

I am very sorry for not writing sooner but my wife and I only recently returned to Wpg. We both wish to thank you for the kind invitation to stay at the Royal York, unfortunately we went west.

The marks arrived and surprisingly enough I had only two failures. I intend to write one off and carry the other. In this way I will have my year and therefore wish to continue at school. I have written to St. Michael's college requesting their calendar and date of commencement.

I would prefer to play for Marlboros and attend St. Mikes. This way I will undoubtedly have more time for school which is of primary importance to me. Hoping this is satisfactory to you.

Sincerely,

Frank Mathers.

Terry Reardon Was the Heart of Baltimore Clippers

Though Terry Reardon played forward with the Montreal Canadiens (alongside his Hall of Fame brother Ken), won two Stanley Cups with the Boston Bruins, and was player-coach of the 1947 Calder Cup–winning Providence Reds, he is most connected to the AHL's Baltimore Clippers. When he died in 1993, the *Baltimore Sun* paid tribute to "Baltimore's Mr. Hockey" and quoted Ray "Gump" Embro, the Clippers reserve goalie and trainer: "Crowds averaged 7,000 to 9,000. We outdrew the Bullets. Yeah, we were minor league, but we were the best AHL franchise at the time. And it was all because of Terry." Reardon started as the Clippers general manager in 1962, when the team debuted to coincide with the opening of the Civic Center. He was there in 1975, when the team disbanded. In between, he took over coaching duties on occasion and lived through the ups and downs of the franchise, a cheap cigar always near. The hardest times were after the NHL expanded—"It is very difficult for an independent club like ours to get players such as we have been able to do the last two years," Reardon said in 1972. The darkest days were when the World Hockey Association unexpectedly moved the broke Michigan Stags team to Baltimore in 1975, forcing the Clippers to cease operations. Reardon did have a small role with the renamed Blades, but the team only lasted one season. The next year, Reardon was a part-owner in the Clippers return to the AHL, but he left in the fall of 1976, when the team dropped down to the Southern Hockey League for a single season.

Before Terry Reardon ran the team in Baltimore, he was the fiery general manager with the AHL's Providence Reds.

Baltimore Ice Sports, Inc.

CIVIC CENTER, BALTIMORE 1, MARYLAND

Phone: SAratoga 7-0703

R. C. "Jake" EMBRY
President

TERRY REARDON
General Manager

August 10, 1965

Mr. George Imlach, General Manager
Toronto Maple Leafs Hockey Club
Maple Leaf Gardens
60 Carlton Street
Toronto, Ontario, CANADA

Dear Punch:

This is to confirm the Baltimore purchase of
Edward Mazur for the sum of forty-two hundred and fifty
($4250.00) dollars.

Purchase is conditional upon Mazur reporting
to the Baltimore training camp.

I talked to Mazur over the weekend. He is
working for Molsons and might possibly retire should the
job become permanent.

Yours truly,

Terry Reardon
General Manager

Ray Miron ran teams and leagues.

Ray Miron: The Man Who Owned a League

In 2004, Ray Miron was presented with the Lester Patrick Trophy for his contributions to hockey in the United States. "It was the climax of my career," recalled Miron from his nursing home in Tulsa, Oklahoma. Miron's journey from an arena manager in his hometown of Cornwall, Ontario, to hockey executive, to league owner, is one for the ages. He was a key man in the Toronto Maple Leafs organization, running the team's farm club in Tulsa in the original Central Hockey League, which operated as a league from 1963 to 1984. In 1992, Miron teamed with Bill Levins to form a *second* Central Hockey League. "It was unique that we owned all the teams, so we were able to control costs a lot better," said Miron. The league still runs today, though teams are individually owned—but they do compete for the Ray Miron President's Cup. In between his role with the two CHLs, Miron was coach and GM for the CHL's Tulsa Oilers and then the Oklahoma City Blazers for two seasons. He was also the general manager of the woeful Colorado Rockies of the NHL, starting from the franchise's original 1976 shift from Kansas City up until 1981. "It took me a long time to get to the majors, but I finally made it. I had a chance for the New York Islanders job, I had a chance for the St. Louis Blues job, I had a chance for the Buffalo job, I had a chance for the Atlanta job. I probably came in second for every one of them," he said.

TULSA HOCKEY CLUB, INC.

CIVIC CENTER • TULSA, OKLAHOMA 74103 • 582-8283

March 18, 1969

I hereby agree to play five (5) games for the
Toronto Maple Leafs Hockey Club and its affiliates.
It is understood that this will in no way affect
my amateur standing in accordance with the National
Hockey League and C.A.H.A. Pro-Amateur Agreement.

[signature]

[signature]
Witness

CENTRAL HOCKEY LEAGUE

KANSAS CITY • FT. WORTH • DALLAS • MEMPHIS • OMAHA • TULSA • HOUSTON • OKLAHOMA CITY • AMARILLO

The Coach that Died Before the Team Did

E. J. Powers, centre, stands next to his Toronto Marlboro players, George "Punch" Imlach and Ernie Dickens.

E. J. Powers was a coach until his last day, and that happened to coincide with the last game that his team played. It all happened on January 17, 1943. Powers was the coach of the AHL's New Haven Eagles, a squad that was calling it quits because war-time restrictions on transportation had cut attendance. With the finale set for that evening, Powers went out to buy a newspaper, suffered a heart attack, and died on the way to New Haven's Grace Hospital. The game went on as scheduled, and the Eagles won, beating the Providence Reds, 9–4. Growing up in Toronto, Powers excelled at hockey and lacrosse, which was another sport that he coached at a high level, winning national championships. Though he only coached two full seasons in the NHL, with the Toronto St. Patricks (the predecessor of the Toronto Maple Leafs), he made an impact. "I started hockey under Eddie Powers, and I don't think I have ever met a finer fellow," Hockey Hall of Famer Hap Day was quoted as saying after Powers's sudden death. "Everyone was always willing to do a little bit more for Eddie, because he was Eddie. He was a fine, likeable person. In addition, he was one of the best hockey players, and it would be difficult to ask for a better coach." For many years, Powers was a scout for the Maple Leafs and, for a time, was in charge of Toronto's farm system. When he was laid to rest at Toronto's Mount Hope Cemetery on January 20, 1943, his pallbearers were prominent hockey names Eddie Convey, Harold Ballard, Joe Primeau, Charlie Watson, Ace Bailey, and Hap Day.

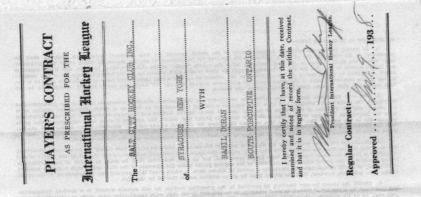

PLAYER'S CONTRACT

AS PRESCRIBED FOR THE

International Hockey League

The...... SALT CITY HOCKEY CLUB, INC. ....

of...... SYRACUSE NEW YORK ......

WITH

...... BASIL DORAN ......

...... SOUTH PORCUPINE ONTARIO ......

I hereby certify that I have, at this date, received examined and noted of record the within Contract, and that it is in regular form.

...... President International Hockey League.

Regular Contract:—

Approved ...... Nov 7 193...

☞ **IMPORTANT NOTICE TO PLAYERS AND CLUB PRESIDENTS** ☜

Every player before signing a contract should carefully scrutinize the same to ascertain whether all of the conditions agreed upon between the Player and Club President have been incorporated therein, and if any have been omitted, the player should insist upon having all the terms, conditions, promises and agreements inserted in the contract before he signs the same. It is understood that the name INTERNATIONAL AMERICAN HOCKEY LEAGUE is to be considered as substituted wherever INTERNATIONAL HOCKEY LEAGUE appears

---

INTERNATIONAL HOCKEY LEAGUE

PLAYER'S CONTRACT (REGULAR)

Articles of Agreement between the ....

.......SALT CITY HOCKEY CLUB INC...............................

of the City of....... SYRACUSE ......, in the {State/Province} of...... NEW YORK ......

a club member of a League known as the "International Hockey League," party of the first part, hereinafter called the Club

and .... BASIL DORAN ....

of the City of....... SOUTH PORCUPINE ......, in the {State/Province} of....... ONTARIO ......

party of the second part, hereinafter called the Player.

Witnesseth:

That in consideration of the mutual obligations herein and hereby assumed, the parties to this contract severally agree as follows:

1. The club agrees to pay the player for the season of 1938-39, beginning on or about the...... 1st

day of...... November ...... 1938, and ending on or about the...... 15th

day of...... April ...... 1939, a salary at the rate of $...... Fourteen hundred dollars - - - -

- for such reason; and an additional sum at the rate of

$ One hundred dollars - - - - -

for such season said additional sum being in consideration of the option herein reserved to the club in Clause 10 hereof; said additional sum to be paid whether said option is exercised or not, making the total compensation to the player for the season

herein contracted for $ Fifteen hundred dollars ($1,500.00).

It is understood that the name INTERNATIONAL AMERICAN HOCKEY LEAGUE is to be considered as substituted wherever INTERNATIONAL HOCKEY LEAGUE appears

14. The "NOTICE" printed at the head of this contract is hereby made a part hereof.

In Testimony Whereof, the parties hereunto have executed this contract, this...... 29th

day of...... October ...... A.D. 193 8.

SALT CITY HOCKEY CLUB INC.

E. J. Vowers

(Seal)

By .... for the President.

WITNESS: J. J. Irvin

Basel Oran Player.

It is understood that the name INTERNATIONAL AMERICAN HOCKEY LEAGUE is to be considered as substituted wherever INTERNATIONAL HOCKEY LEAGUE appears

Hockey Hall of Fame

Imperial Oil – Turofsky/Hockey Hall of Fame

George Mara Says No to Pros, Yes to Olympics

History may have been different had George Mara needed the money to play professionally. The son of George Mara Sr., a famed Toronto athlete turned business icon, Mara Jr. grew up in privilege. A skilled centre, Mara was approached about playing in the NHL by the hometown Leafs (for which he later served on the board of directors), the New York Rangers, and the Detroit Red Wings. His single game in 1946 with the Rangers' farm club, the Rovers, didn't go well, wrote columnist Jim Coleman: "The New Yorkers gave a bit of heckling to George Mara when he made his debut with the Rovers the other day. . . . They were unaware of the fact that he was playing in a pair of borrowed skates and was experiencing some difficulty in navigating successfully."

Mara's decision to keep his amateur status was Canada's gain—he was first a member of the Canadian Navy during the Second World War, suiting up for Navy teams in Toronto and Halifax, and then he was also a last-minute addition to the 1948 RCAF Flyers for the Olympics in St. Moritz, Switzerland. Mara ended up leading the team as captain and as a scorer, with 17 goals in only eight games as the Canadians rolled to a gold medal. Post hockey, Mara was a successful businessman, but he kept his ties to the Olympics and was one of the people who established the fundraising arm of the Canadian Olympic Committee, known as the Olympic Trust. For his commitment to the Olympics, he was made a member of the Order of Canada in 1976, and he was subsequently inducted into the Canadian Olympic Hall of Fame in 1989, as both an athlete and a builder, and then to Canada's Sports Hall of Fame in 1993.

Before he was captain of the 1948 Olympic gold medal–winning Team Canada, George Mara was a Toronto Marlboro.

CANADIAN PACIFIC TELEGRAPHS

C.D. 2X

CLASS OF SERVICE
Full Rate
Day Letter
Night Message
Night Letter

Please mark an X opposite the class of service desired

MONEY TRANSFERRED BY TELEGRAPH TO PRINCIPAL POINTS IN CANADA AND THE UNITED STATES

CANADIAN PACIFIC COMMUNICATIONS

CABLE CONNECTIONS TO ALL PARTS OF THE WORLD RADIOGRAMS TO SHIPS

TIME FILED

CHECK

Send the following message, subject to the conditions on the back thereof, which are hereby agreed to.

W. D. NEIL, General Manager of Communications, Montreal

Report delivery.

COPY—January 28. 1942-US.

Mr. Frank Calder,
910 Sun Life Building,
Montreal, Canada.

January 6, 1942. 10.35 a.m.

Please put William Shill of Young Rangers Toronto on our negotiation list replacing Mara negotiations abandoned.

C. H. Day.

Chg. Maple Leaf Gdns.

C.P.T. reported delivered 10.30 a.m. standard.

October XX 9, 1945.

Mr. Jack Adams,
Detroit Hockey Club,
Grand River at McGraw,
Detroit, Illinois.

Dear Jack:

Please find enclosed assignment agreements transferring the rights to service of Eric
Prentice to the Detroit Hockey Club in return for which
the Detroit Hockey Club gives the Toronto Maple Leaf
Hockey Club the rights to service of George Mara.

Will you kindly sign and return at your
convenience.

Yours truly,

CHD/LP
Enc. 4

The Marshall Plan Didn't Work Out

The reunion with the old documents from his days at St. Michael's College couldn't have come at a better time for Willie Marshall. The talented playmaker, who is the all-time leading scorer in American Hockey League history, is working on his autobiography. Harkening back to 1950, he recalls the push and pull that went on over his services and how he believes it affected the rest of his career. Like most things, it came down to money. Since he was not excelling in his schooling, as he confessed to Father Flanagan, Marshall signed with another junior team, the Guelph Biltmores. "I went to Guelph and had the highest contract in junior history that year," Marshall said. He played four games for his new team. "The OHA had so much pressure from [NHL president] Clarence Campbell and [Leafs owner] Conn Smythe. They took my contract away and sent me back to St. Mike's." The promising junior centreman (85 goals in 126 junior games) angered the wrong people, namely the one that controlled his destiny: Conn Smythe. Still, he's in the AHL Hall of Fame, and to this day, the league's leading goal-scorer gets the Willie Marshall Award. No one is likely to ever challenge Marshall's 1,375 points over 20 seasons (1952 to 1972). Regrets? "You're disappointed [at] not getting to the National League. I had 33 games, but I don't think I played three minutes in any game." Marshall only counted one goal in the NHL—a Tim Horton shot from the point that he tipped in. You'll be able to read about it soon.

Willie Marshall with the Hershey Bears.

June 22nd, 1950

Mr. Willie Marshall
43 First Street
Kirkland Lake, Ontario

Dear Willie:

I was wondering what your plans are for next
season. I would like you to come back to St. Michael's next
year again and help us win the OHA. Fr. Regan has made it
clear to me that you are in good standing and would be
welcome back.

I do think that we have a very good chance of
winning and that we will definitely be the team to beat.
We have a strong nucleus from last year's team and we have
a number of good players coming in. Our new coach will be
announced early in July.

I would like to hear from your regarding your
plans and if there is any way in which I can be of help
to you please let me know.

Hope you are enjoying the summer; or do you get
any summer in Kirkland?

Regards to your family.

Yours sincerely,

Director of Athletics

43 First Street,
Kirkland Lake, Ontario.
July 25, 1950

Dear Father:

I received your letter a few weeks back and
after careful consideration I have decided it useless
for me to attend College this coming year as you know
through no fault of the College, I have not done so well
the past two years. I regret very much under the
circumstances I will not be able to play for St. Mike's
this coming winter for I believe as you say with good
replacements for the boys that are leaving we should be
able to cop that cup this coming season. I have had
several good offers for the coming season but do not
know where I will be going, but I can assure you that
I would like to play my last season in Junior with
St. Mike's if arrangements could be made financially
but my schooling would be a bygone conclusion. I
would attend school though and do the best I could
but it doesn't seem to be in me to grasp the work
as quickly as lots of the other boys. Of course you
know I am on the Leafs sponsored list and I think probably
it would be wise for me to play for them if satisfactory
arrangements can be made. I would be glad to hear from
you at your convenience.

Best regards to you from mother and father
and say hello to everyone for me,

Yours sincerely,

(Sgnd) Willie

Reid Aimed for Big Five, Settled for Big Four

The Calgary Tigers in 1924, with Charlie Reid fourth from the right.

While Charlie Reid carved out a pretty decent career as a goaltender and then as a coach, the really fascinating thing about his contract is that it is for the Big Five Hockey League—a league that never existed. But there was a short-lived Big Four Hockey League in Alberta, which ran from 1919 to 1921. "Nowhere was the line between pro and amateur more blurred than in the Big Four League, launched in 1919 with two teams each in Calgary and Edmonton," writes Steven Sandor in *The Battle of Alberta*. "The Big Four attempted to become the Big Five before the 1920–21 season. Discussions were held with Saskatoon, but league president Allan McCaw could not put a deal together to bring in the expansion club from Saskatchewan." The paperwork is pretty good evidence that McCaw expected to succeed with the eastern expansion. As for Reid, he was a Western boy for the most part; he played in the various Alberta leagues from 1919 to 1924, and had two stints in the Pacific Coast Hockey League with the Vancouver Maroons. PCHL's president Frank Patrick praised Reid in 1922: "There is no doubt at all, but that Reid is a high-class goalkeeper." Reid made the NHL, sort of, as a backup with the 1926–27 Detroit Cougars, but he never saw action. As his career wound down, Reid turned to coaching, where he helmed minor league teams in Niagara Falls, Ontario, and Pittsburgh, Pennsylvania.

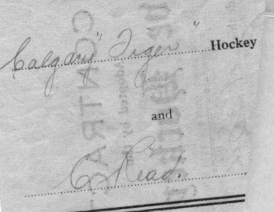

Big Five Hockey League

CONTRACT

Between

Calgary "Tiger" Hockey

and

C. Reid.

Received, Approved and Rec

CONTRACT
Adopted by the
Big Five Hockey League

This Agreement made this _30th_ day of _November_ 192_1_

between _Charlie Reid._ .... party of the first part, and

Calgary Hockey Club Ltd party of the second part, Witnesseth:

FIRST. Said party of the second part agrees to devote his entire time and services, as a hockey player, to said party of the first part, to play all league and exhibition games during the hockey season of _1921-1922_

SECOND. Said party of the second part agrees to conform to all the rules and regulations now adopted, or which may be hereafter adopted by the Big Five Hockey League, or by the party of the first part, appertaining to his services aforesaid.

THIRD. Said party of the second part agrees not to render any services as a hockey player during the time of this contract to any other person, corporation or association, other than the party of the first part, without the written consent of the party of the first part so to do.

In consideration of the foregoing premises the party of the first part agrees:

of now $300. paid in advance. **FIRST.** To pay to the party of the second part the sum of $_1000.00_ to be paid in equal weekly instalments, during the hockey season of the Big Five Hockey League.

Season starts Dec. 12th

SECOND. Said party of the first part agrees to pay the travelling expenses, board and lodging _; ends March 15th_ of said party of the second part whenever said party of the second part may be travelling in the service of the said party of the first part during the hockey season, and when not so travelling the party of the second part will pay all his own expenses.

THIRD. Said party of the first part agrees to furnish the said party of the second part with one, only, complete outfit, for his use while employed with the party of the first part, the same to be returned at the termination of his contract.

It is hereby mutually agreed by the parties hereto, in consideration of the premises hereinbefore set forth, that should the party of the second part, at any time or times, or in any manner, fail to comply with the covenants and agreements herein contained, or any of them, or with any of the rules and regulations of the Big Five Hockey League, or of the party of the first part, which are now or may hereafter from time to time be made, or should the said party of the second part at any time or times be intemperate, immoral, careless, indifferent, or conduct himself in such a manner, whether on or off the ice, as to endanger or prejudice the interest of the said party of the first part, or prove incompetent in the judgment of the party of the first part, then the said party of the first part hereunto shall have the right to discipline, suspend, fine or discharge the said party of the second part in such manner as to it, the said party of the first part, shall seem fit and proper, and in case of fine imposed, it is agreed by said party of the second part that he will pay the same, or that the same may be withheld, as and for liquidated damages.

In order to enable the party of the second part to fit himself for the duties necessary under the terms of this contract, the said party of the first part may require the said party of the second part to report for practice one week prior to the opening of the hockey season.

It is further agreed that if the said party of the first part should desire the services of the said party of the second part for any period of time after the date mentioned for the expiration of the term mentioned herein, or which may be mentioned in renewal hereof, said first party shall have the right to the same by paying compensation to the said second party for each game at a pro-rata rate of regular salary.

IN WITNESS WHEREOF, the said party of the first part has caused these presents to be signed by its officer thereunto duly authorized, and the said second party has affixed his hand and seal on the day and year first above written.

By _Fred Johnson_ Pres.

Chas. E. Reid

Player sign here.

Marcetta Unravels Mystery Letter

Just a month before he died at age 78, in September 2014, Milan Marcetta helped answer some of the questions that arose because of a letter dated December 5, 1962, that was found in his file from Maple Leaf Gardens and reproduced here. The first answer was obvious: The Society for International Hockey Research database has no record of the Syracuse Braves Hockey Club existing that season in the Eastern Professional Hockey League. It turns out, the team moved. "It was Syracuse first. They moved from Syracuse to St. Louis," said Marcetta. But he didn't move with the team. "I started out in Syracuse, then I got traded to Calgary and went back to Calgary in the Western Hockey League." Originally from Cadomin, Alberta, Marcetta was one of those WHL mainstays, returning to various teams in between brief stints in the NHL—seven games total for the Maple Leafs and North Stars in the three seasons after the 1967 expansion. "It was a little too late for a lot of us. I was in my mid-30s then," he said. Marcetta also solved another mystery: whom the other two people who wrote and received the letter were. Gus Kyle was running the St. Louis Braves team, albeit not all that successfully. "I played for him before in Calgary, and I didn't get along with him. He didn't get along with a lot of guys," said Marcetta. "He was a bad coach and he had a bad attitude." Alf Pike, at the helm with the Calgary Stampeders, was better. "He was a good coach. He knew the game quite well. His only problem was he didn't trust the young guys. He didn't give the young guys much of a shot," explained Marcetta. "Anybody that was young, he would just bark at them. He didn't give you much ice time."

Milan Marcetta skates alongside Larry Hillman.

PHONE 472-7029

Syracuse Bra... ey Club, Inc.

WA... IAL
ROOM 234

315 MONTGOMERY STREET -:- SYRACUSE 3. NEW YORK

5th December 62.

Mr. Alf PIKE,
Calgary,Alberta.

Dear ALF:

    Just a few lines regarding the contract of Milan MARCETTA.
His contract is for $4250.00 for 171 days, amounting to $24.85 per day.

    I had a bonus for him of $250.00, should the club make the
playoff finals.

    He has been paid up to and including 5th December, and
wants to drive out to Calgary, so He is on his own until He
arrives there, as far as we are concerned.

    Trusting this is all the information you require and
I hope things are well with you. We are running a promotion for
tonights game, which we started 5 weeks ago, and are all sold
out. Up until now we have been drawing terrible. Hockey has been
out of here for 9 years, and our coming in so late, with little
time for promotion, has made it real rough. However, it has been
a tremendous experience for myself, and I am enjoying the experience, which keeps me busy as hell all the time. No time for a few
laughs or anything.

    Kindest personal regards to Lloyd and the boys, I remain,

Sincerely,

Gus KYLE.

Milan Marcetta,
Suite 14, 309 -- 3rd Ave. N. E.,
Calgary, Alberta

Imperial Oil – Turofsky/Hockey Hall of Fame

Hockey Hall of Fame

HOWIE MEEKER'S HOCKEY BASICS

Howie Meeker has always loved sharing his knowledge of hockey.

Meeker's Pro-Tips Required Stickhandling with Management

Howie Meeker's "Pro-Tips" segments on *Hockey Night in Canada* were a popular part of the intermissions for a few years as the 1970s went into the early 1980s. Meeker always promised that the NHL stars would "show you what to do and how they got to do it." The players always seemed to be having a blast, hamming it up while also demonstrating their skills. The veteran instructor and commentator, reminiscing about the show, said that lining up talent was never the issue. "All the players wanted to come. When you phoned and talked to them personally on the telephone [they'd say], 'Sure, sure, just get me permission and I'll be there!'" Meeker recalled. The problem was management. "It was tough to sell to the general managers that guys might be away for a week or 10 days," explained Meeker, who filmed the segments in Newfoundland. To help with the paperwork, Meeker relied on his agent, Jerry Petrie, who also represented the likes of Gary Carter, Jean Béliveau, and Guy Lafleur through the years. "I did all the legwork and everything else. Jerry just looked after the complications that might come from the NHL," said Meeker, whose 1973 book, *Howie Meeker's Hockey Basics*, was named one of the most important Canadian books by the Literary Review of Canada in 1999.

HOWIE MEEKER ENTERPRISES LTD.

Suite 205,
6600 Trans Canada Hwy.,
Pointe Claire, Québec H9R 4S2
Tel.: (514) 694-4025

July 31, 1981.

Mr. George Imlach,
General Manager,
Toronto Maple Leafs,
Maple Leaf Gardens,
60 Carlton Street,
Toronto, Ontario M5B 1L1.

Dear Punch:

This letter will confirm our discussions re: the participation of Laurie Boschman of the Toronto Maple Leafs in my Pro-Tips hockey series. It also is understood that Laurie had permission to utilize the Toronto Maple Leaf Uniform in this production.

Punch, the Pro-Tips series is designed to teach some of the basics of hockey to the coaches and youngsters watching Hockey Night In Canada, as well as to provide entertainment and insight to the normal fan. Laurie did an outstanding job in Pro-Tips, and helped us achieve our goals.

I truly appreciate your and Mr. Ballards support all these years, and particularly with my Pro-Tip project.

If you could confirm the above to me in a brief letter, it would be greatly appreciated.

I wish you and the Toronto Maple Leafs the best of luck for the 1981-82 season.

Thank you again for your help.

Yours very truly,

Howie Meeker,
President.

/mw

Punch - would APPRECIATE A LETTER like THIS ONE ENCLOSED BUT ON MAPLE LEAF STATIONARY THANKS. "Howie"

August 11, 1981

Mr. Howie Meeker
Suite #205
6600 Trans Canada Hwy.
Pointe Claire, Quebec
H9R 4S2

Dear Howie:

This letter will confirm the approval of the Toronto Maple Leaf Hockey Club in having Laurie Boschman appear in the television production of "Pro-Tips" which will be shown on Hockey Night in Canada during the 1981-82 season.

This permission will also allow Laurie Boschman to wear the Toronto Maple Leaf uniform during the production and eventual showing on Canadian and United States television.

Sincerely,

GEORGE "PUNCH" IMLACH
General Manager

GI:gs

THE ORIGINAL SIX ERA

Gagnon Was a Speedy Black Cat

Given his success in the NHL, it's surprising to learn that Johnny "Black Cat" Gagnon was reluctant to sign with the Montreal Canadiens. Already a star around *La Belle Province* for the likes of the Quebec Bulldogs, Chicoutimi Bleuets, Trois-Rivières Renards, and the Quebec Sons of Ireland, he said no when the Habs came calling in the spring of 1926. As reported by the *Globe*: "I am still a minor and therefore could not sign a contract even if I wished to do so," he said, denying he had signed a contract. "I am but 20 years of age, and if I wished to join the pros, I would have to get permission from my father in Chicoutimi, and he is opposed to my jumping to pro ranks." After three seasons with the Providence Reds, the 5-foot-5, 150-pounder finally joined Montreal in the fall of 1930. The fans loved the speedy right winger, as did the press, especially when he lined up alongside Howie Morenz and Aurèle Joliat. "Only a master of broken French could hope to duplicate Gagnon's rare stories and characteristic remarks. He was a whole show in himself," raved Mike Rodden in his "Highways of the Sport" column in the *Globe and Mail*, quoting Gagnon's happiness about being traded back to Montreal from the Bruins in January 1935. "Dose Canadien owners relize now dey mak' a mistak'. It is good, too, because witout myself in de lineup dat team might fall right out of de league. Me, I'm one of dose good playaires you can't never kept down." His one Stanley Cup came in 1931, and the Society for International Hockey Research retroactively named him the playoff MVP in its study of pre–Conn Smythe Trophy postseasons. After he hung up his skates in 1945, Gagnon was a scout for Providence of the AHL and then the NHL's Rangers, and he stayed on an NHL payroll until his death in 1984.

Johnny "Black Cat" Gagnon actually standing still.

QUEBEC PROVINCIAL HOCKEY LEAGUE
PLERS CONTRACT

◆

Chicoutimi Nov. 26th 1922

I, _J. M Gagnon_ hereby bind myself to play for _the Chicoutimi_ Hockey Club during the season 192 2 192 3 . I agree to remain the property of this club after playing season of 192 192 ; unless a written release is granted by the management of the above named club.

NOTICE.—Should a player sign for two different clubs he will be barred to compete in this league.

J. M Gagnon
Player

T. E. Joron
Witness

-215

Approved by _R. W. Halpin_
President

The Unappreciated Lorne Chabot

The file on Lorne Chabot in the Hockey Hall of Fame archives contains a number of pitches for his induction. To date, they have been in vain. In 1991, famed scribe Jim Coleman made his case for the keeper, who played for the Rangers, Maple Leafs, Canadiens, Black Hawks, and Maroons between 1926 and 1937. "Lorne Chabot was an unjustly ignored man. Never has he been elected to the Hall of Fame; despite his All-Star selection, his Vezina Trophy, and his two Stanley Cup championships. In 11 NHL seasons, he yielded an average of only 2.12 goals per game. In nine years of Stanley Cup playoffs, he earned an average of only 1.73 goals per game. He had a total of 78 shutouts," stated Coleman. The Rangers signed Chabot, a native of Montreal, as a free agent after he led the Port Arthur (now Thunder Bay), Ontario, squad to the Allan Cup. The Blueshirts subsequently tried to promote him as Lorne Chabotsky to try to attract Jewish fans to Madison Square Gardens. After being struck in the eye, he was dealt by the Rangers to Toronto in October 1928, along with $10,000 for goalie John Ross Roach. Chabot played five seasons with the Leafs, helping the team win the 1932 Stanley Cup. On endurance alone, Chabot deserves recognition: he was the keeper in the longest game in NHL history (March 24–25, 1936, Montreal Maroons versus Detroit, when Mud Bruneteau scored on Chabot and the Wings won 1–0 after 176 min and 30 seconds), and the second longest game (April 3–4, 1933, Toronto versus Boston, when his Leafs won 1–0 on a Ken Doraty goal after 164 minutes and 46 seconds).

Lorne Chabot was one of hockey's early goaltending superstars.

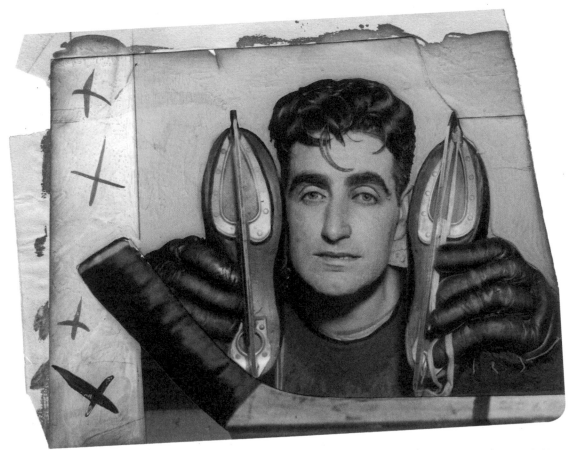

☞ IMPORTANT NOTICE TO PLAYERS AND CLUB PRESIDENTS ☜

Every player before signing a contract should carefully scrutinize the same to ascertain whether all of the conditions agreed upon between the Player and Club President have been incorporated therein, and if any have been omitted, the player should insist upon having all the terms, conditions, promises and agreements inserted in the contract before he signs the same.

NATIONAL HOCKEY LEAGUE

PLAYER'S CONTRACT (REGULAR)

Articles of Agreement between the NEW YORK RANGERS PROFESSIONAL

HOCKEY CLUB, INC.

of the City of NEW YORK , in the { State / Province } of NEW YORK

a club member of a League known as the "National Hockey League," party of the first part, hereinafter called the Club and

LORNE CHABOT

of the City of PORT ARTHUR , in the { State / Province } of ONTARIO

party of the second part, hereinafter called the Player.

Witnesseth:

That in consideration of the mutual obligations herein and hereby assumed, the parties to this contract severally agree as follows:

1. The club agrees to pay the player for the season of 192 8-9 , beginning on or about the 10th

day of October 192 8 , and ending on or about the 10th

day of April , 192 9 a salary at the rate of $ 4,900.00 (Four Thousand

Nine Hundred Dollars. for such season; and an additional sum at the rate of

$ 100.00 (One Hundred Dollars)

for such season said additional sum being in consideration of the option herein reserved to the club in Clause 10 hereof; said additional

sum to be paid whether said option is exercised or not, making the total compensation to the player for the season herein contracted

for $ 5,000.00 (Five Thousand Dollars)

...ment of the period covered by this contract, unless this contract shall be ter... the club for the purpose of playing games, in which event the instalment then return "home" of the club. Provided, however, that if the player is not in receive such proportion of the season's salary (or of the monthly salary mul... days of actual employment bears to the number of days in the season or the ...of days for which the player is held, provided he be not held more than four

...ntinuance of this contract establish reasonable rules for the government of ...be a part of this contract as fully as if herein written and binding upon the ...mpairing the faithful and thorough discharge of the duties incumbent upon ...player and deduct the amount thereof from any money due or to become ...for violation of any rules so established, and during such suspension the ...contract. When the player is fined or suspended, he shall be given notice ...of the suspension and the reason therefor.

...form his duties be impaired at any time during the term herein prescribed, ...ne due under this contract, such proportion thereof as the period of said ...ibed; but no such deduction shall be made by reason of any accident or ...lar duties under the direction of the club, unless such injury or accident ...fteen days, in which event this contract may be terminated at the option ...written notice thereof by the club.

...the preceding section, he will submit himself to a medical examination ...elected by the club, such examination when made at the request of the ...ct or conduct of the player contrary to the terms of this agreement or

...uniform, the player making a deposit of $30.00 therefor, which deposit ...termination of this contract, upon the surrender of the uniform by him

...ties necessary under the terms of this contract, the club may require ...designate, and to participate in such exhibition contests as may be

.................................days prior to the...

...lling expenses, and meals en route of the player from his home city

...rect or by way of the city of...................................... ...nd participate in the exhibition games, as provided for, a penalty ...ucted from the compensation stipulated herein.

... to the completion of the period of this contract, give the player ...ligations hereunder, in which event the liabilities and obligations, ...of said one day. The player, at the expiration of said one day ...to the club. If such notice be given to the player while "abroad"

...the player agrees to perform for the club, and for no other party, during the period of this contract (unless with the written consent of the club), such duties pertaining to the exhibition of the game of hockey as may be required of him by said club, at such reasonable times and places as said club may designate for the National Hockey League season for the year 1928-9 beginning on

or about the 10th day of October 192 8 , and ending on or

about the 10th day of April, 192 9 , unless sooner terminated in accordance with other provisions hereof.

9. The player will not, either during the playing season, or before the commencement or after the close thereof, participate in any exhibition hockey games, indoor baseball, basketball or football, unless the written consent of the club has first been given to him.

10. The player will, at the option of the club, enter into a contract for the succeeding season upon all the terms and conditions of this contract, save as to Clauses One and Ten, and the salary to be paid the player in Clause One hereof unless it be increased in event of such renewal shall be the same as the total compensation provided for the player in Clause One hereof unless it be increased or decreased by mutual agreement.

11. The club shall not transfer the services of the player to any other club without furnishing the player in writing all of the conditions under which said transfer is made and showing what team has claim to his services, and what claim is.

12. The "NOTICE" printed in red ink at the head of this contract is hereby made a part hereof.

In Testimony Whereof, the parties hereunto have executed this contract, this.................

day of.................October.................A.D. 192 8

(SEAL)

NEW YORK RANGERS PROFESSIONAL HOCKEY CLUB, INC.

By John S Hammond
President.

Lorne E. Chabot
Player.

WITNESSES:

What If Jacques Plante Had Ended Up a Ranger?

Writers love to play, "What if?" Todd Denault, author of the acclaimed biography, *Jacques Plante: The Man Who Changed the Face of Hockey*, is no different. He has seen Allan Stitt's 1947 paperwork where the New York Rangers, under the steward-ship of Frank Boucher, laid claim to Plante, and there is evidence that the Toronto Maple Leafs had their eyes on "The Snake" as well. "Had Plante been declared Rangers property in 1948, his career may have followed a similar trajectory as what played out in Montreal, in that he would have found his path to the NHL blocked by a Hall-of-Fame goaltender," speculated Denault. "From 1948 to 1953 Chuck Rayner patrolled the New York goal, and from 1948 to 1951 he was at the peak of his own Hall-of-Fame career (as witnessed by the Rangers appearance in the 1950 Stanley Cup Final and Rayner claiming the Hart Trophy that year). As a result, I don't think that Plante would have emerged as the Rangers full-time starter until about 1953, which was ironically right around the same time he took control of the Canadiens net." (He had been blocked by Bill Durnan and Gerry McNeil in Montreal.) In the end, NHL president Clarence Campbell confirmed that Plante was indeed Canadiens property. From there, Plante took matters into his own hands, and many consider him the greatest goaltender ever. There are the seven Vezina Trophies, the Hart Memorial Trophy in 1962, his three appearances as the NHL's First All-Star Team goalie (1956, 1959, 1962) and his four showings on the second team (1957, 1958, 1960, 1971), and his six Stanley Cups. Plante was elected to the Hockey Hall of Fame as an Honoured Member in 1978. But he was an innovator too, with his goalie mask, his style of play and handling of the puck, his influential book, *On Goaltending*, and his time as a goalie coach.

Jacques Plante as a teenage goaltending phenom.

Re: Player JACQUES PLANTE

       This player was a registered member of
Canadiens Junior Hockey Club. During the last week
of the Training Camp, he went home to Quebec to see
his father and while at home, he was contacted to
play with Quebec. Without the authority and against
the ruling of the Junior Group, he agreed to play in
Quebec. This was brought up at a Meeting of the
Quebec Junior Hockey Association and the Quebec Club
was ordered to return Plante to Canadiens. Mr.
Campbell was notified of this and the situation was
explained to him.

       After a lot of pressure, Plante came
back to Canadiens, but political pressure was exerted
so that Canadiens were forced to return him to Quebec.
However, he signed Option Agreement Form "B" before
he left.

       This player accepted money from Canadiens.

DP:AG

January 14, 1948.

January 20, 1948.

Mr. Frank Boucher,
Madison Square Garden Corporation,
307 West 49th Street,
NEW YORK 19, N.Y., U.S.A.

J-2

Dear Mr. Boucher: RE: Jacques Plante

Further to our conversation at your office recently reference the above-named player, I have now had the opportunity of examining the entire file at this office and likewise have had access to the files of the Registrar of the Quebec Amateur Hockey Association. I think that you will understand the situation best if I report the events in chronological order. This I have done in the enclosed statement.

I feel sure you will agree that there can be no doubt as to the correctness of Plante's being placed on the Sponsorship List of the Canadiens Juniors Hockey Club.

With further reference to your letter of December 18th directed to Miss Pinard, examination of our files shows that Toronto made an even earlier inquiry and claim of this player's services (December 17th), which claim they abandoned when it was confirmed that he was properly a member of a Sponsored Club.

May I also add this observation, that I do not think your scout, Mr. Hebert, was entirely frank with you in representing the status of this player because as a member of the Junior League, and having attended the meetings, he must have known of the decision of the League and that Plante was a member of the Canadiens Junior Hockey Club. By sending you simply a notification from the Quebec Registrar dated December 17th showing the release from Quebec on December 5th and registration on December 6th, he was only giving you a very small part of the facts. However, he is your representative and you can deal with that situation yourself.

Yours very truly,

NATIONAL HOCKEY LEAGUE

CSC/EM   President
Encl.

LOG OF CORRESPONDENCE AND EVENTS
REFERENCE JACQUES PLANTE

Plante was a resident of Shawinigan Falls, and played with
Shawinigan Falls Junior Hockey Club in the season 1946-47.

In late September or early October, pursuant to an arrangement
made through a Mr. Racette, Plante came to Montreal and
trained with the Canadiens Junior Hockey Team until the ice
was taken out of the Forum for some kind of a circus, at
which time he returned to his home in Shawinigan Falls for a
holiday.

While in Shawinigan Falls, around the third week of October,
he was persuaded not to return to Montreal but to go to Quebec.
This action led to a dispute between Quebec Citadels and
Montreal Canadiens Juniors, which dispute came up for
consideration at a meeting of the Quebec Junior Amateur
Hockey Association on October 27th. At this meeting a motion
was passed with only one dissenting vote in which it was
decided that Plante was the property of Canadiens Juniors
Hockey Club, and he was ordered to return to Montreal.
Plante and the Quebec Club disobeyed the order of the League
and on November 18th the Registrar of the Quebec Amateur Hockey
Association wrote a letter to Plante at Quebec advising him
of the request for his suspension by the Canadien Junior Hockey
Club for his failure to return, and warned him that if he did
not return by the 22nd of November he would be suspended.

This notice was not immediately acted on, and negotiations
continued back and forth between the clubs until finally the
Quebec Junior Hockey Club was threatened with expulsion from
the Junior League unless they complied with the terms of the
League resolution. Thereupon Quebec Junior Hockey Club on
December 5th relinquished their claim to Plante and agreed
to abide by the order of the League. This was arranged by
telegram from the Manager of the Quebec Citadels to Frank Selke
on December 5th.

On December 6th, the dispute having been finally settled, the
Registrar, Mr. Dilio, issued the playing certificate for Plante
to the Canadiens Juniors Hockey Club.

Subsequently, political pressure from several sources was brought
to bear on the Montreal Canadiens Professional Hockey Club to
secure Plante's release and return to Quebec, but before they
agreed to this release they secured from Plante a Form "B" Option
which was properly registered and reported in Bulletin No. 401.

Subsequently, Plante was released by Canadiens Juniors Hockey
Club, and his name was removed from the Sponsorship List.

Montreal, January 20, 1948

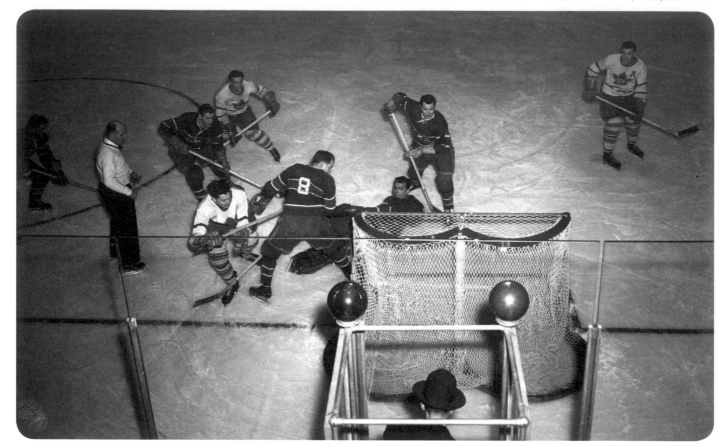

A Great Defenceman Requires Great Goaltenders

Talk about a bonus clause that is almost guaranteed to come true. As per his 1948–49 contract with the Montreal Canadiens, defenceman Doug Harvey would receive a $500 bonus should Bill Durnan win the Vezina Trophy as the goalie with the lowest goals-against average in the league. That year was Harvey's second with the club, but Durnan was a veteran who had already won the previous four Vezinas—and he would win the next two, enriching the pockets of his protectors, like Harvey, Butch Bouchard, Ken Reardon, and Glen Harmon. The other clause in the contract, making the All-Star Team, went unfilled for Harvey until he made the NHL's First All-Star Team in 1951–52. Harvey was actually the last Hab to sign a contract for the 1948 season, and the Canadiens left training camp in Sainte-Hyacinthe, Quebec, with everyone signed but their young D-man from Montreal's West End. "His signing should be a mere formality," said Frank Selke Jr., general manager of the Canadiens in September 1948. "Harvey has always appeared content with his contract." At the end of his career, which included stints with the New York Rangers and the St. Louis Blues, Harvey could admire his six Norris Trophies, as the league's best defenceman, next to his six Stanley Cups. He was elected to the Hockey Hall of Fame as an Honoured Member in 1973.

There are a lot of bodies in front of goaltender Bill Durnan during a game at Maple Leaf Gardens on January 19, 1949, including his defencemen Glen Harmon (No. 8) and Doug Harvey to his right.

STANDARD
PLAYER'S CONTRACT
National Hockey League

The
DOUGLAS HARVEY
of MONTREAL WITH
CLUB DE HOCKEY CANADIEN

I hereby certify that I have, at this date, received, at this date, examined and noted of record that it is in regular form.

President National Hockey League.

Dated _____ 19__

IMPORTANT NOTICE TO PLAYER

Before signing this contract you should carefully examine it to be sure that all terms and conditions agreed upon have been incorporated herein, and if any has been omitted, you should insist upon having it inserted in the contract before you sign.

NATIONAL HOCKEY LEAGUE
STANDARD PLAYER'S CONTRACT

This Agreement

BETWEEN: CLUB DE HOCKEY CANADIEN
hereinafter called the "Club",
a member of the National Hockey League, hereinafter called the "League".

— AND —

DOUGLAS HARVEY
hereinafter called the "Player".

of Montreal in {Province}/{State} of Quebec

Witnesseth:

That in consideration of the respective obligations herein and hereby assumed, the parties to this contract severally agree as follows:—

1. The Club hereby employs the Player as a skilled Hockey Player and agrees to pay the Player for the season of 1948/49 ("season" meaning the period commencing the date on which the Player reports to the Club at its training camp or other place designated by the Club, and ending on the completion of the Club's games in the National Hockey League Championship Schedule, Play-off and Stanley Cup Series) a salary of

Seven thousand Dollars ($7,000.).

If Goalkeeper William Durnan wins the Vezina Trophy Douglas Harvey will receive a bonus of $500.

If Douglas Harvey is named on either "All Star" team he shall receive a bonus of $500.

Payment of such salary shall be in semi-monthly instalments following the commencement of the regular League Championship Schedule of Games or following the date of reporting, whichever is later. Provided, however, that if the player is not in the employ of the Club for this entire period, then he shall receive such proportion of the salary as the number of days of actual employment bears to the total number of days in the said period.

And it is further mutually agreed that if the contract and the rights to the services of the player are assigned, exchanged, loaned or otherwise transferred to a club in another league, the player shall only be paid at the rate of

_____ Dollars for the season in the _____ League;
_____ Dollars for the season in the _____ League.

or_____

2. The Player agrees to give his services and to play hockey in all League Championship, Exhibition, Play-Off and Stanley Cup games to the best of his ability under the direction and control of the Club for the said season in accordance with the provisions hereof.

The Player further agrees:

(a) to report to the Club training camp at the time and place fixed by the Club, in good physical condition,
(b) to keep himself in good physical condition at all times during the season,
(c) to give his best services and loyalty to the Club and to play hockey only for the Club unless his contract is released, assigned, exchanged or loaned by the Club,
(d) to co-operate with the Club and participate in any and all promotional activities of the Club and the League which will in the opinion of the Club promote the welfare of the Club or professional hockey generally,
(e) to conduct himself on and off the rink according to the highest standards of honesty, morality, fair play and sportsmanship, and to refrain from conduct detrimental to the best interests of the Club, the League or professional hockey generally.

3. In order that the Player shall be fit and in proper condition for the performance of his duties as required by this contract the Player agrees to report for practice at such time and place as the Club may designate and participate in such exhibition games as may be arranged by the Club within thirty days prior to the first scheduled Championship game. The Club shall pay the travelling expenses and meals en route from the Player's home to the Club's training camp. In the event of failure of the player to so report and participate in exhibition games a fine not exceeding Five Hundred Dollars may be imposed by the Club and be deducted from the compensation stipulated herein.

4. The Club may from time to time during the continuance of this contract establish rules governing the conduct and conditioning of the Player, and such rules shall form part of this contract as fully as if herein written. For violation of any of such rules or for any conduct impairing the thorough and faithful discharge of the duties incumbent upon the Player, the Club may impose a reasonable fine upon the Player and deduct the amount thereof from any money due or to become due to the Player. The Club may also suspend the Player for violation of any such rules. When the Player is fined or suspended he shall be given notice in writing stating the amount of the fine and/or the duration of the suspension and the reason therefor.

---

5. Should the Player be disabled... tion and treatment by a physician select... shall be at its expense unless made necess... or the rules established under Section 4.

If the Player, in the sole judgment... of the season or at any subsequent time d... as to render him unfit to play skilled hocke... period of disability or unfitness, and no com...

If the Player is injured as the result... discharged from the hospital, and his medic... and provided further that the Club's obligat... injury.

It is also agreed that if the Player's i... Club's physician, unfit to play skilled hockey... unfit, but in no event beyond the end of the c... Player releases the Club from any and every ac...

6. The Player represents and agrees th... of which cannot be estimated with certainty ar... that the Club shall have the right, in addition... proceedings from playing hockey for any other t...

7. The Player and the Club recognize ar... and skill as a hockey player. Accordingly the Pl... newal thereof engage or participate in football, b... written consent of the Club.

8. The Player hereby irrevocably grants t... exclusive right to permit or authorize any person,... television of himself, and agrees that all rights in... distributed or otherwise disseminated by the Club...

The Player further agrees that during the p... appearances, participate in radio or television prog... articles, or sponsor commercial products without th...

9. It is mutually agreed that the Club will not... for winning any particular game or series of games ex...

10. The Player agrees that during the curren... player under contract or reservation to any Club of t... written consent of the Club with which such player is co...

11. It is mutually agreed that the Club shall... Player's services to any other professional hockey club,... transfer or loan, and will faithfully perform and carry on... the Player and such other Club.

It is further mutually agreed that in the event tha... the Club shall, by notice in writing delivered personally t... the Player of the name and address of the Club to which... to such club. If the Player fails to report to such other Cl... him during the period of such suspension.

12. If the Club shall default in the payments to t... obligation agreed to be performed by the Club hereunder,... default, and if the Club shall fail to remedy the default withi... ated, and upon the date of such termination all obligations o... compensation to that date.

13. The Club may terminate this contract upon wri... League clubs) if the player shall at any time:
(a) fail, refuse or neglect to obey the Club's rules gov...
(b) fail, refuse or neglect to render his services hereund...
(c) fail, in the opinion of the Club's management, to ex... as a member of the Club's team.

In the event of termination under sub-section (a) or (b)... such notice is delivered to him or the date of the mailing of such... In the event of termination under sub-section (c) it shall t... to the Player, and the Player shall only be entitled to the compen... In the event that this contract is terminated by the Club... games the instalment then falling due shall be paid on the first w...

14. The Player further agrees that the Club may carry on... for his suspension or expulsion and that in the event of suspension... expulsion this contract, at the option of the Club, shall terminate...

15. The Player further agrees that in the event of his suspen... deducted from the salary stipulated in Section 1 bear an amount... suspension bears to the total number of days of the League Champi...

16. If because of any condition arising from a state of war or c... be deemed advisable by the League or the Club to suspend or cease o...
(a) in the event of suspension of operations, the Player shall b... pension,
(b) in the event of cessation of operations, the salary stipulated... cessation, and
(c) in the event of reduction of operations, the salary stipulated i... between the Club and the Player.

17. The Club agrees that it will on or before October 1st next fol... personally or by mail directed to the Player at his address set out below... contract save as to salary.

The Player hereby undertakes that he will at the request of the Cl... the same terms and conditions as this contract save as to salary which sha... Player and the Club do not agree upon the salary to be paid the matter sh... agree to accept his decision as final.

18. The Club and the Player severally and mutually promise and ag... the League and by all the terms and provisions thereof, a copy of which shal... and officers, and the Player, at the main office of the League and at the main...

The Club and the Player further agree that in case of dispute between t... date it arose to the President of the League as an arbitrator and his decision s...

19. The Player agrees that the Club's right to renew this contract as... play hockey only with the Club, or such other club as provided in Section 2 an... to televise the Player as provided in section 8 have all been taken into consider... Section 1 hereof.

20. The Player hereby authorizes and directs the Club to deduct and pa... National Hockey League Pension Society, out of the salary stipulated in Section... dred Dollars ($500.00) or such lesser proportion thereof as the number of days... bears to the number of days of the League Championship Schedule of games, an... Society a proper receipt for such sum in the name of the Player.

21. It is severally and mutually agreed that the only contracts recogni... Player's Contracts which have been duly executed and filed in the League's office an... the entire agreement between the Parties and there are no oral or written inducem...

In Witness Whereof, the parties have signed this 25th
of September A.D. 1948 day

WITNESSES:

Margaret McInnes

Margaret McInnes

CLUB DE HOCKEY CANADIEN

By D. Raymond
President

Douglas N. Harvey
Player

2288 Harvard Avenue, Montreal
Home Address of Player

Béliveau's Early Days All Aces

In retrospect, it's hard to believe that the mighty Montreal Canadiens had to wait to get Jean Béliveau into their lineup on a regular basis. Though he was in their system and had played games with the big club while still skating with the Victoriaville Tigres and the Quebec Citadelles in the juniors, Béliveau didn't become a starter until 1953–54. Instead, he was the top player for the Quebec Aces. "The Aces had money in the till to trump the Canadiens," wrote Béliveau in *My Life in Hockey*. "In Quebec, senior hockey didn't take a back seat to the professional ranks. The Colisée was filled to capacity night after night." According to Béliveau, he made $10,000 his first season with the Aces, at least $3,000 more than he would have in the NHL. Punch Imlach, the coach and general manager of the Aces, later wrote that politics played a big part in Béliveau remaining in the provincial capital, and he pegged the salary of *le Gros Bill* closer to $20,000 given his wages from a job in a dairy and other sources. Béliveau was a star in Quebec, and his ascendancy was inevitable. While contemporaries like Boom-Boom Geoffrion and Dickie Moore went straight from junior to the Habs, Béliveau believes his time with the Aces served him well—beyond setting a high price for his promotion. "The extra time in Quebec helped me acclimatize to the demands of city life and to grow up gradually, more normally, than I would have had I been a 20-year-old Montreal Canadien." Hard to argue with his 10 Stanley Cup rings as a player and his election to the Hockey Hall of Fame as an Honoured Member in 1972.

Jean Béliveau, as a member of the QSHL's Quebec Aces, signs autographs for some fans.

HON. D. RAYMOND
PRESIDENT

D. C. COLEMAN
VICE-PRESIDENT

F. J. SELKE
GENERAL MANAGER

"DICK" IRVIN
COACH

CLUB DE HOCKEY CANADIEN INC.

Membre de la—National Hockey League—Member
2313 ST. CATHERINE ST. WEST

TEL. WILBANK 6131

MONTREAL,

October 17th, 1951

Mr. Jack Latter,
Quebec "Aces" Hockey Club,
Quebec, Que.

Dear Jack:

    Enclosed are assignments for Jean
Beliveau from Canadiens to Quebec "Aces" with
right of repurchase by Canadiens.

    You should sign and send all copies
to Central Registry for registration and dis-
tribution.

                Yours very truly,
                CLUB DE HOCKEY CANADIEN

                Frank J. Selke

                FRANK J. SELKE
                MANAGING DIRECTOR

FJS*mjm

cc: Central Registry

Encl.

MEMBER — MEMBRE
OF THE   DE LA
QUEBEC SENIOR HOCKEY LEAGUE

TEL. 4-2424

THE QUEBEC ACES INC.
les As de Québec Inc.

P. O. BOX 1487

QUEBEC
August 5th. 1952

Mr. Jean-Marc Béliveau,
148, Fraser Street,
Quebec, Que.

Dear Mr. Béliveau:-

        The Quebec Aces Hockey Club
hereby exercises its option to renew its C.A.H.A.
Standard Player's Contract with you for the
season 1952-53 at a salary of THREE HUNDRED DOLLARS
($300.00) per week, income tax to be deducted at
source.

        We would appreciate it if you
would sign the enclosed four copies of Standard
Player's Contract "A" and return to us the four
copies at your earliest convenience.

        We expect to open our training
camp on September 22nd.

            Yours very truly,

            THE QUEBEC ACES INC.

            George Imlach,
            Coach

:jm
encl. 4

The Rookie Deal of Henri Richard

As the little brother of the iconic Maurice "Rocket" Richard, Henri was always on the radar of the Montreal Canadiens, even though there was a 15-year age gap between them. At 19 years of age, with a year of junior eligibility still available, the diminutive 5-foot-7 centre was invited to the Canadiens training camp in 1955, though some saw this as a publicity stunt. "During this camp, I practised with the team and I think that I did well, but the management sent me back anyway to the juniors," Henri told *United Athletes* magazine in February 2011. Playing with the Montreal Royals, Henri impressed with a couple of goals during an exhibition game against the senior club. So, three games into the 1955–56 season, Canadiens GM Frank Selke signed Henri—on a calendar page. The proper paperwork was done up and submitted to the league two days later. "I went up with Maurice to see Mr. Selke in his office," Henri told Dick Irvin in *The Habs*. "He asked Maurice if I was ready and Maurice said, 'Sure. He's ready to play and he's ready to sign.' So I signed, but they gave me a two-way contract. If I didn't make it I would be sent to the Royals for less money." Henri became known as "The Pocket Rocket" and established a legacy of his own—a speedy playmaker with top-notch skills and an ability to make those around him even better. He didn't especially like the nickname though: "I didn't mind, but when people ask me to sign it, I never do," he said in 2009.

A rookie Henri Richard tries to elude the Leafs defender to get a shot on Harry Lumley.

HON. D. RAYMOND
PRESIDENT

D. C COLEMAN
VICE-PRESIDENT

F. J. SELKE
MANAGING DIRECTOR

"TOE" BLAKE
COACH

CLUB DE HOCKEY CANADIEN INC.

Membre de la—National Hockey League—Member
2313 ST. CATHERINE ST. WEST
MONTREAL 25. P.Q.
TEL. WILBANK 6131

October 14, 1955

Central Registry
603 Sun Life Building
Montreal

Gentlemen:

We are sending you herewith National Hockey League contract between Club de Hockey Canadien Inc. and Henri Richard and shall appreciate receiving one copy for our records in due course.

Very truly yours,

CLUB DE HOCKEY CANADIEN INC.

R-148

Removed from Jr Canadien E. S. L.

Frank J. Selke/D

Frank J. Selke,
Managing Director.

CENTRAL REGISTRY
REC'D | SEEN
Oct 15 12 08 PM '55

ACTION

1953 NOVEMBER 1953 | 1953 DECEMBER 1953 | 1954 JANUARY 1954

DECEMBER **14** MONDAY

9:00 Henri Richard

10:00 Bonus for signing 5000.00

11:00 Salary with Canadiens for 1955-56 season 7000.00

12:00 for 1956-57 " 8000.00

1:00

2:00 If Henri plays with Royals he will be paid at the rate of 5000.00 per season.

3:00 Henri Richard Selke Oct 12-1955

4:00

5:00

Fires cost money!!!
Fire Alarm Systems can reduce this loss

A NATIONAL ELECTRICAL SERVICE
Northern Electric COMPANY LIMITED

Eleven Stanley Cups for One Man

By 1968, when he was in negotiations for a new contract, Henri Richard had completely escaped the shadow of his older brother, Maurice "Rocket" Richard. The siblings had played five seasons together, and Maurice often said he played longer just for the opportunity to play with his brother. Comparing them is difficult, as The Rocket, during his 18 campaigns, was a fiery goal-scoring winger, who finished with 544 goals and 965 points. The Pocket Rocket, a centre, was all about skating skills, dazzling stickwork, and leadership during his 20 seasons, with 358 goals and 688 assists. Both were elected to the Hockey Hall of Fame as Honoured Members, but Henri has his brother—and everyone else in history—beat on one important fact: his name is etched on the Stanley Cup a record 11 times. Chances are, it's a mark that will never be broken. In an interview between Henri Richard and Kevin Shea of the Hockey Hall of Fame, Richard gave credit to teammates rather than brag: "Again, I'd tell you that I was in the right place at the right time. A hockey team needs great defencemen to win, and that's what we had all the 20 years I was there. After (Doug) Harvey and (Tom) Johnson, we had (Serge) Savard, (Guy) Lapointe, and (Larry) Robinson." Retiring as captain of *le bleu, blanc, et rouge*, the Cup once again in his hands, Henri ran a tavern until 1985, and then worked as an ambassador for his beloved Canadiens.

Henri Richard celebrates with the Stanley Cup during one of his 11 championships.

CLUB DE HOCKEY CANADIEN INC.

2313 St. Catherine St. West · Tel. Wellington 2-6131 · Montreal 25, P.Q.

Personal & Confidential   October 16, 1968

Mr. Henri Richard
2000 Boulevard de la Concorde,
Duvernay,
Cite Laval, Quebec.

Dear Henri:

This letter is simply to confirm my brief conversation
with you yesterday morning when I told you we will pay
you a salary of $37,500.00 for the 1968/69 season in-
stead of what is called for in your contract.

Also, as mentioned to you, on checking your records for
the past thirteen years, your average number of points
during the regular season has been fifty-seven points
and that takes last season into account. If you are
successful in attaining fifty-seven points this season
we are going to pay you an additional $2,500.00 bonus.

In addition last season, as per League records during
the regular season, you were a plus four player, which
was not up to your regular potential. We are going to
pay you an additional $1,000.00 bonus if you are plus
ten or better during the regular season this year and a
further $1,000.00 bonus if you are plus twenty or better
during the regular season.

We are so happy with your training camp that I am looking forward to your having one of your finest years and
in this respect we are also prepared to pay you $1,500.00
bonus if you make the third All-Star team and an additional $1,500.00 if you make the second All-Star team and an
additional $2,000.00 if you make the first All-Star team,
making a total possible bonus of $5,000.00 if you make the
first All-Star team in the National Hockey League.

Good luck for the coming season.

Sincerely yours,

Sam Pollock

Sam Pollock,
Vice President & General Manager.

SP:D

Attach to Richard Contract

CLUB DE HOCKEY CANADIEN INC.

2313 St. Catherine St. West · Tel. WEllington 2-6131 · Montreal 25, P.Q.

Le 16 octobre 1968

PERSONNELLE & CONFIDENTIELLE

Monsieur Henri Richard,
2,000, boulevard de la Concorde,
Duvernay,
Cité Laval, Québec.

Cher Henri,

La présente fait suite à notre conversation d'hier matin relativement à l'ajustement apporté à votre salaire, soit de $37,500.00 pour la saison 1968-69 au lieu de ce qui était stipulé sur votre contrat.

Aussi, tel que je vous ai mentionné, après avoir vérifié vos records, établis au cours des treize (13) dernières années, votre moyenne de points durant une saison régulière se chiffrerait à 57, et ce tout en incluant la saison dernière. Ainsi, si vous atteigniez 57 points au cours de la présente saison, nous vous remettrions un boni additionnel de $2,500.00.

De plus, l'an dernier, d'après les statistiques de la Ligue, au cours de la saison régulière, vous vous classiez en tant que joueur d'ordre 'plus quatre', ce qui est inférieur à votre potentiel habituel. Nous vous accorderons un boni additionnel de $1,000.00 si vous vous classez en tant que joueur d'ordre 'plus dix' ou mieux au cours de la saison régulière cette année et, encore, un second boni de $1,000.00 vous sera remis si vous atteignez l'ordre 'plus vingt' ou mieux, au cours de la saison régulière.

Nous sommes tellement satisfaits de votre camp d'entraînement que je suis persuadé que vous aurez une de vos meilleures saisons. A cet effet, nous sommes également disposés à vous accorder un boni de $1,500.00 si vous parvenez à vous mériter un poste avec la troisième équipe étoile, $1,500.00 de plus si vous vous classez avec la deuxième équipe étoile et enfin un autre boni de $2,000.00

....../2

Monsieur Henri Richard,
Page 2,
Le 16 octobre 1968.

si vous vous alignez avec la première équipe, pour un total possible de $5,000.00 de bonis si vous faites parti de la première équipe étoile de la ligue de hockey Nationale.

Bonne chance.

Sincèrement,

Sam Pollock

Sam Pollock,
Vice-président et gérant général.

SP:dc

CLUB DE HOCKEY CANADIEN INC.

2313 St. Catherine Street West   Tel.: 932-6131   Montreal 25, P.Q.

November 13, 1968

Mr. C.S. Campbell, President,
National Hockey League,
922 Sun Life Building,
Montreal 110.

Dear Mr. Campbell:

You will probably want to attach the enclosed copy

of letter to Henri Richard's contract.

Very truly yours,

Sam Pollock,
Vice President &
General Manager.

Encl.
SP:D

Established 1909—More than a half century of professional hockey leadership

Hockey Hall of Fame

Imperial Oil – Turofsky/Hockey Hall of Fame

Spot the Hall of Famers

Hockey Hall of Fame

To keep teams in the loop, every week the National Hockey League would circulate a bulletin that detailed the comings and goings of players, who had signed, who had their amateur status reinstated, and other goodies. Bulletin No. 236, dated November 14, 1945, was dramatically different from earlier bulletins in the year, when so much of it involved players serving Canada or the United States during the Second World War. It's also dramatically different because of two names buried in the bulletin that went on to legendary status. There are two important notes from Olympia Incorporated, the parent company of the Detroit Red Wings: (1) Gordon Howe had been moved from the reserve list of Indianapolis Capitals of the AHL (where he never played a game) to the Omaha Knights of the USHL; and (2) Terrance G. Sawchuk had been moved from Indianapolis's reserve list to that of the Knights as well. But how's this for a comparison? Howe went on to play 1,167 regular season games in the NHL, and Sawchuk tended goal for 971 NHL games. Of the other players named on the NHL portion of the bulletin, in total, the 68 skaters played 2,566 NHL games—and the few other major names, such as John Sorrell and Hec Kilrea, never made it back to the big league. As for the netminders, there's only a handful listed, and combined, they played 302 games.

Terry Sawchuk (top left) as a member of the Indianapolis Capitals. In action from December 19, 1946 (top right), rookie Gordie Howe (also pictured above) maintains his balance after a hit by Howie Meeker, at Maple Leaf Gardens.

BULLETIN NO. 236   Montreal, November 14th, 1945

The NATIONAL HOCKEY LEAGUE advises:

Suspension of Player Tony Demers has been lifted by Club de Hockey Canadiens Inc.

Players Archie Wilder, Tony Demers, Frank Bennett, Arthur Shoquist, Leslie Ramsay, Douglas Webster, Kenneth McAuley and Cyril Rouse have been reinstated as amateurs by the C.A.H.A.

Player William A. Carse has been unconditionally released by Chicago National Hockey Team Inc. and his name removed from their Special Reserve List.

Players Roy Hawkey, David Heath and John Hrushka having been given their outright release, their names have been removed from the Contingent Reserve List of Chicago National Hockey Team Inc.

Player Arthur Wiebe having been given his unconditional release, his name has been removed from the Suspended List of Chicago Black Hawks.

Suspension of Player Herman Gruhn has been lifted and he has been given his release by Club de Hockey Canadien Inc.

Notice of Negotiation with Players Vernon Smith and George Robinson has been filed by New York Rangers.

Player Ralph Nattrass and Goalkeeper Douglas Jackson are on loan from Chicago National Hockey Team Inc. to the Kansas City Club and their names have been returned to the Reserve List and Goalkeepers Reserve List respectively of Chicago Black Hawks.

Player Bert

Player Will
Team Inc. for failure

Suspension
to the Reserve List o

Goalkeeper

Players Ed
from Organized hockey

Goalkeeper
Reserve List to the

Goalkeeper
Reserve List of Ind

Goalkeeper
Reserve List of Det

---

(2)

NATIONAL HOCKEY LEAGUE (Cont'd)

Player Robert Thorpe has been transferred from the Contingent Negotiation List of Detroit Red Wings to the Reserve List of the Omaha Club.

Player Eric Prentice has been transferred from the Contingent Reserve List of Pittsburgh to the Reserve List of Toronto Maple Leaf Hockey Club Ltd.,

Player Eric Prentice has been transferred from the Reserve List of Toronto Maple Leaf Hockey Club Ltd. to the Reserve List of Detroit Red Wings.

Player Geo. Mara has been transferred from the Contingent Negotiation List of Detroit Red Wings to the Reserve List of Toronto Maple Leafs.

Player George Mara has been removed from the Reserve List of Toronto Maple Leafs.

Olympia Incorporated advise per Reserve List, Form "D", as follows:

Player Gordon Howe has been transferred from the Reserve List of Indianapolis to the Reserve List of Detroit Red Wings.

Player Gerald Brown has been transferred from the Contingent Reserve List to the Reserve List of Detroit Red Wings.

Players Norman McAtee and Roly McLenahan have been transferred from the Reserve List of Indianapolis to the Reserve List of Detroit Red Wings.

Player Gordon Petrie has been transferred from the Contingent Reserve List of Indianapolis to the Reserve List of the Omaha Club.

Player Barry Sullivan has been transferred from the Reserve List of Omaha to the Reserve List of the Indianapolis Club.

Players Patrick A. Lundy and Rod F. Morrison have been transferred from the Contingent Reserve List to the Reserve List of the Indianapolis Club.

OLYMPIA INCORPORATED advise per Reserve List, Form "D":

Players Keith Burgess, Morden Skinner and Rudy J. Migay have been removed from the Reserve List of the Indianapolis Club.

Players Jas. D. Skinner, Geo. Edwards, Roy C. Tingren, Lee Foglin, Jas. Uniac, Fred A. Glover, Benedict Woit, Joseph R. Mayer, Donald M. Morrison, Conrad Poitras, Maxwell Quackenbush and Geo. William Yorke have been transferred from the Reserve List of Indianapolis to the Reserve List of the Omaha Club.

Players Cecil H. Allen, Hector Kilrea, Wm. Jacobson, Gordon Barefoot, W. A. Brennan, Roy H. Glover, Wilfred McManus, Mirco Narduzzi, Jack T. O'Mara, Gerald Olinski, Wm. Parsons and Fred Sparks have been removed from the Contingent Reserve List of the Indianapolis Club.

Goalkeepers Thos. McGrattan and Terance G. Sawchuk have been transferred from the Goalkeepers Reserve List of Indianapolis to the Goalkeepers Reserve List of the Omaha Club.

Goalkeeper Jas. W. Grenway has been removed from the Goalkeepers Reserve List of the Indianapolis Club.

Player John Sorrell has been removed from the Voluntarily Retired List of the Indianapolis Club.

---

(3)

Y LEAGUE (CONT'D)

A INC. Advise per Reserve List, Form "D" (Cont'd):

s Armand Dufault and Bernard McCarthy have been transferred from the erve List of Indianapolis to the Reserve List of the Omaha Club.

KEY LEAGUE advises:

Armand Lemieux has been transferred from the Contingent Reserve List eserve List of the Providence Club.

Jas. C. MacIntosh, John Baby and John Horeck have been transferred List of St. Louis to the Reserve List of the Buffalo Club.

oger Gabana has been transferred from the Reserve List of the o the Reserve List of the Pittsburgh Club.

red from the Contingent Reserve List to
b.

from the Reserve List of the
Club.

as been lifted and his name returned
List of the Buffalo Club.

oved from the Goalkeepers Reserve

McKay have been transferred
serve List of the Buffalo Club.

l Thurier and Louis Trudel
re on loan from Chicago National
serve List of that Club.

ally released by the Indianapolis

by the Hershey Club and his name

l from the Contingent Reserve
a Club.

from the Reserve List of

from the Reserve List of Hershey

om the Contingent Reserve List
atement as an amateur.

the Reserve List of the Detroit
b.

Polo Goes to Camp

That the coach's letter is sincere and welcoming, there is no doubt. But being nice is one thing, and winning is another. Ted Garvin was the coach of the Detroit Red Wings in 1973–74 and lasted 11 games into the season, going 2–8–1, before being replaced by Hall of Famer Alex Delvecchio. "I don't imagine [Garvin] ever watched me play," said Dennis Polonich, reflecting on being taken in the 1973 draft, in the eighth round, 118th overall. "He didn't last very long, so I never got to know him other than training camp." The rookies from Western Canada were flown into Winnipeg for a meet-and-greet of sorts, and "Polo" remembers a fruit basket awaiting him, with a message that said, "Welcome to the Red Wings organization." Wearing a new suit and new tie, Polonich welcomed the adventure, having grown up on a farm in Foam Lake, Saskatchewan. "That was one of my first airplane flights as well, from Saskatoon to Winnipeg, and then there were many more after that," he said. Ned Harkness, GM of the Wings, presented him with a contract. "I think I got a $7,500 signing bonus. They asked if I wanted it then, and I said, 'No, I'll get it when I go to training camp,' because I was being Mr. Nice Guy. I had money in the bank, because I worked in Flin Flon in the mine. I had spending money. I got home, and I told my friends and my father that I'd signed for $7,500. My dad said, 'Where's the money?' I said, 'I'll get it when I go to training camp.' He said, 'No, you'll get it now.' So I sheepishly called them from my grandma's house, because we never had a phone on the farm, and I got them to send me $3,500 and I got the other $4,000 when I went to training camp." Polonich spent the season in London, England, with the Wings-affiliated Lions club, and he cracked the big-league roster for 1974–75 and played pro hockey until 1987.

Dennis Polonich started his NHL career in Detroit.

DETROIT HOCKEY CLUB, INC.

Member of the National Hockey League

OLYMPIA STADIUM / 5920 GRAND RIVER, DETROIT, MICHIGAN 48208 / TELEPHONE (313) 895-7000

June 12, 1973

Mr. Denis Polonich
Box 176
Foam Lake, Saskatchewan

Dear Denis:

I would like to take this opportunity to welcome you to the
Detroit Red Wings' organization and to let you know that I am
looking forward to meeting you at training camp this fall.

If you have any questions or problems before that time, please
feel free to contact me. I'm sure you'll find that I'm a very easy
guy to talk to. With regard to my coaching, I consider myself a
very fair but firm coach to play for and I only know one thing and
that is to win. I think Detroit has lost long enough and so, from
now on - we win!

We felt you were worth drafting, so we must have thought a
"helluva" lot of you. Positions are open on every club in the
Detroit organization, so come into camp prepared to give it your
best effort and you will most certainly be rewarded for your effort
and hard work.

So, once again Denis, welcome to the club and we'll see you in
the fall.

Sincerely,

DETROIT HOCKEY CLUB, INC.

Ted Garvin
Coach

TG/11

DETROIT RED WINGS

Terrible Ted Turns Management

There is no doubt that Ted Lindsay was a great hockey player. Aggressive and determined, he's in the Hockey Hall of Fame for a reason. Born in Renfrew but raised in Kirkland Lake, Ontario, Lindsay played a year at St. Michael's College in Toronto, and he was a part of a 1944 Memorial Cup win as a loaner to the Oshawa Generals. He was fortunate to end up in the Detroit Red Wings organization, where the left winger was always at the top of the point standings during his heyday of the 1940s and 1950s. Behind the scenes, it was not an easy ride as Lindsay clashed with management and tried to start the first NHL Players' Association. After his playing days, Lindsay worked as a TV commentator until the Red Wings repatriated him, hiring him to be the club's general manager in March 1977. For someone so outspoken during his career, Lindsay found the transition—and competition—a challenge. "The World Hockey [Association] was still in existence. You couldn't penalize anybody, because if you penalized them, or fined them, they'd quit you and go to the World Hockey," he said. "I recognized very quickly that you can't put a real winning team together when the World Hockey was in existence." When the Wings were struggling in March 1980, Lindsay stepped behind the bench and replaced coach Bobby Kromm. After he was dumped as GM on April 11, he stuck around as coach until he was fired in November 1980. Lindsay did get a kick out of the gushing fan-letter portion of the note from Leafs GM Jim Gregory over the exchange of Dan Maloney for Errol Thompson and a host of draft picks. "Jim is a great, great gentleman, and I look forward to seeing him all the time." Lindsay was elected to the Hockey Hall of Fame as an Honoured Member in 1966.

There was a lot of hockey for Ted Lindsay between his time playing at St. Michael's College and as an executive with the Detroit Red Wings.

MAPLE LEAF GARDENS LIMITED

60 CARLTON STREET, TORONTO, ONTARIO M5B 1L1 · (416)368-1641

March 16th, 1978

Mr. Ted Lindsay
General Manager
Detroit Red Wings Hockey Club
5920 Grand River at McGraw
DETROIT, Michigan 48208

Dear Ted,

Hope this finds you in good health and enjoying the NHL wars as we wend our way to the playoffs.

May I take this opportunity to tell you that, since my St. Mike's days, I have been an ardent fan of yours and I couldn't resist writing this letter to tell you how much I enjoyed our discussions regarding our recent trade. There is no doubt in my mind that Detroit's future is in the best of hands.

In regards to our trade, my wish is that both of us come out, 'smelling like roses', and I mean that sincerely. I am enclosing a copy of Errol's contract and Standard Assignment Forms, which I would ask that you sign and forward on to Central Registry at your convenience. Would you please forward a copy of Dan Maloney's contract to our office. Should you desire any medical information we have in our files on Errol, we would be happy to forward it to you.

Also, it is my understanding, although I would need your confirmation on this, that the first round draft choice is to be used by you either in 1979, 1980 or 1981. I would appreciate your comments on this.

If there is ever anything I can do to assist you in any way, kindly do not hesitate to call. Looking forward to seeing you soon.

Yours very truly,

J. M. GREGORY
GENERAL MANAGER

JMG/ps
encl.

JUL 25 1978

DETROIT HOCKEY CLUB, INC.

Member of the National Hockey League

OLYMPIA STADIUM / 5920 GRAND RIVER, DETROIT, MICHIGAN 48208 / TELEPHONE (313) 895-7000

July 18, 1978

Mr. Jim Gregory
Maple Leaf Gardens, Ltd.
60 Carlton St.
Toronto, Ont. M5B 1L1

Dear Jim:

RE: DAN MALONEY TRADE

Thanks for your letter of June 30th, and this will confirm that my understanding of our deal is as outlined in your letter. To repeat:

1. Detroit may notify you in any year prior to March 15th of our intention to take the first round selection. *1979 1980 1981*

2. If you have not heard from us by March 15th, you may trade the draft choice at any time after that date.

3. The year we decide to make the selection, you will receive our 2nd round draft choice.

We've forwarded Don Ellis a copy of this letter. Best regards.

Sincerely,

DETROIT HOCKEY CLUB, INC.

Ted Lindsay
General Manager

TL/rh

Stanfield Leaves Boston with a New Deal, Two Rings

Fred Stanfield heads over the boards.

Looking back on the May 1973 trade that took him from Boston to Minnesota in exchange for goaltender Gilles Gilbert, forward Fred Stanfield can't help but consider the behind-the-scenes manoeuvrings on all sides. For one thing, Stanfield had a no-trade contract, but he'd had enough of butting heads with Bruins GM Harry Sinden. Yet, their relationship was amicable enough that, just before the deal was made, Sinden extended Stanfield's contract with some bonuses. "Harry kind of outsmarted Wren Blair a little bit," surmised Stanfield, referring to the GM of the North Stars. "Blair was getting older, and Harry kind of took advantage of that, and he played around with Wren Blair, and I think he tricked him into making the trade." With Gerry Cheevers in the net, Stanfield and the Bruins won two Stanley Cups—in 1970 and 1972—but "Cheesy" jumped to the WHA, and Boston used four different goalies in 1972–73 trying, unsuccessfully, to win again. "Harry needed a goaltender really bad for the Bruins, and he wanted Gilles Gilbert," said Stanfield. "I was disappointed because of him trying to get rid of me after what I'd done for him.... That was my own opinion, but sometimes that's part of hockey, the way they treat you." On lesser teams in Minnesota and then Buffalo, Stanfield's numbers dropped off from his Beantown consistency as a 20-goal-a-year man. He was a player-coach in his final season, 1978–79 with the AHL's Hershey Bears, and then tried coaching junior, with the OHA's Niagara Falls Flyers the following year, but found it wasn't for him. Settling in Buffalo, Stanfield owned a business that sold new and used office furniture for 20 years.

BOSTON BRUINS

BOSTON PROFESSIONAL HOCKEY ASSOCIATION, INC.
150 CAUSEWAY ST. BOSTON, MASS. 02114

TELEPHONES (AREA CODE 617) 227-0277, 227-3206

EXECUTIVE OFFICES

May 24, 1973

Mr. Wren Blair
General Manager
Minnesota Northstars
7901 Cedar Avenue South
Bloomington, Minnesota 55420

Dear Wren:

      Enclosed please find Standard Assignment Agreement papers
with regard to Fred Stanfield. Please sign and forward to Central Registry
for registration.

      With best regards, I am

                   Sincerely yours,

                   Harry Sinden
                   Managing Director

HS:cm
Enclosures 3

BOSTON BRUINS

BOSTON PROFESSIONAL HOCKEY ASSOCIATION, INC.
150 CAUSEWAY ST. BOSTON, MASS. 02114

TELEPHONES (AREA CODE 617) 227-0277, 227-3206

EXECUTIVE OFFICES

May 24, 1973

Mr. Wren Blair
General Manager
Minnesota Northstars
7901 Cedar Avenue South
Bloomington, Minnesota 55420

Dear Wren:

      I am writing to memorialize our negotiations of May 22, 1973 with respect to the
trade which took place between your club, the Minnesota Northstars, and the Boston Bruins.

      It is my understanding that the Boston Bruins have the following obligations in respect
to that transaction:

    A. A $5,000.00 cash settlement to Stanfield.

    B. A $10,000.00 increase to his salary for the years 1973-74 and 1974-75.

    C. A $7,500.00 increase to his salary for the years 1975-76 and 1976-77.

It is also my understanding that the Minnesota Northstars are obligated to a $25,000.00
payment, as a signing bonus, to Gilbert. If the foregoing represents our mutual understanding
of the transaction, kindly write me a letter so indicating.

      I want to take this opportunity to thank you for the very professional way in which you
conducted your part of the Stanfield/Gilbert deal. I know you feel, as I do, that to all parties
concerned, everything was saved out of an apparently hopeless situation.

      Looking forward to seeing you at the draft meetings in Montreal, I remain

                   Sincerely yours,

                   Harry Sinden
                   Managing Director

HS:cm

Trouble Bruin

Being traded is one thing, but getting the finances straight afterward is another. After trading Jacques Plante to the Bruins, the Leafs furnished a copy of the contract and asked Boston to cut a cheque for $13,446.32, "which covers twenty-eight (28) days' salary for him." The Bruins did that, but a complication arose at the end of the season. Plante wrote to Bruins GM Harry Sinden on August 8, 1973, asking, "What happened to my share of the money for the second-place finish, the playoffs, and my expense money to go to Boston from Toronto ($100-plus) and to come back home in Magog. Please ask your accountant." Not having heard from Sinden, Plante wrote again on December 6, but to Weston Adams, the president of the Bruins. In March 1974, Plante escalated the gripe, writing to NHL president Clarence Campbell on the letterhead of the WHA Quebec Nordiques, for whom Plante was coach and general manager. The Leafs had paid for his accommodations in the past, and he expected the Bruins to pay for his stay at the Sonesta Hotel: "Mr. Sinden then agreed to pay for my meals at the hotel since this is much more expensive than eating at home.... The hotel bill came to $1,010.44 in all, including my meals and phone calls." Campbell sent it all back to the Bruins, prompting Sinden's letter. It was all settled on August 7, 1974, when Sinden admitted that the playoff share was never paid to Plante, and he was due a "check equal to 14/78ths of $2,500 representative of the number of games he was with our team." Plante still was not quite satisfied, though, and wrote a long handwritten letter to Campbell further expressing his frustrations.

Jacques Plante in net during his short stay in Boston.

September 16, 1974

Mr. C.S. Campbell, president,
National Hockey League
9h0 Sunlife Building,
Montreal, P.Q.

Dear Mr. Campbell,

You are an honest man and a fair man. This you have provent
during your many years as president of the National Hockey
League.
In your letter dated September 5, 1974 you tell me that I
received my share of Championship money; I beleive
you. If I demanded it at first, it was because Boston told
me that they sent the money to Toronto. In my life I
never knew how much we received for finishing money
or playoff wins.
My basic salary I knew and from then on, I played
to win each gagme and championship. Each lost I took
upon myself as I was the last man before a goal.
When I left New-York in 1965 I told them it was not
a salary matter and that if I ever came back, I would
go to them before doing something else; which I did.
Since they knew I needed a knee operation before
returning to action, (I told them) they did not sign me.
So I went to St-Louis, where Scotty Bowman knew
also I needed an operation. I did not want to sign a
contract under false pretention and not play if the
operation went wrong.
I did with Boston what I did in New-York and told
Harry Sinden the same thing about a come back.
Like in New-York, I told Boston in plenty of time for
them to get another goalie (May 2, 1973).
They signed Gilles Gilbert who is a good goalie and
will be better in the coming years. He will be in Boston
for the next 15 years --- so they gain by me retiring
instead of staying. Had I stayed, Minnesota would
not have traded Gilbert this year.

3---

2

I did not leave Boston for money either. I was
offered $90,000 for 1974 and made $60.000.ºº in
Quebec, less the playoff share the Bruins made.
This I knew before hand.

I had no choice, like in New.York and took the
only decision I could make.

When an employe leaves his job, the company does
not fine him but after his week or two notice,
they pay him his 4%.

I gave a long enough notice to Boston and they
signed a good young goalie.

New York brought up Eddie Giacomin, kept me on
their list and gave me my equipment (not sold).
Boston on the other hand got mad at me. Kept my
equipment and said they lost it (have you ever in
your life heard of this in pro hockey) and if you
look at the protected list of June 1973, you will
not see my name on the Boston rosters.

May I also ask you to see the receit the post-office
gives the sender of a register letter. "The letter the
Bruins are saying they sent me in the fall of 1973".

And I have to come back to my traveling money.
Boston never told me I had to fill in an expense
sheet of paper. Harry Sinden only told me to give
my sheet of expenses to his secretary...which I
did, with him looking on.

If I need to fill in the form, I can still do it,
but there is no way they can get out of this in
giving such an excuse.

The league sais they pay the expenses to and from
the home rink and they did not do it. If a move is
made during the season they move the furniture,
which I did not charge them.

To end this long letter; Mr. Campbell please tell
Boston to pay me my due. How can they find
me for not going to their camp when I was not on
their list, was not protected and was not invited.

---3

You told me to write you if you could be of some help. I am doing so since my problems started with Boston.

I would not want to go to court for a mere $600.00, but if your answer is again negative, I will not bother you anymore and hire a lawyer.

Wether you can do this for me or not. I thank you for taking time to answer my too many letters and I wish you long life and a healthy one in whatever you chose to do from now on. I remain,

Yours sincerely,

[signature: Jacques Plante]

My new address is
Jacques Plante
10127 - 121 st. Apt. 180,
Edmonton, Alberta.

What the Dickens

From November 2, 1947 forward, Ernie Dickens's name would forever be tied to the other six names involved in a massive trade between Toronto and Chicago. Going to the Black Hawks were Gus Bodnar, Bud Poile, Gaye Stewart (who formed an entire line known as The Flying Forts, since they were all from Fort William, Ontario), and Bob Goldham, and heading north to the Leafs were Cy Thomas and future Hall of Famer Max Bentley. Said NHL president Clarence Campbell at the time: "Chicago needs manpower, and they certainly will benefit by getting such NHL calibre players from the Leafs. The trade indicates that Toronto is willing to sacrifice the players for a man like Bentley, who can give the Leafs the nucleus for a top-notch third line." Contrast that to the thoughts of Poile years later: "It wasn't a bad deal—for Toronto. After they got Bentley, the Leafs won maybe 20 Stanley Cups." Essentially, Dickens was a throw-in from the Leafs' minor-league system. But in the late 1930s, the fleet defenceman was a hot prospect out of Winnipeg. In 1939, future sportswriting legend Scott Young wrote about Dickens in the *Winnipeg Free Press*: a "black-haired blue line bouncer . . . who has been compared to the best ever produced by local hockey competition." The strength of the Leafs blue line made it tough for Dickens to move up the depth chart, and he played only 25 games for the team in 1941–42 and 1945–46, with three years of military service in between. But he faced no such playing-time issues in Chicago with the woeful Hawks, and he was a solid part of the team from the trade through to 1951. His last full season came in 1951–52 with the Pacific Coast League's Calgary Stampeders, and then he acted as a player-coach for a single year with the Oshawa Truckmen of Ontario's senior "B" league. Dickens, a member of the Manitoba Hockey Hall of Fame, settled in nearby Bowmanville and ran a fish business.

Ernie Dickens was a part of one of the biggest trades in NHL history.

NATIONAL HOCKEY LEAGUE

PRESIDENT
FRANK CALDER
910 SUN LIFE BUILDING
TEL., MARQUETTE 3438
RESIDENCE, ELWOOD 5917

MONTREAL,   September 19th 1938

RECEIVED

SEP 20 1938

Connie Smythe Esq.,
Maple Leaf Gardens,
Toronto.

Dear Mr Smythe:-

At your request the name of player Ernie
Dickens, Falcon Rangers Juniors, of Winnipeg,
has to-day been placed on the Negotiation List
of Toronto Maple Leaf Hockey Club Limited
replacing that of Webster, with whom negotiations
have been abandoned.

Sincerely yours,

Frank Calder

---

*This application must
be completed and signed
in duplicate*

ORIGINAL

CANADIAN AMATEUR HOCKEY ASSOCIATION
Professional Try-out Application Form
SEASON 1938-1939

The undersigned player hereby applies to the Canadian Amateur Hockey Association for permission to try-out
with the Toronto Maple Leaf Hockey Club of the _____ National _____ Professional Hockey
League under the conditions set out below.

The undersigned player may try-out and practice providing no contract has been signed and no money taken
outside of legitimate travelling and living expenses.

The player granted this privilege may not, under any circumstances, take part in a professional league game.

Upon the issue of this sanction the player shall be debarred from participation in amateur games and before
being again permitted to participate in amateur competition, such player must return to the Branch from which he
set out unless he has already given notice of his intention to transfer to another Branch, in which case his application shall be subject to the regular transfer rules.

If a player does not conform with these regulations in trying out with a professional team, he is automatically
suspended.

Date of signing *Sept 19th* 1938   *Ernie Dickens*
                                                              (Player sign here)

Countersigned,   *1488 Elgin Ave. Winnipeg.*
                                                              Address

_____
Registrar-Treasurer
CANADIAN AMATEUR HOCKEY ASSOCIATION

_____
C.A.H.A. Branch

Trade Ends Mortson's Championship Ways

Gus Bodnar, Al Rollins, Cal Gardner, and Gus Mortson pose as Black Hawks on their return to at Maple Leaf Gardens in January 1953.

When "Old Hardrock" Gus Mortson was traded to the Chicago Black Hawks on September 11, 1952, he was joining a sad-sack team that hadn't made the playoffs since 1946, a rough change of events for Mortson after four Stanley Cups in six seasons with the Maple Leafs. Toronto GM Conn Smythe had made the deal—Mortson, Ray Hannigan, Cal Gardner, and goalie Al Rollins for keeper Harry Lumley—and actually admitted it could help the other squad: "Anyway, it wouldn't be bad to see Chicago in the playoffs after their lean years," Smythe told Al Nickleson of the *Globe and Mail*. In the same story, Mortson assessed the deal: "Four-for-one trade, eh? Guess I can't be very good. I just returned from a trip in Chicago where I heard some rumours about this. So I started making some friends there. It might be a sign of good luck. Ever since juvenile hockey, I've had the good fortune to be on championship teams or on teams that were eliminated by the eventual champions. The change might be good." The Hawks did make the playoffs in 1953, but they lost in the semis to the Montreal Canadiens, that year's Cup winner. A tough defenceman who led the league in penalty minutes four times in his career, Mortson was named captain of the Hawks in 1954, but he never made the NHL playoffs again, not even in his final season in 1958–59 with the Detroit Red Wings. Upon Mortson's retirement, Chicago beat writer Bud Booth praised Mortson: "Hockey players that are both good and colourful are rare discoveries."

May 5, 1953

Chicago National Enterprises,
North LaSalle St.,
CHICAGO, Illinois,
U. S. A.

Dear Sirs:

This will be your authority to forward my next

salary cheque c/o The Royal Bank of Canada, Bay & Wellington Sts.,

Toronto, Ontario.

Yours truly,

J. A. Mortson

J A Mortson

May 13, 1953

Mr. Gus Mortson
47 Rossland Drive
Toronto, Ont., Canada

Dear Gus:

I wish to acknowledge yours of May 5th authorizing me to send your
next salary check to the Royal Bank of Canada, Bay & Wellington Sts.,
Toronto, Ont., Canada. Would you please be more explicit and advise
as to whether you mean your Play-off check or your first salary
check for next year and if the check should be made payable to the
Royal Bank of Canada. In any event, we would much prefer that the
check be made payable to you as customary and mail it to the Royal
Bank of Canada where you could go in and endorse it if you want the
check turned over to the bank. Will you please advise.

Kind regards and hoping you are enjoying a pleasant summer.

Very truly yours,

CHICAGO BLACK HAWKS

WJT:fn

A Happy Dea Just Wanted to Play

In retrospect, Billy Dea is honest about his talents and the way his 20-year pro-hockey career turned out. He started in the old WHL with Saskatoon and Vancouver before making the NHL with the Rangers. After a season and a half in Detroit, he was dealt to Chicago but ended up buried with the AHL's Buffalo Bisons for a decade. "I was happy to be in the league, but I never considered myself a great player, so I never, ever felt that I had a lot of bargaining power," admitted Dea. GM Tommy Ivan signed him to a 1959–60 contract with the Black Hawks, but negotiated similarly to Jack Adams of the Red Wings. "They just basically said, 'Here's the figure' and maybe a few bonuses or something," said Dea. "I was no negotiator, I'll tell you that." With the 1967 expansion looming, the Hawks put Dea on the playoff roster, where he was paid $100 a game. "I only got two or three shifts a game. It was nice. Of course, I think that's what helped me get drafted the next year," he said. The Penguins took Dea in the expansion draft, and he stuck around there for two seasons, finishing his career back in Detroit with more stints in the AHL and CHL. Post hockey, Dea was a scout and was a part of the Red Wings staff that drafted Steve Yzerman. "He really fell into our lap. Steve was rated number four," said Dea, rhyming off the first three draftees: Brian Lawton, Sylvain Turgeon, Pat LaFontaine. "[Wings owner] Mr. Illich wanted Pat LaFontaine, because he was a local kid, but we were happy we got Steve."

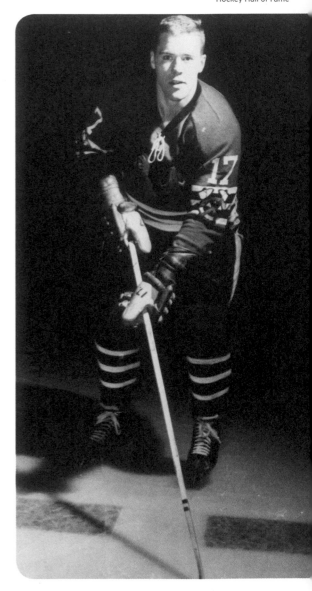

Billy Dea played in Chicago and was a mainstay of the club's AHL affiliate in Buffalo.

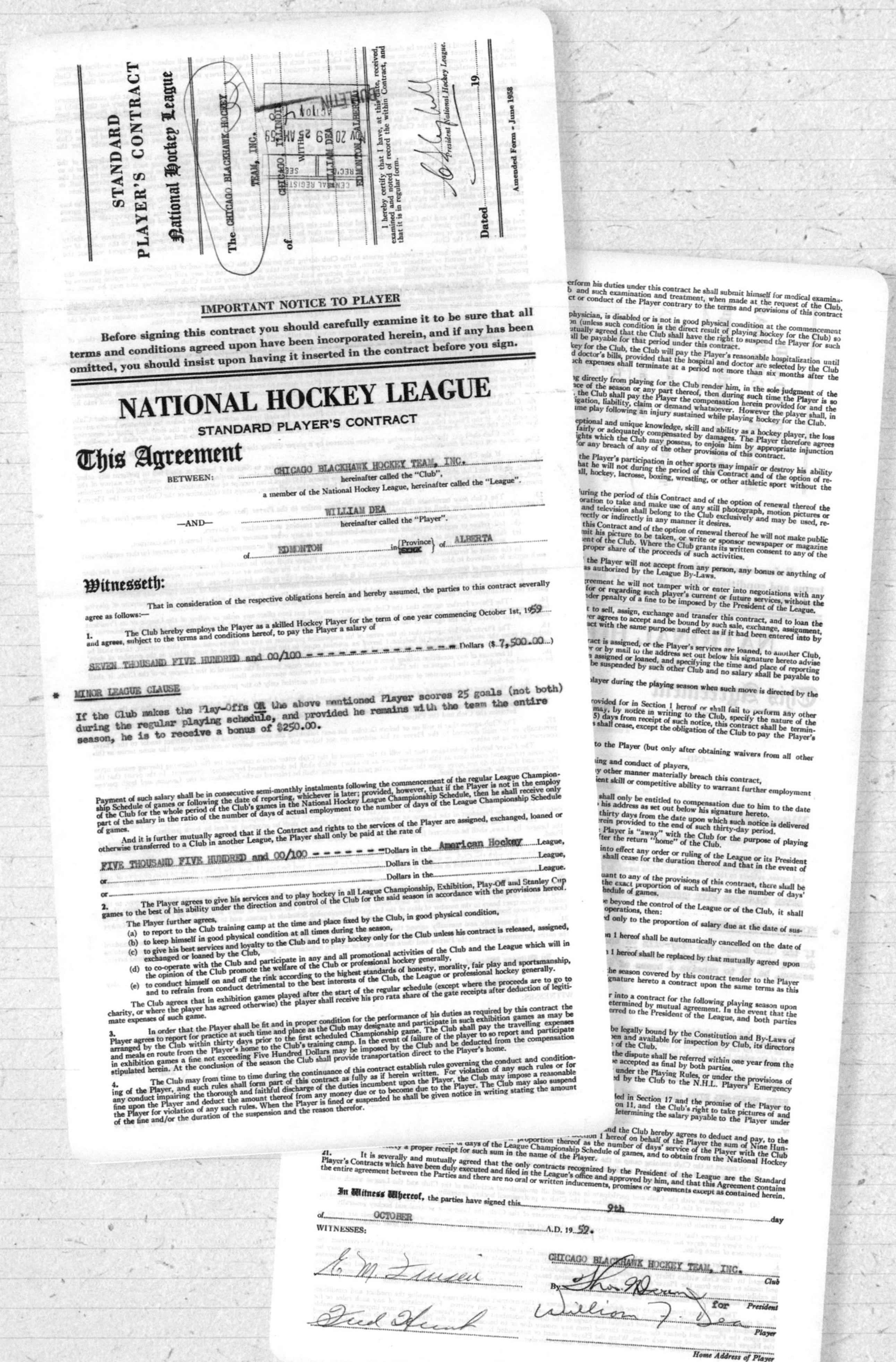

IMPORTANT NOTICE TO PLAYER

Before signing this contract you should carefully examine it to be sure that all terms and conditions agreed upon have been incorporated herein, and if any has been omitted, you should insist upon having it inserted in the contract before you sign.

NATIONAL HOCKEY LEAGUE

STANDARD PLAYER'S CONTRACT

This Agreement

BETWEEN: CHICAGO BLACKHAWK HOCKEY TEAM, INC.
hereinafter called the "Club",
a member of the National Hockey League, hereinafter called the "League".

—AND—

WILLIAM DEA
hereinafter called the "Player".

of   EDMONTON   in {Province} of   ALBERTA

Witnesseth:

That in consideration of the respective obligations herein and hereby assumed, the parties to this contract severally agree as follows:—

1. The Club hereby employs the Player as a skilled Hockey Player for the term of one year commencing October 1st, 1959, and agrees, subject to the terms and conditions hereof, to pay the Player a salary of

SEVEN THOUSAND FIVE HUNDRED and 00/100 ————————— Dollars ($ 7,500.00)

MINOR LEAGUE CLAUSE

If the Club makes the Play-Offs OR the above mentioned Player scores 25 goals (not both) during the regular playing schedule, and provided he remains with the team the entire season, he is to receive a bonus of $250.00.

Payment of such salary shall be in consecutive semi-monthly instalments following the commencement of the regular League Championship Schedule of games or following the date of reporting, whichever is later; provided, however, that if the Player is not in the employ of the Club for the whole period of the Club's games in the National Hockey League Championship Schedule, then he shall receive only part of the salary in the ratio of the number of days of actual employment to the number of days of the League Championship Schedule of games.

And it is further mutually agreed that if the Contract and rights to the services of the Player are assigned, exchanged, loaned or otherwise transferred to a Club in another League, the Player shall only be paid at the rate of

FIVE THOUSAND FIVE HUNDRED and 00/100 ————— Dollars in the   American Hockey   League,
or ———————————————————— Dollars in the .... League.
or ———————————————————— Dollars in the .... League.

2. The Player agrees to give his services and to play hockey in all League Championship, Exhibition, Play-Off and Stanley Cup games to the best of his ability under the direction and control of the Club for the said season in accordance with the provisions hereof.

The Player further agrees,
(a) to report to the Club training camp at the time and place fixed by the Club, in good physical condition,
(b) to keep himself in good physical condition at all times during the season,
(c) to give his best services and loyalty to the Club and to play hockey only for the Club unless his contract is released, assigned, exchanged or loaned by the Club,
(d) to co-operate with the Club and participate in any and all promotional activities of the Club and the League which will in the opinion of the Club promote the welfare of the Club or professional hockey generally,
(e) to conduct himself on and off the rink according to the highest standards of honesty, morality, fair play and sportsmanship, and to refrain from conduct detrimental to the best interests of the Club, the League or professional hockey generally.

The Club agrees that in exhibition games played after the start of the regular schedule (except where the proceeds are to go to charity, or where the player has agreed otherwise) the player shall receive his pro rata share of the gate receipts after deduction of legitimate expenses of such game.

3. In order that the Player shall be fit and in proper condition for the performance of his duties as required by this contract the Player agrees to report for practice at such time and place as the Club may designate and participate in such exhibition games as may be arranged by the Club within thirty days prior to the first scheduled Championship game. The Club shall pay the travelling expenses and meals en route from the Player's home to the Club's training camp. In the event of failure of the player to so report and participate in exhibition games a fine not exceeding Five Hundred Dollars may be imposed by the Club and be deducted from the compensation stipulated herein. At the conclusion of the season the Club shall provide transportation direct to the Player's home.

4. The Club may from time to time during the continuance of this contract establish rules governing the conduct and conditioning of the Player, and such rules shall form part of this contract as fully as if herein written. For violation of any such rules or for any conduct impairing the thorough and faithful discharge of the duties incumbent upon the Player, the Club may impose a reasonable fine upon the Player and deduct the amount thereof from any money due or to become due to the Player. The Club may also suspend the Player for violation of any such rules. When the Player is fined or suspended he shall be given notice in writing stating the amount of the fine and/or the duration of the suspension and the reason therefor.

[right column — partially obscured]

... perform his duties under this contract he shall submit himself for medical examination ... and such examination and treatment, when made at the request of the Club ... or conduct of the Player contrary to the terms and provisions of this contract ...

... physician, is disabled or is not in good physical condition at the commencement ... (unless such condition is the direct result of playing hockey for the Club so ... mutually agreed that the Club shall have the right to suspend the Player for such ... for that period under this contract. ... key for the Club, the Club will pay the Player's reasonable hospitalization until ... d doctor's bills, provided that the hospital and doctor are selected by the Club ... ch expenses shall terminate at a period of not more than six months after the ...

... d directly from playing for the Club render him, in the sole judgment of the ... nce of the season or any part thereof, then during such time the Player is so ... the Club shall pay the Player the compensation herein provided for and the ... gation, liability, claim or demand whatsoever. However the player shall, in ... me play following an injury sustained while playing hockey for the Club.

... ptional and unique knowledge, skill and ability as a hockey player, the loss ... fairly or adequately compensated by damages. The Player therefore agrees ... hts which the Club may possess, to enjoin him by appropriate injunction ... for any breach of any of the other provisions of this contract.

... the Player's participation in other sports may impair or destroy his ability ... that he will not during the period of this Contract and of the option of re- ... ball, hockey, lacrosse, boxing, wrestling, or other athletic sport without ...

... during the period of this Contract and of the option of renewal thereof the ... oration to take and make use of any still photograph, motion pictures or ... and television shall belong to the Club exclusively and may be used, re- ... rectly or indirectly in any manner it desires.

... this Contract and of the option of renewal thereof he will not make public ... mit his picture to be taken, or write or sponsor newspaper or magazine ... ent of the Club. Where the Club grants its written consent to any of the ... proper share of the proceeds of such activities.

... the Player will not accept from any person, any bonus or anything or ... as authorized by the League By-Laws.

... greement he will not tamper with or enter into negotiations with any ... r regarding such player's current or future services, without the ... der penalty of a fine to be imposed by the President of the League.

... er to sell, assign, exchange and transfer this contract, and to loan the ... er agrees to accept and be bound by such sale, exchange, assignment, ... act with the same purpose and effect as if it had been entered into by ...

... act is assigned, or the Player's services are loaned, to another Club, ... or by mail to the address set out below his signature hereto advise ... n assigned or loaned, and specifying the time and place of reporting ... e suspended by such other Club and no salary shall be payable to ...

... layer during the playing season when such move is directed by the ...

... provided for in Section 1 hereof or shall fail to perform any other ... may, by notice in writing to the Club, specify the nature of ... 5) days from receipt of such notice, this contract shall be termin- ... shall cease, except the obligation of the Club to pay the Player's ...

... to the Player (but only after obtaining waivers from all other ...

... ing and conduct of players, ... ny other manner materially breach this contract, ... ient skill or competitive ability to warrant further employment ...

... shall only be entitled to compensation due to him to the date ... his address as set out below his signature hereto. ... thirty days from the date upon which such notice is delivered ... erein provided to the end of such thirty-day period. ... Player is "away" with the Club for the purpose of playing ... fter the return "home" of the Club.

... into effect any order or ruling of the League or its President ... shall cease for the duration thereof and that in the event of ...

... rsuant to any of the provisions of this contract, there shall be ... the exact proportion of such salary as the number of days' ... schedule of games.

... be beyond the control of the League or of the Club, it shall ... operations, then: ... ed only to the proportion of salary due at the date of sus- ...

... 1 hereof shall be automatically cancelled on the date of ...

... 1 hereof shall be replaced by that mutually agreed upon ...

... the season covered by this contract tender to the Player ... signature hereto a contract upon the same terms as this ...

... er into a contract for the following playing season upon ... determined by mutual agreement. In the event that the ... erred to the President of the League, and both parties ...

... be legally bound by the Constitution and By-Laws of ... pen and available for inspection by Club, its directors ... t of the Club.

... the dispute shall be referred within one year from the ... se accepted as final by both parties.

... led in the Playing Rules, or under the provisions of ... by the Club to the N.H.L. Players' Emergency ...

... led in Section 17 and the promise of the Player to ... on 11, and the Club's right to take pictures of and ... determining the salary payable to the Player under ...

... and the Club hereby agrees to deduct and pay, to the ... portion thereof as the number of days' service of the Player with the Club ...

... days of the League Championship Schedule of games, and to obtain from the National Hockey ... a proper receipt for such sum in the name of ...

11. It is severally and mutually agreed that the only contracts recognized by the President of the League are the Standard Player's Contracts which have been duly executed and filed in the League's office and approved by him, and that this Agreement contains the entire agreement between the Parties and there are no oral or written inducements, promises or agreements except as contained herein.

In Witness Whereof, the parties have signed this .... 9th .... day of .... OCTOBER .... A.D. 19 52.

WITNESSES: CHICAGO BLACKHAWK HOCKEY TEAM, INC.

....   By .... for President

....   William T. Dea .... Player

         Home Address of Player

A First Class Family

What's written on the page is all well and good, but it's sometimes the handshake deals that make all the difference. Bill Gadsby, originally hailing from Edmonton, began his career with nine seasons in Chicago. The family's first daughter was born in 1953, not long after Gadsby was named to the NHL Second All-Star Team, his first such honour. Gadsby asked for a raise from Hawks GM Bill Tobin, who wrote back: "Bill, you must be walking the baby late at night." The memories make both Bill and Edna, who were married in 1952, laugh. "That's a true story," confirmed Edna. "But he did get the raise. Bill Tobin was quite a nice man." In 1954, as he sat negotiating deals with Rangers GM Muzz Patrick, he made sure to include discussion of getting his growing family to and from the Big Apple. "We called those our Productive Years, because I went [to New York] with one small child—she was only a year and a half— and I was expecting my second when we got traded from Chicago," recalled Edna Gadsby. "Then when we left New York for Detroit, we had four young children." To deal with the move, Gadsby asked for first-class travel for his family. "It was a verbal situation," confirmed the defenceman. The Hockey Hall of Fame inducted Gadsby as an Honoured Member in 1970, and he passed away in March 2016.

Toronto's swimming sensation Marilyn Bell drops the puck in a ceremonial face-off between Bill Gadsby and Teeder Kennedy on October 9, 1954, at Maple Leaf Gardens.

SEP 12 1957

STANDARD
PLAYER'S CONTRACT

National Hockey League

IMPORTANT NOTICE TO PLAYER

Before signing this contract you should carefully examine it to be sure that all terms and conditions agreed upon have been incorporated herein, and if any has been omitted, you should insist upon having it inserted in the contract before you sign.

NATIONAL HOCKEY LEAGUE

STANDARD PLAYER'S CONTRACT

This Agreement

BETWEEN:

NEW YORK RANGERS, INC.
(New York Rangers Hockey Club)
hereinafter called the "Club",
a member of the National Hockey League, hereinafter called the "League".

— AND —

WILLIAM GADSBY
hereinafter called the "Player".

10956 - 131st Street
Edmonton   in (Province/State) of Alberta

Witnesseth:

That in consideration of the respective obligations herein and hereby assumed, the parties to this contract severally agree as follows:—

1. The Club hereby employs the Player as a skilled Hockey Player for the term of one year commencing October 1st, 19...57 and agrees, subject to the terms and conditions hereof, to pay the Player a salary of

FOURTEEN THOUSAND and No/100 - - - - - - - - - - - - - - - Dollars ($ 14,000.00)

(A) The Player is to be paid an additional sum of FIVE HUNDRED and No/100 DOLLARS ($500.00) if the Club (N.Y. Rangers H. C.) finishes second (2nd) or better in the final N.H.L. Championship Schedule for the 1957-58 Season, provided the Player remains with the Club (N. Y. Rangers H. C.) for the full 1957-58 Season.

Payment of such salary shall be in consecutive semi-monthly instalments following the commencement of the regular League Championship Schedule of games or following the date of reporting, whichever is later; provided, however, that if the Player is not in the employ of the Club for the whole period of the Club's games in the National Hockey League Championship Schedule, then he shall receive only part of the salary in the ratio of the number of days of actual employment to the number of days of the League Championship Schedule of games.

And it is further mutually agreed that if the Contract and rights to the services of the Player are assigned, exchanged, loaned or otherwise transferred to a Club in another League, the Player shall only be paid at the rate of

.... Dollars in the...League.
or,... Dollars in the...League.
or,... Dollars in the...League.

2. The Player agrees to give his services and to play hockey in all League Championship, Exhibition, Play-Off and Stanley Cup games to the best of his ability under the direction and control of the Club for the said season in accordance with the provisions hereof.

The Player further agrees:

(a) to report to the Club training camp at the time and place fixed by the Club, in good physical condition,
(b) to keep himself in good physical condition at all times during the season,
(c) to give his best services and loyalty to the Club and to play hockey only for the Club unless his contract is released, assigned, exchanged or loaned by the Club,
(d) to co-operate with the Club and participate in any and all promotional activities of the Club and the League which will in the opinion of the Club promote the welfare of the Club or professional hockey generally,
(e) to conduct himself on and off the rink according to the highest standards of honesty, morality, fair play and sportsmanship, and to refrain from conduct detrimental to the best interests of the Club, the League or professional hockey generally.

3. In order that the Player shall be fit and in proper condition for the performance of his duties as required by this contract the Player agrees to report for practice at such time and place as the Club may designate and participate in such exhibition games as may be arranged by the Club within thirty days prior to the first scheduled Championship game. The Club shall pay the travelling expenses and meals en route from the Player's home to the Club's training camp. In the event of failure of the player to so report and participate in exhibition games a fine not exceeding Five Hundred Dollars may be imposed by the Club and be deducted from the compensation stipulated herein.

4. The Club may from time to time during the continuance of this contract establish rules governing the conduct and conditioning of the Player, and such rules shall form part of this contract as fully as if herein written. For violation of any of such rules or for any conduct impairing the thorough and faithful discharge of the duties incumbent upon the Player, the Club may impose a reasonable fine upon the Player and deduct the amount thereof from any money due or to become due to the Player. The Club may also suspend the Player for violation of any such rules. When the Player is fined or suspended he shall be given notice in writing stating the amount of the fine and/or the duration of the suspension and the reason therefor.

21. It is severally and mutually ... Player's Contracts which have been duly executed and filed in the ... approved by him, and that this Agreement contains the entire agreement between the Parties and there are no oral or written inducements, promises or agreements except as contained herein.

In Witness Whereof, the parties have signed this ....12th............ day

of ......September...... A.D. 19....57.

WITNESSES: NEW YORK RANGERS, INC.
                                             (New York Rangers Hockey Club)
                                                                        Club

                                             By Murray Patrick, Gen'l Manager
                                                                     President

                                             William Gadsby
                                                                        Player
                                             10956 - 131st St., Edmonton, Alberta
                                                          Home Address of Player

Pilote Learns to Deal with Ivan

By the time he was negotiating his contract for the 1967–68 and 1968–69 campaigns, Pierre Pilote had a pretty good idea of how to interact with his boss, Tommy Ivan. As the general manager of the Chicago Black Hawks since 1954, Ivan was set in his ways, and Pilote, a trusted rushing defenceman, had been with the club since 1955, just a year after Ivan had arrived. "It got easier because maybe I got smarter," said Pilote. "You get more established, so you can figure out maybe what you're worth. Instead of going in there and asking for something, you just let him talk. Basically, you don't want to say, 'I've done this, I've done that.' After a while, he'll say, 'What else have you done?' You go there two or three times and compromise." With a place in the Hockey Hall of Fame and his number hanging in the rafters at the United Center, Pilote considered how the general managers in the six-team NHL must have figured out pay scales. "I'd say the standard was set with other hockey players, say, in Montreal and Detroit, so they all knew what everybody else was getting. There's no way you could double your salary compared to another star." Unlike a lot of rearguards, Pilote's contract doesn't make note of his plus/minus stats. "I don't think it was brought up to me that I was a minus player. In those days, I wasn't going for plus/minus, I was trying to get as many points as I could—but at the same time, play defence." Pilote was elected to the Hockey Hall of Fame as an Honoured Member in 1975.

Pierre Pilote protects his goalie, Dave Dryden, from Frank Mahovlich at Maple Leaf Gardens during the 1967-68 NHL season.

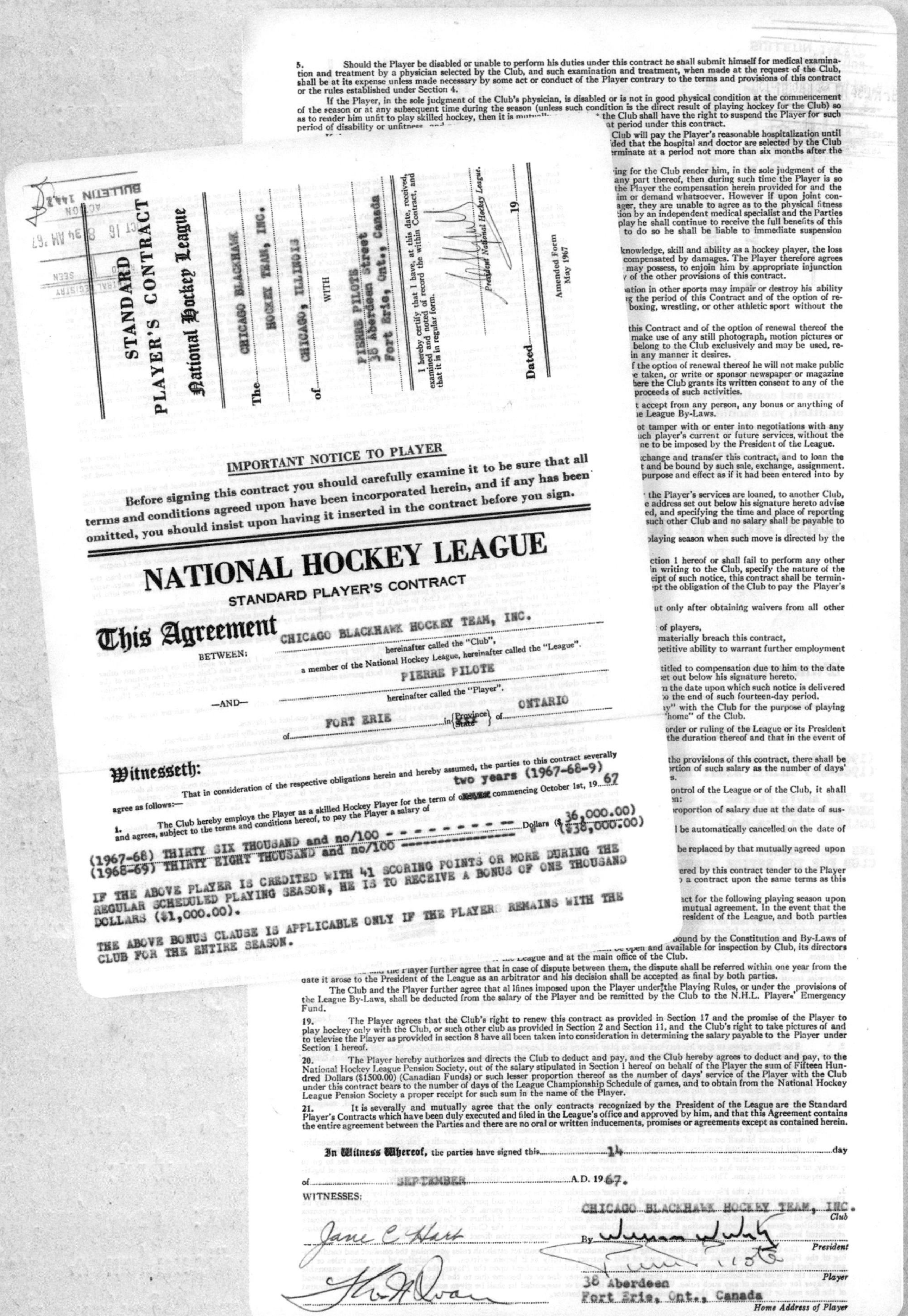

STANDARD
PLAYER'S CONTRACT
National Hockey League

The CHICAGO BLACKHAWK HOCKEY TEAM, INC.
CHICAGO, ILLINOIS

WITH

PIERRE PILOTE
38 Aberdeen Street
Fort Erie, Ont., Canada

I hereby certify that I have, at this date, received,
examined and noted of record the within Contract, and
that it is in regular form.

President National Hockey League.

19

Dated

Amended Form
May 1967

IMPORTANT NOTICE TO PLAYER

Before signing this contract you should carefully examine it to be sure that all
terms and conditions agreed upon have been incorporated herein, and if any has been
omitted, you should insist upon having it inserted in the contract before you sign.

NATIONAL HOCKEY LEAGUE
STANDARD PLAYER'S CONTRACT

This Agreement CHICAGO BLACKHAWK HOCKEY TEAM, INC.

hereinafter called the "Club",

BETWEEN: a member of the National Hockey League, hereinafter called the "League".

PIERRE PILOTE

hereinafter called the "Player".

—AND—

FORT ERIE in Province of ONTARIO
of State

Witnesseth:

That in consideration of the respective obligations herein and hereby assumed, the parties to this contract severally agree as follows:

That in consideration of the respective obligations herein and hereby assumed, the parties to this contract severally agree as follows: two years (1967-68-9)

commencing October 1st, 19 67

1. The Club hereby employs the Player as a skilled Hockey Player for the term of years commencing October 1st, 19....
and agrees, subject to the terms and conditions hereof, to pay the Player a salary of ....Dollars ($ 36,000.00)
($38,000.00)

(1967-68) THIRTY SIX THOUSAND and no/100 ——————————————
(1968-69) THIRTY EIGHT THOUSAND and no/100 ——————————————

IF THE ABOVE PLAYER IS CREDITED WITH 41 SCORING POINTS OR MORE DURING THE
REGULAR SCHEDULED PLAYING SEASON, HE IS TO RECEIVE A BONUS OF ONE THOUSAND
DOLLARS ($1,000.00).

THE ABOVE BONUS CLAUSE IS APPLICABLE ONLY IF THE PLAYER REMAINS WITH THE
CLUB FOR THE ENTIRE SEASON.

(partially visible second page, behind)

5. Should the Player be disabled or unable to perform his duties under this contract he shall submit himself for medical examination and treatment by a physician selected by the Club, and such examination and treatment, when made at the request of the Club, shall be at its expense unless made necessary by some act or conduct of the Player contrary to the terms and provisions of this contract or the rules established under Section 4.

If the Player, in the sole judgment of the Club's physician, is disabled or is not in good physical condition at the commencement of the season or at any subsequent time during the season (unless such condition is the direct result of playing hockey for the Club) so as to render him unfit to play skilled hockey, then it is mutually...
period of disability or unfitness, and ...

...Club will pay the Player's reasonable hospitalization until ...ded that the hospital and doctor are selected by the Club ...erminate at a period not more than six months after the

...ing for the Club render him, in the sole judgment of the ...any part thereof, then during such time the Player is so ...the Player the compensation herein provided for and the ...im or demand whatsoever. However if upon joint con- ...ager, they are unable to agree as to the physical fitness ...tion by an independent medical specialist and the Parties ...play he shall continue to receive the full benefits of this ...to do so he shall be liable to immediate suspension

...knowledge, skill and ability as a hockey player, the loss ...compensated by damages. The Player therefore agrees ...may possess, to enjoin him by appropriate injunction ...of the other provisions of this contract.

...ation in other sports may impair or destroy his ability ...the period of this Contract and of the option of re- ...boxing, wrestling, or other athletic sport without the

...this Contract and of the option of renewal thereof the ...make use of any still photograph, motion pictures or ...belong to the Club exclusively and may be used, re- ...in any manner it desires.

...the option of renewal thereof he will not make public ...e taken, or write or sponsor newspaper or magazine ...here the Club grants its written consent to any of the ...proceeds of such activities.

...t accept from any person, any bonus or anything of ...e League By-Laws.

...ot tamper with or enter into negotiations with any ...uch player's current or future services, without the ...ne to be imposed by the President of the League.

...xchange and transfer this contract, and to loan the ...t and be bound by such sale, exchange, assignment, ...purpose and effect as if it had been entered into by

...the Player's services are loaned, to another Club, ...e address set out below his signature hereto advise ...ed, and specifying the time and place of reporting ...such other Club and no salary shall be payable to

...playing season when such move is directed by the

...ction 1 hereof or shall fail to perform any other ...in writing to the Club, specify the nature of the ...eipt of such notice, this contract shall be termin- ...pt the obligation of the Club to pay the Player's

...ut only after obtaining waivers from all other ...of players.

...materially breach this contract, ...petitive ability to warrant further employment

...titled to compensation due to him to the date ...et out below his signature hereto.

...n the date upon which such notice is delivered ...o the end of such fourteen-day period.

..."y" with the Club for the purpose of playing ..."home" of the Club.

...order or ruling of the League or its President ...the duration thereof and that in the event of

...the provisions of this contract, there shall be ...rtion of such salary as the number of days'

...control of the League or of the Club, it shall

...roportion of salary due at the date of sus-

...l be automatically cancelled on the date of

...be replaced by that mutually agreed upon

...red by this contract tender to the Player ...o a contract upon the same terms as this

...ct for the following playing season upon ...mutual agreement. In the event that the ...resident of the League, and both parties

...be bound by the Constitution and By-Laws of ...the League and at the main office of the Club.
...be open and available for inspection by Club, its directors

...and the Player further agree that in case of dispute between them, the dispute shall be referred within one year from the date it arose to the President of the League as an arbitrator and his decision shall be accepted as final by both parties.

The Club and the Player further agree that all fines imposed under the Playing Rules, or under the provisions of the League By-Laws, shall be deducted from the salary of the Player and be remitted by the Club to the N.H.L. Players' Emergency Fund.

19. The Player agrees that the Club's right to renew this contract as provided in Section 17 and the promise of the Player to play hockey only with the Club, or such other club as provided in Section 2 and Section 11, and the Club's right to take pictures of and to televise the Player as provided in section 8 have all been taken into consideration in determining the salary payable to the Player under Section 1 hereof.

20. The Player hereby authorizes and directs the Club to deduct and pay, and the Club hereby agrees to deduct and pay, to the National Hockey League Pension Society, out of the salary stipulated in Section 1 hereof on behalf of the Player the sum of Fifteen Hundred Dollars ($1500.00) (Canadian Funds) or such lesser proportion thereof as the number of days' service of the Player with the Club under this contract bears to the number of days of the League Championship Schedule of games, and to obtain from the National Hockey League Pension Society a proper receipt for such sum in the name of the Player.

21. It is severally and mutually agree that the only contracts recognized by the President of the League are the Standard Player's Contracts which have been duly executed and filed in the League's office and approved by him, and that this Agreement contains the entire agreement between the Parties and there are no oral or written inducements, promises or agreements except as contained herein.

In Witness Whereof, the parties have signed this.............14.............day

of.............SEPTEMBER.............A.D. 19 67 .

WITNESSES:

CHICAGO BLACKHAWK HOCKEY TEAM, INC.
Club

Jane C. Hart

By... President

.... Player

38 Aberdeen
Fort Erie, Ont., Canada
Home Address of Player

Moose Vasko's Weighty Issues

When asked about his defensive partner, Elmer "Moose" Vasko, and his battles with the bulge, Pierre Pilote said, "Elmer's approach to early weigh-in was to *pray* he was close to his playing weight." After Vasko and Pilote started anchoring the Black Hawks blue line in 1956, big things were expected of the 6-foot-3, 210-pound Vasko: "I would compare his style to Kenny Reardon of the Canadiens a few years ago," said Hawks GM Tommy Ivan. "He carries the puck with elbows flying and knees high. There's lots of action when he goes down the ice. He carries along the boards a lot. He's not a real hard hitter but more of a blocker." While Pilote sparked the offence, getting around Vasko was "like trying to wrestle a bear." Throughout his career, Moose had issues with his weight, and he often wore a heavy sweat jacket under his uniform during practice. After a decade of service, Vasko walked away from the Hawks, weighing 228 pounds. During a sabbatical year from hockey, he worked in Chicago at a liquor store that he co-owned. Left unprotected in the expansion draft, Moose was claimed by the Minnesota North Stars, and in his second season there, he was named team captain. Come the 1969–70 training camp, however, he had ballooned up to 242 pounds. In Vasko's final season, he got into just three games for the North Stars, spending most of the time with the WHL's Salt Lake Golden Eagles.

Moose Vasko as a North Star.

GENERAL MILLS, INC. · GENERAL OFFICES · 9200 Wayzata Boulevard · Minneapolis, Minnesota 55440

October 10, 1969

Mr. Wren Blair
General Manager
Minnesota North Stars Hockey
7901 Cedar Avenue
Bloomington, Minnesota 55423

Dear Mr. Blair:

I have read with some interest about Moose Vasko's exile
due to excess poundage. Having somewhat the same problem
with my own flights into obesity, but with an easy solu-
tion for what ails me -- calories -- I thought I'd share
my secret.

Coming to you for forwarding to Moose is a case of
'total'. This product has 100% of the minimum daily
adult vitamin and iron requirements now officially
established. Yet it has only 101 calories per serving.
All the energy of Wheaties -- but with the best combin-
ation of nutrients available in any cereal. I can get
a wholesome, filling breakfast with 'total'. In fact,
it watches my vitamins while I watch my weight. When
combined with hard exercise, it will help peel the
pounds off fast.

I hope Moose enjoys his 'total' and a quick return to
playing weight.

                              Sincerely,

                              Bob Rowe

                              Robert W. Rowe
                              Product Manager
                              General Mills, Inc.

RWR:mms

October 15, 1969

Mr. Robert W. Rowe
Product Manager
General Mills, Inc.
9200 Wayzata Boulevard
Minneapolis, Minnesota 55440

Dear Mr. Rowe:

Thank you for your letter of October 10 and your
generous offer of a case of "Total" for Mr. Vasko.

I would venture to say, though, however great your
product is, unless Moose cuts down on items containing malt nobody is going to have much success
in this problem area.

We do appreciate your interest in our problem and
in our organization.

Kindest personal regards.

                         Yours very truly,

                         Wren A. Blair
                         General Manager-Coach

WAB:mv

Black Hawks 'Steal' Nylund from Leafs

Today, fans accept July 1 as free-agent frenzy day, in which teams can ink unsigned players without any compensation, but that was not always the case. As the 1980s progressed, the NHL was attempting to establish rules and consistency for free agency. On August 27, 1986, the Chicago Black Hawks signed defenceman Gary Nylund to a deal, snatching him away from the Maple Leafs, the team that had drafted and nurtured him. Toronto GM Gerry McNamara was tasked with putting together a package to present to arbitrator E.J. Houston about compensation for Nylund. "In those days, it was something new. I think it probably was my first and only arbitration. You had to make a pitch," recalled McNamara. The Leafs had asked for centre Ed Olczyk in return, but were awarded Jerome Dupont, Ken Yaremchuk, and the fourth pick in the 1987 Entry Draft. "Chicago really stole him. The arbitrator happened to be the ECHL [East Coast Hockey League] commissioner, Houston, who was a judge, and I never forgave him for that," said McNamara. "I thought that they kowtowed to [Hawks owner Bill] Wirtz. I thought we got very bad compensation for Gary Nylund, we didn't get our money's worth out of him. In the end, [Nylund] was a mistake right off the handle. He was a pretty good player, but he had a devastating knee injury and he was never the same player." A year later, the Leafs did acquire Olczyk in a trade, along with Al Secord, for Rick Vaive, Steve Thomas, and Bob McGill.

O-Pee-Chee/Hockey Hall of Fame

Gary Nylund began his NHL career as a Maple Leaf.

MAPLE LEAF GARDENS LIMITED

60 CARLTON STREET, TORONTO, ONTARIO M5B 1L1 • (416) 977-1641

September 5, 1986

TORONTO REBUTTAL RE: CHICAGO ARBITRATION PROPOSAL

In my first discussion with Ed Houston regarding the arbitration, he advised me to be realistic and fair in what I submitted as compensation. Immediately, I re-evaluated the compensation with my staff. The conclusion was the same. The idea of one quality player from Chicago in return for a quality player from Toronto was fair. Ed Olczyk from Chicago for Gary Nylund from Toronto was fair.

Next, I asked my scouts to provide me with the reports from the N.H.L. Central Scouting Bureau on Nylund and Olczyk. I felt that this would be a good unbiased report from an independent source. As the enclosed reports illustrate, Nylund grades as a much better N.H.L. prospect than Olczyk with Central Scouting. Even in the area of skating, Nylund is graded as excellent while Olczyk does not receive as favorable comments with even a mention of a "hitch in his skating." This further enhanced my opinion that we were complying with the wishes of the Arbitrator and being realistic and fair in what we submitted for compensation.

I was advised yesterday that Chicago in return for Nylund had offered Jerome Dupont, Ken Yaremchuk and a fourth-round selection in the 1987 Entry Draft. I thought that they must be kidding. In the three days that Bob Pulford and I had talks regarding compensation prior to arbitration, he offered me the likes of Keith Brown or Behn Wilson. I turned both those offers down, but at least those two player's were regulars on his team. His formal offer is totally unsatisfactory.

I suppose that the idea is that Dupont will replace Nylund on our defense. If Dupont is that good, why would Chicago sign Gary Nylund? Dupont was also a first-round draft choice. Again, no comparison. Dupont played a full season in the minors (1982-83) and even saw time in the minors in his second season (1983-84). Nylund was never even close to playing in the minors. At one point I know that Dupont was considering retirement and going back to school.

I consider Dupont as Chicago's seventh defenseman. He saw 75 games of action during the regular season only because of injuries to other defensemen. For the Playoffs, he didn't even dress for the first two games of their series against us. He was added to the lineup for the third game, due to an injury to Behn Wilson, and we won 7-2.

I also suppose that Ken Yaremchuk is being pushed as a first-round draft pick. Again, there is no comparison with Nylund. Yaremchuk wasn't able to make the jump from junior to the N.H.L. In his first season, he remained with Portland. He has still never made it as an N.H.L. regular in three seasons with Chicago. He even had a stint in the minors in 1984-85.

Toronto Rebuttal....2

When he joined Chicago, he was a center. Then he was moved to the wing and he hasn't been able to establish himself there. Our time sheets for the four games that Yaremchuk played in Toronto this season bear out the fact that he is a spare forward (6:30, 4:25, 12:00, 5:55).

A player that I can compare to Yaremchuk is Dan Hodgson. Hodgson had much more impressive scoring statistics as a junior than Yaremchuk. And in his first N.H.L. season with us he had 25 points (13 goals, 12 assists) in 40 games which compares more favorably than Yaremchuk's third N.H.L. season totals of 34 points (14 goals, 20 assists) in 78 games. And Hodgson couldn't even play on our team, I sent him to the minors in February.

The clincher is the fourth-round draft choice. The new Collective Bargaining Agreement limits the selection of players after the first three rounds to those who have played three years of Canadian Junior experience. This makes the fourth-round pick a diluted draft choice.

The Chicago offer reminds me of the one situation that you told us to avoid. The Vachon-McCourt arbitration. Detroit made an unreasonable offer of a backup goaltender (Jim Rutherford) and a first-round "disappointment" (Bill Lochead). Here we have an offer of a backup defenseman (Dupont) and a first-round disappointment (Yaremchuk).

These are two players that Pulford has tried to trade to every N.H.L. team over the last two seasons. Gary Nylund is one player that I have absolutely never offered to anyone in a trade. Dupont and Yaremchuk are two players that I have serious doubts about them making our team. I don't want to be "stuck" with two players who I might have to play in Newmarket and pay U.S. dollar contracts. An additional financial risk occurs with Dupont who has a "one-way" N.H.L. salary.

Chicago has signed a quality player from us. Now they are trying to steal their 15th and 18th players on their team (excluding goaltenders). If Chicago had called me a month ago and offered Dupont, Yaremchuk and a fourth-round selection for Nylund, I would have laughed. If, on the other hand, I had offered Nylund to Chicago for Dupont, Yaremchuk and a fourth-round selection, they would have chartered a plane to come down to pick Nylund up. The term fair and equal compensation cannot be applied to their offer.

Chicago is trying to make Olczyk out to be a superstar while undervaluing Nylund. Too much is being made of Olczyk being a Chicago-born player and his public relations stature. His off-ice value can't be mixed up with his on-ice value. He has shown good potential over his first two N.H.L. seasons, but he had played on a line with proven N.H.L. veterans. He is not a superstar player at this point.

We do not feel that we are being unfair in our submission. Instead of having a veteran defense partner to bring him along, Nylund has had to play with every defense partner imaginable. He has played in all critical game situations, killed penalties and even played on the power play. Other intangibles like his imposing physical presence and toughness cannot be accurately gauged. We must be compensated with a player of equal value from Chicago. When looking over their lineup we consider a Troy Murray, a Al Secord, a Doug Wilson, but the "fairest" we viewed as being Ed Olczyk.

Toronto Rebuttal....3

We won six of our eight regular season meetings against Chicago this past season and swept them in three straight games in the Playoffs. It was the first time in many years that we had enjoyed any kind of success against them. Obviously, Nylund was a key factor in our recent success. Now they are trying to make us pay with this injustice.

I feel that their offer is an insult to the Toronto Maple Leafs, an insult to the Arbitrator and an insult to the N.H.L. free agent provisions. If they are successful in "stealing" Nylund with the lure of U.S. dollars, then the mass exodus that I alluded to in my initial presentation will soon occur. This is a direct challenge to the Canadian N.H.L. teams.

If Chicago had offered one "quality" player and we had asked for another "quality" player, then we would have been close and I could live with the verdict either way. But they have tried to insult us with an offer of two "fringe" players and a "worthless" draft selection for a key player from our team.

GERRY McNAMARA
General Manager

Imperial Oil – Turofsky/Hockey Hall of Fame

Frank Prazak/Hockey Hall of Fame

Bobby Hull Never Met a Product He Couldn't Endorse

Bobby Hull's contract with the House of Masters to push the hair replacement procedure in 1990 made sense for the follicly challenged Golden Jet. While his hair had long ago gone into early retirement, Hull had not, and it was just one more in a very long line of products he endorsed. In 1991, the *Globe and Mail*'s William Houston summed up Hull as "part icon, part clown, all showman . . . everything a sports celebrity is supposed to be." In the same article, Dick Lucas of House of Masters called Hull a "'wonderful' pitchman: 'He commands so much respect.'" The roster of Hull's deals is almost as impressive as his statistics on the ice: Milk Duds, Bauer, Miller Lite (and then later Northern Algonquin Brewing Company), Jantzen Actionwear, Philco Television, Fox 40 Power Puck, and don't forget the Bobby Hull skate sharpener, produced by McIntyre Aluminum. But hey, if expressionist painter LeRoy Neiman paints your likeness—in action yet—for the cover of *TIME Magazine* (March 1, 1968), then it's fair to say that you are a notable figure that the public can buy into. [Note: Allan Stitt's collection includes a LeRoy Neiman watercolour of the Golden Jet.] Not every product was successful, however. While Hull's signing in 1972 was credited as the reason the World Hockey Association gained any respectability, he was hired as commissioner of a reincarnated World Hockey Association in 2004, which fell flat on its face. "We are going to let the star players entertain," Hull said when the latter-day WHA was announced. "We are not going to let people inhibit them from doing their stuff." The same could be said about Bobby Hull.

Jukka Rautio/HHOF-IIHF Images

The changing hair of Bobby Hull includes being young with the Black Hawks and addressing an even younger audience, hugging goaltender Vladimir Dzurilla of Czechoslovakia after the 1976 Canada Cup, and in 2008, at a reunion of the 1976 Canada Cup winning team.

AGREEMENT

BETWEEN

HOUSE OF MASTERS

AND

BOBBY HULL

Where as the above named parties agrees as follows.

For the consideration of the sum, fifty thousand dollars ($50,000.00), paid by the House of Masters to Mr. Hull, Mr. Hull agrees to the following:

1) to be available to the House of Masters as a model for their commercials of which content has to be agreeable to both parties.

2) Mr. Hull must avail Himself, on reasonable notice, four times per year for commercial productions as a model.

3) Mr. Hull is to avail Himself, on reasonable notice, four times per year for special personal appearances, at the place of business of the House of Masters, or any such place they choose.

4) Mr. Hull agrees to act as an official spokesperson for the House of Masters and at all times act in the best interest of the House of Masters.

5) Mr. Hull, in His capacity as official spokesperson for the House of Masters, agrees to be model and spokesperson to produce a sales presentation video tape having a maximum length running time of twenty (20) minutes.

6) Mr. Hull further agrees to model for the production of one special commercial per year for which additional renumerations will be paid to Him.

Payments

Mr. Hull will receive twenty five thousand dollars ($25,000.00) upon execution of this contract . The balance of $25,000.00 will be paid in three installments of $8,500.00 each. Mr. Hull will receive additional payments of $5,000.00 plus reasonable expenses for any special commercial in which the House of Masters may ask him to be a model and spokesperson, from time to time. Further payments of 15% of each Hairpiece sold during any of Mr. Hull's personal appearances and where Mr. Hull had a personal contact with the client of the House of Masters, shall be paid to Mr. Hull once the sale is completed.

It is to be clearly understood that Mr. Hull grants the exclusive use and irrevocable right of his image to the House of Masters and any of their subsidiaries for the purpose of hair replacement advertising to be used by them exclusively in any media the House of Masters choose. Furthermore, the House of Masters is given this exclusive right for one year from the date of this contract for both the Canadian and American market, save and except the metro Chicago, U.S.A. area.

This contract shall be renewable for an additional year once the terms of this contract are ended. All terms and conditions shall remain as is in the original contract, save and except for renumerations, which shall be negotiated and agreed to by both parties.

This contract is the entire agreement between the parties, but for the purpose of clarity, no further payment other than those stated herein shall be made from the House of Masters to Mr. Hull, other than if a separate agreement for additional work and payment is agreed upon, between the parties.

Witness _____ Per House of Masters _____

Dated 05/12/90 Dated 05/12/90

Witness _____ Bobby Hull _____

Dated 05/12/90 Dated 05/12/90

Page 2

Shoot, Shibicky, Shoot!

Alex Shibicky was one of the pioneers of the slap shot, and he was undoubtedly one of the first to use the high-powered blast on a regular basis. Playing for the New York Rangers from 1935 to 1942, and then briefly after World War II, the left winger was asked to describe his shot: "It's just like a bullet. Then, when you follow through, it's the most beautiful shot you'd ever want to see." The Winnipeg native, nicknamed "Shoe," scored 110 goals and had 91 helpers over eight seasons. Hall of Famer Frank Boucher, who played alongside and then coached Shibicky on the 1940 Stanley Cup–winning Rangers, thought Shibicky should have gotten more goals, especially teaming with brothers Neil and Mac Colville, as he did for so many years in the minors and NHL. "He'd hold it too long, seeking a little better position, and you'd hear the gang on the bench go through a ritual when Alex waited, 'Shoot, Shibicky . . . Shoot, Shibicky . . . Ah, shit, Shibicky,'" Boucher wrote in his autobiography. The Colvilles and Shibicky were graduates of a hockey camp that Rangers GM Lester Patrick held at Winnipeg Amphitheatre in 1934. The trio made up a rare line with three right-handed shots, and Shibicky told the *Winnipeg Free Press* in 1994 that the move to left wing worked for him. "It was the best move I ever made. As a right-hand shot coming off left wing, it gave me a better shooting angle."

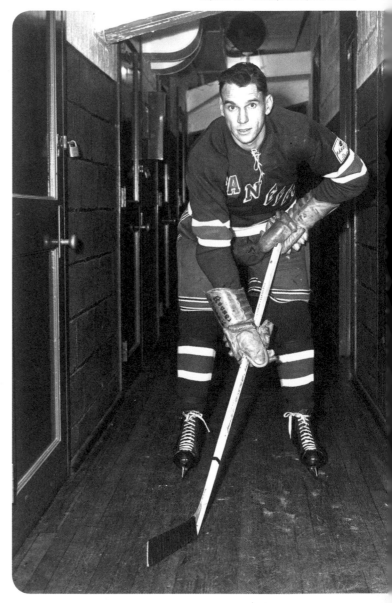

Alex Shibicky poses in the hallway.

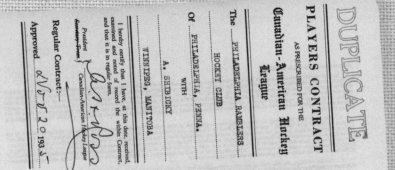

DUPLICATE

PLAYERS CONTRACT
AS PRESCRIBED FOR THE
Canadian-American Hockey League

The PHILADELPHIA RAMBLERS
HOCKEY CLUB
Of PHILADELPHIA, PENNA.
WITH
A. SHIBICKY
WINNIPEG, MANITOBA

Regular Contract:—
Approved, Nov 20 193 5

President
Secretary-Treas.
Canadian-American Hockey League

I hereby certify that I have, at this date, received, examined and made of record the within Contract, and that it is in regular form.

IMPORTANT NOTICE TO PLAYERS AND CLUB PRESIDENTS

Every player before signing a contract should carefully scrutinize the same to ascertain whether all of the conditions agreed upon between the Player and Club President have been incorporated therein, and if any have been omitted the player should insist upon having all the terms, conditions, promises and agreements inserted in the contract before he signs the same.

CANADIAN-AMERICAN HOCKEY LEAGUE

PLAYER'S CONTRACT (Regular)

Articles of Agreement between the PHILADELPHIA RAMBLERS

HOCKEY CLUB

of the City NEW YORK , in the State or Province of NEW YORK

a club member of a League known as the "Canadian-American Hockey League," party of the first part, hereinafter called the Club and

A. SHIBICKY of the City of

WINNIPEG in the State or Province of MANITOBA party of the second

part, hereinafter called the Player.

Witnesseth:

That in consideration of the mutual obligations herein and hereby assumed, the parties to this contract severally agree as follows:

1. The club agrees to pay the player for the season of 193 5-36 beginning on or about the FIRST day of NOVEMBER , 193 5 , and ending on or about the TENTH day of APRIL 193 6

a salary at the rate of $ 900.00 (NINE HUNDRED DOLLARS)

for such season; and an additional sum at the rate of $ 100.00 (ONE HUNDRED DOLLARS)

for such season said additional sum being in consideration of the option herein

reserved to the club in Clause 10 hereof; said additional sum to be paid whether said option is exercised or not, making the total compensation to the player for the season herein contracted for $ 1,000.00 (ONE THOUSAND DOLLARS)

... commencement of the period covered by this contract, unless this contract shall be terminated ... the club for the purpose of playing games, in which event this contract shall be terminated ... "home" of the club. Provided, however, that if the player is not in the service of the ... such proportion of the season's salary, (or of the monthly salary multiplied by four), stated ... al employment bears to the number of days in the season or the number of days in the ... uch the player is held, provided he be not held more than four months from the beginning

... the continuance of this contract establish reasonable rules for the government of its ... shall be a part of this contract as fully as if herein written and binding upon the player; ... impairing the faithful and thorough discharge of the duties incumbent upon the player, ... yer and deduct the amount thereof from any money due or to become due to the player; ... of any rules so established, and during such suspension the player shall not be entitled ... the player is fined or suspended, he shall be given notice in writing, stating the amount ... e reason therefor.

... y to perform his duties be impaired at any time during the term herein prescribed, the ... come due under this contract, such proportion thereof as the period of said disability ... ed; but no such deduction shall be made by reason of any accident or injury received ... uties under the direction of the club, unless such injury or accident shall wholly or ... days, in which event this contract may be terminated at the option of the club, pro... n notice thereof by the club.

... ided in the preceding section, he will submit himself to a medical examination and ... to be selected by the club, such examination when made at the request of the club ... ter act or conduct of the player contrary to the terms of this agreement or rules and

... plete uniform, the player making a deposit of $30.00 therefor, which deposit shall ... termination of this contract, upon the surrender of the uniform by him to the club,

... elf for the duties necessary under the terms of this contract, the club may require the ... such places as the club may designate, and to participate in such exhibition contests as may be arranged

by the club for a period of Fifteen days prior to the First day of

November , the club to pay the travelling expenses, and meals en route of the player from his home

city to the training place of the club, whether he be ordered to go there direct or by way of the city of

In the event of the failure of the player to so report for practice and participate in the exhibition games, as provided for, a penalty of at least $100.00 may be imposed by the club, the same to be deducted from the compensation stipulated herein.

7. The club may, at any time, after the beginning and prior to the completion of the period of this contract, give the player one day's written notice to end and determine all its liabilities and obligations hereunder, in which event the liabilities and obligations undertaken by the club shall cease and determine at the expiration of said one day. The player, at the expiration of said one day, shall be freed and discharged from all obligations to render service to the club. If such notice be given to the player while "abroad" with the club, he shall be entitled to his travelling expenses to the city of

8. The player agrees to perform for the club, and for no other party, during the period of this contract (unless with the written consent of the club), such duties pertaining to the exhibition of the game of hockey as may be required of him by said club, at such reasonable times and places as said club may designate for the Canadian-American Hockey League season for the year 193 5-36

beginning on or about the First day of November 193 5

and ending on or about the Tenth day of April 193 6 unless sooner terminated in accordance with other provisions hereof.

9. The player will not, either during the playing season, or before the commencement or after the close thereof, participate in any exhibition hockey games, indoor baseball, basketball or football, unless the written consent of the club has first been given to him.

10. The player will, at the option of the club, enter into a contract for the succeeding season upon all the terms and conditions of this contract, save as to Clauses One and Ten, and the salary to be paid the player in event of such renewal shall be the same as the total compensation provided for the player in Clause One hereof unless it be increased or decreased by mutual agreement.

11. The club shall not transfer the services of the player to any other club without furnishing the player in writing all of the conditions under which said transfer is made and showing what team has claim to his services and what that claim is.

12. The "NOTICE" printed at the head of this contract is hereby made a part hereof.

In Testimony Whereof The parties hereunto have executed this contract and copies thereof, each of which shall be considered an original, one copy being retained by the club and one copy by the player, this 14th day of Nov. A.D. 193 5

(Seal)

WITNESSES:

PHILADELPHIA RAMBLERS HOCKEY CLUB.

By _Lester Patrick_ President.

Alex Shibicky Player.

Rangers and Boucher Inseparable for 30 Years

Frank Boucher and the New York Rangers went together like peanut butter and jam. Already a star in the young NHL, the native of Ottawa, Ontario, was an original with the club in its debut season of 1926, and he remained a part of the team until 1955, as a player, coach, and in management. Consider the contract and letter reproduced here; there's a stamp on the second page of the 1937–38 contract addressing the switch in ownership, "Transferred to Madison Square Garden Corporation." Boucher took less money that season as a player—he made $5,800 in 1934–35, and $6,000 in the following two campaigns—but took another $1,500 to act as assistant to general manager Lester Patrick while still playing. He retired from on-ice action after the 1937–38 campaign (though he returned during the war) and coached the Rangers' amateur farm club, New York Rovers of the Eastern League, for a championship season in 1938–39. In his first year behind the bench of the NHL club in 1939–40, the Rangers won the Stanley Cup. On Valentine's Day in 1951, the team threw a love-in for Boucher, the only original Ranger still with the team. That night, New York City mayor Vincent R. Impellitteri said that Boucher "prompted good sportsmanship and, in doing that, made for better citizens tomorrow." After receiving all of the gifts, including a black Studebaker sedan from the fans, Boucher said that he and wife would "cherish this the rest of our lives." Another good example of how well respected he was: he was given the original Lady Byng Memorial Trophy permanently in 1935 after claiming the award seven times in eight seasons for his fair play, and a new trophy was donated to be given to future Lady Byng winners.

September 10, 1937

Mr. Frank Boucher
197 Crichton Street
Ottawa, Ont.
Canada

Dear Frank:

This letter will serve to confirm verbal agreement with you whereby you are to receive in addition to your contract as a player, the Sum of Fifteen Hundred ($1500.00) Dollars, said sum to be compensation for your services as my assistant during the playing season of 1937/38.

Yours sincerely,

Lester Patrick

LESTER PATRICK

LP AZ

Imperial Oil – Turofsky/Hockey Hall of Fame

Frank Boucher, right, gives an interview on Jack Dennett's radio show on CFRB in Toronto.

PLAYER'S CONTRACT

AS PRESCRIBED FOR THE

National Hockey League

The NEW YORK RANGERS PROFESSIONAL

HOCKEY CLUB, 苑.

of NEW YORK N. Y.

WITH

FRANK BOUCHER

of OTTAWA ONT.

I hereby certify that I have, at this date, received,
examined and noted of record the within Contract, and
that it is in regular form.

Frank Calder
President National Hockey League.

Regular Contract:—

Approved _November 6_ 193 7.

☛ **IMPORTANT NOTICE TO PLAYERS AND CLUB PRESIDENTS** ☚

Every player before signing a contract should carefully scrutinize the same to
ascertain whether all of the conditions agreed upon between the Player and Club
President have been incorporated therein, and if any have been omitted, the player
should insist upon having all the terms, conditions, promises and agreements inserted in the contract before he signs the same.

NATIONAL HOCKEY LEAGUE

PLAYER'S CONTRACT (REGULAR)

Articles of Agreement between the NEW YORK RANGERS

PROFESSIONAL HOCKEY CLUB, 苑.

of the City of NEW YORK , in the State/Province of NEW YORK

a club member of a League known as the "National Hockey League," party of the first part, hereinafter called the Club and

FRANK BOUCHER

of the City of OTTAWA , in the State/Province of ONTARIO

party of the second part, hereinafter called the Player.

Witnesseth:

agree as follows: That in consideration of the mutual obligations herein and hereby assumed, the parties to this contract severally

1. The club agrees to pay the player for the season of 1937/38, beginning on or about the FIRST

day of NOVEMBER , 193 7, and ending on or about the TENTH

day of APRIL , 193 8, a salary at the rate of $ 3,400. (THREE THOUSAND FOUR

HUNDRED DOLLARS)

$ 100.00 (ONE HUNDRED DOLLARS) for such season; and an additional sum at the rate of

for such season said additional sum being in consideration of the option herein reserved to the club in Clause 10 hereof; said additional

sum to be paid whether said option is exercised or not, making the total compensation to the player for the season herein contracted

for $ 3,500. (THREE THOUSAND FIVE HUNDRED DOLLARS)

All payments to be made as follows:

1. In semi-monthly instalments after the commencement
terminated by the club while the player is "abroad" with the club
falling due shall be paid on the first week-day after the return
the service of the club for the entire season, then he shall receive
tiplied by four), stated in this contract, as the number of days o
number of days in the season plus the additional number of day
months from the beginning of the season.

2. The club may from time to time during the continu
its players "at home" and "abroad," and such rules shall be a
player; and for violation of such rules or for any conduct impa
the player; the club may impose reasonable fines upon the pla
due to the player. The club may also suspend the player fo
player shall not be entitled to any compensation under this co
in writing, stating the amount of the fine or the duration of th

3. Should the player be disabled, or his ability to perfo
the club may deduct from the amount then due, or to becom
disability or impairment may bear to the term herein presc
injury received by the player while in performance of his re
shall wholly or partly incapacitate the player for a period of
of the club, provided, however, that the player shall be giv

4. Should the player become disabled, as provided
and treatment by a regular physician, in good standing, to
club shall be at its expense, unless made necessary by som
rules and regulations made under it.

5. The club shall furnish the player with one comp
shall be returned to him at the end of the season or upon
to the club.

6. In order to enable the player to fit himself for
the player to report for practice at such places as the cl

arranged by the club for a period of FIFTEEN

NOVEMBER , the club to

to the training place of the club, whether he be ordered
In the event of the failure of the player to so report fo
of at least $100.00 may be imposed by the club, the sam

7. The club may, at any time, after the begin
one day's written notice to end and terminate all its lia
undertaken by the club shall cease and terminate at
shall be freed and discharged from all obligations to re

with the club, he shall be entitled to his travelling ex

8. The player agrees to perform for the club,
consent of the club), such duties pertaining to the ex
reasonable times and places as said club may designa

or about the FIRST

about the TENTH

visions hereof.

9. The player will not, either during the p
in any hockey, baseball, indoor baseball, basketball
consent of the club has first been given to him.

10. The player will, at the option of the clu
of this contract, save as to Clauses One and Ten,
the total compensation provided for the player in

11. The club shall not transfer the servic
conditions under which said transfer is made and

12. In consideration of the salary to be p
cably authorizes the Club to make or to authorize a
firms or corporations may see fit, of his photographs or of any reprodu
ing or publicity.

13. The player agrees and covenants that during the life of this contract he will not tamper with or enter into negotiati
any other player under contract or reservation to any club, member of this League, for, or regarding, his future or present services without
written consent of the club of which the player negotiated with is a member, under penalty of a fine.

14. The "NOTICE" printed in red ink at the head of this contract is hereby made a part hereof.

In Testimony Whereof, the parties hereunto have executed this contract, this _First_

day of _November_ A.D. 193 _7_

NEW YORK RANGERS PROFESSIONAL HOCKEY CLUB, 苑.

By _Leslie Saunders_ Vice President.

Frank Boucher Player.

(SEAL)

WITNESSES:

Adrienne Zains

Adrienne Zains

TRANSFERRED TO MADISON SQUARE GARDEN CORPORATION

Leslie Saunders

Promotion Suited Coulter

According to centreman and teammate Frank Boucher, it wasn't until Art Coulter was made captain of the New York Rangers that he really started to make a difference. Coulter, a puck-moving defenceman from Winnipeg, arrived in the Big Apple in a January 1936 deal with Chicago, for Earl Seibert, a rare one-for-one trade of future Hall of Famers. "I suggested that Art, being a man of tall pride, should be made captain of the team," wrote Boucher in *When the Rangers Were Young*. "If Lester did this and took Art into his confidence, I was convinced the change would benefit Coulter psychologically." For the 1937–38 campaign, Coulter was named captain, replacing the retired Bill Cook. He took to the role, said Boucher: "He lent strength to our smaller players, always on the spot if opposing players tried to intimidate them, responding beautifully to his new responsibilities." A $500 bonus was written into his 1940–41 contract. The captain of the Stanley Cup–winning team in 1940, Coulter left the Rangers, and professional hockey, after the 1941–42 season, serving in the United States Coast Guard during the Second World War. He played in 466 games, was named to the NHL's Second All-Star Team four times, and was elected to the Hall of Fame as an Honoured Member in 1974.

Muzz Patrick, captain Art Coulter, Ott Heller, and Babe Pratt on November 1, 1940, at Maple Leaf Gardens.

☞ IMPORTANT NOTICE TO PLAYERS AND CLUB PRESIDENTS ☜

Every player before signing a contract should carefully scrutinize the same to ascertain whether all of the conditions agreed upon between the Player and Club President have been incorporated therein, and if any have been omitted, the player should insist upon having all the terms, conditions, promises and agreements inserted in the contract before he signs the same.

NATIONAL HOCKEY LEAGUE

PLAYER'S CONTRACT (REGULAR)

Articles of Agreement between the MADISON SQUARE GARDEN CORPORATION (NEW YORK RANGERS PROFESSIONAL HOCKEY CLUB)

of the City of NEW YORK, in the State/Province of NEW YORK a club member of a League known as the "National Hockey League," party of the first part, hereinafter called the Club and

ARTHUR COULTER

of the City of CHICAGO, in the State/Province of ILLINOIS party of the second part, hereinafter called the Player.

Witnesseth:

agree as follows: That in consideration of the mutual obligations herein and hereby assumed, the parties to this contract severally

1. The club agrees to pay the player for the season of 19 40/41 beginning on or about the First day of November 19 40, and ending on or about the Fifteenth day of April 19 41, a salary at the rate of $ 5,400. (Five Thousand Four Hundred Dollars) for such season; and an additional sum at the rate of $ 100. (One Hundred Dollars)

for such season said additional sum being in consideration of the option herein reserved to the club in Clause 10 hereof; said additional sum to be paid whether said option is exercised or not, making the total compensation to the player for the season herein contracted for $ 5,500. (Five Thousand Five Hundred Dollars)

   (a) A bonus of $500. is to be paid to the player if he should make an All-star rating either by the Canadian Press or by the Managers of the National Hockey League for season 1940/41.

   (b) An additional bonus of $500. is to be given the player for acting in capacity of Captain on the New York Rangers Club for season 1940/41.

A.C.

L.P.

14. ...

15. If, because of any condition ... ase of war, it shall be deemed advisable by the National Hockey League or by the Club to suspend or curtail operations, then in the event of suspension of operations this contract shall become void and at an end and in the event of curtailment but not suspension of operations the conditions set forth in Clause One hereof shall be automatically cancelled and shall be replaced by others to be mutually agreed upon between the Club and the Player.

In Testimony Whereof, the parties hereunto have executed this contract, this 17th day of October A.D. 19 40.

MADISON SQUARE GARDEN CORP. (NEW YORK RANGERS PROFESSIONAL HOCKEY CLUB)

(Seal)

By *Lester Patrick*
Vice-President

Arthur Coulter
Player.

WITNESSES:

Adrienne Zaino

Frank Boucher

When Father Signs Son

By the time Lester Patrick signed his son, Lynn, to another Rangers contract for the 1941–42 season, any charges of nepotism had long been set aside. Lynn had just finished second in league scoring and would indeed be destined for big things—finishing second again in 1941–42, and fourth the next year, before military commitments derailed his career. In a 1942 interview with the *Winnipeg Free Press*, James C. Hendy, who put together the annual *NHL Guide*, recalled the question marks from Lynn's early days. "Back in 1934, when Lynn Patrick skated out to centre ice for the Rangers, his father, Lester Patrick, came in for a merciless barrage of criticism. The fans did not seem to realize, or care, that Papa Patrick had not been the one who had at first been sold on his son's ability to play NHL hockey," said Hendy. "The presence of Lynn in a Ranger uniform had been entirely because of the enthusiasm of Bill Cook and Frankie Boucher, then reaching the end of their playing careers, and acting in a player-coach capacity for [Lester] Patrick. Both of them saw in the young giant the makings of a star. Perhaps had Lynn not been Lester's son, and there is no more critical man in hockey than Lester, he might have tabbed Lynn as a coming star more quickly than he did." Lynn also got to skate alongside his younger brother, Muzz, with the Rangers. Like his father, Lynn moved behind the bench and into the executive office after his career; also like his father, Lynn's two sons, Craig and Glenn, played in the NHL.

Muzz, Lester, and Lynn Patrick outside the Hockey Hall of Fame.

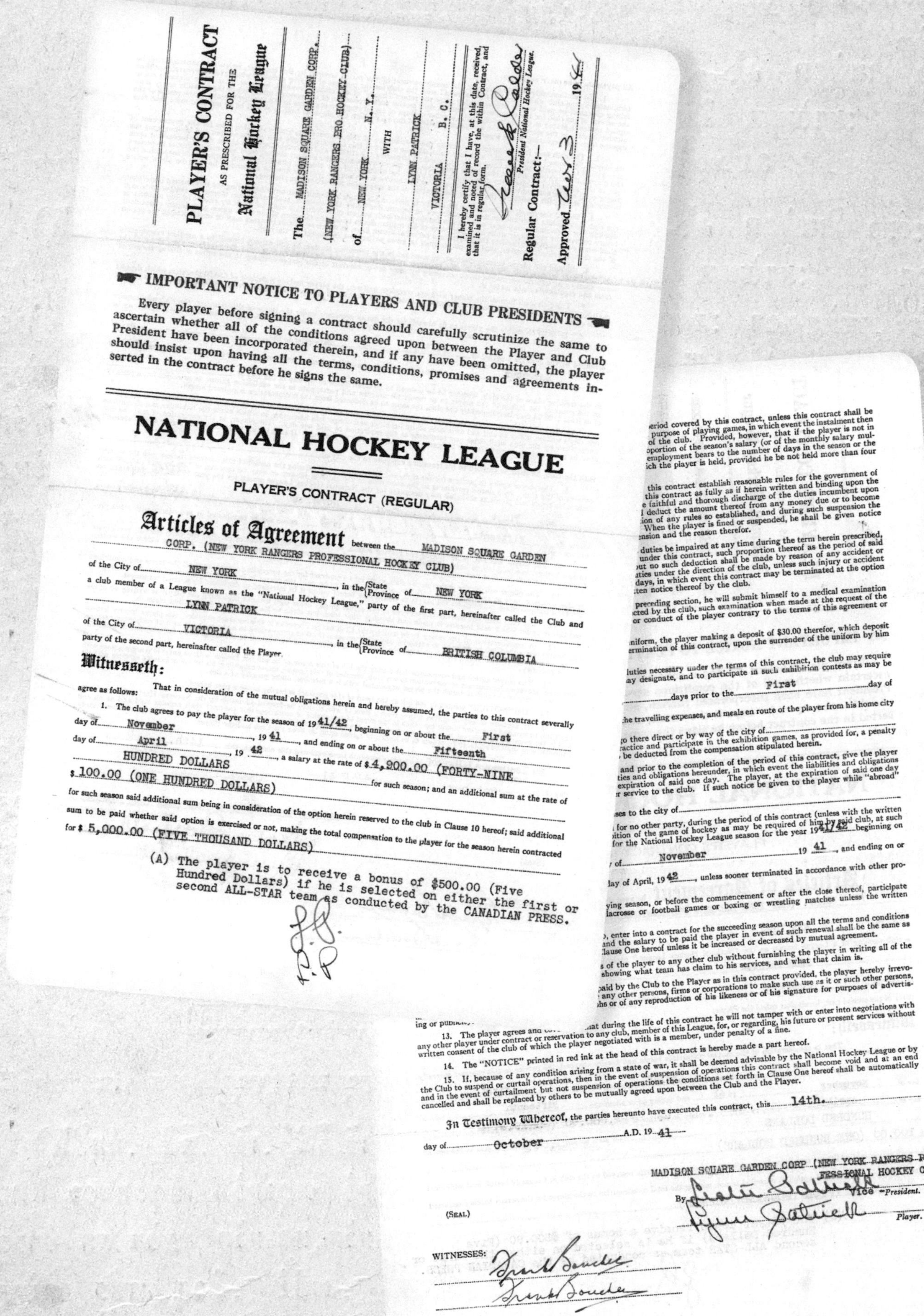

PLAYER'S CONTRACT
AS PRESCRIBED FOR THE
National Hockey League

The MADISON SQUARE GARDEN CORP. (NEW YORK RANGERS PRO. HOCKEY CLUB)
of NEW YORK N. Y.
WITH
LYNN PATRICK
VICTORIA B. C.

I hereby certify that I have, at this date, received, examined and noted of record the within Contract, and that it is in regular form.

Frank Calder
President National Hockey League.

Regular Contract:—
Approved Nov 3 1941

IMPORTANT NOTICE TO PLAYERS AND CLUB PRESIDENTS

Every player before signing a contract should carefully scrutinize the same to ascertain whether all of the conditions agreed upon between the Player and Club President have been incorporated therein, and if any have been omitted, the player should insist upon having all the terms, conditions, promises and agreements inserted in the contract before he signs the same.

NATIONAL HOCKEY LEAGUE

PLAYER'S CONTRACT (REGULAR)

Articles of Agreement between the MADISON SQUARE GARDEN CORP. (NEW YORK RANGERS PROFESSIONAL HOCKEY CLUB) of the City of NEW YORK, in the State/Province of NEW YORK a club member of a League known as the "National Hockey League," party of the first part, hereinafter called the Club and LYNN PATRICK of the City of VICTORIA, in the State/Province of BRITISH COLUMBIA party of the second part, hereinafter called the Player.

Witnesseth:

That in consideration of the mutual obligations herein and hereby assumed, the parties to this contract severally agree as follows:

1. The club agrees to pay the player for the season of 1941/42, beginning on or about the First day of November, 1941, and ending on or about the Fifteenth day of April, 1942, a salary at the rate of $4,900.00 (FORTY-NINE HUNDRED DOLLARS) for such season; and an additional sum at the rate of $100.00 (ONE HUNDRED DOLLARS) for such season said additional sum being in consideration of the option herein reserved to the club in Clause 10 hereof; said additional sum to be paid whether said option is exercised or not, making the total compensation to the player for the season herein contracted for $5,000.00 (FIVE THOUSAND DOLLARS)

(A) The player is to receive a bonus of $500.00 (Five Hundred Dollars) if he is selected on either the first or second ALL-STAR team as conducted by the CANADIAN PRESS.

L.P.
F.P.

...period covered by this contract, unless this contract shall be ... purpose of playing games, in which event the instalment then ... of the club. Provided, however, that if the player is not in ... proportion of the season's salary (or of the monthly salary mul... employment bears to the number of days in the season or the ... which the player is held, provided he be not held more than four

... this contract establish reasonable rules for the government of ... this contract as fully as if herein written and binding upon the ... faithful and thorough discharge of the duties incumbent upon ... deduct the amount thereof from any money due or to become ... of any rules so established, and during such suspension the ... When the player is fined or suspended, he shall be given notice ... pension and the reason therefor.

... duties be impaired at any time during the term herein prescribed, ... under this contract, such proportion thereof as the period of said ... but no such deduction shall be made by reason of any accident or ... duties under the direction of the club, unless such injury or accident ... days, in which event this contract may be terminated at the option ... written notice thereof by the club.

... preceding section, he will submit himself to a medical examination ... ted by the club, such examination when made at the request of the ... or conduct of the player contrary to the terms of this agreement or

... uniform, the player making a deposit of $30.00 therefor, which deposit ... termination of this contract, upon the surrender of the uniform by him

... duties necessary under the terms of this contract, the club may require ... may designate, and to participate in such exhibition contests as may be ... days prior to the First day of

... the travelling expenses, and meals en route of the player from his home city ... to there direct or by way of the city of ... practice and participate in the exhibition games, as provided for, a penalty ... be deducted from the compensation stipulated herein.

... and prior to the completion of the period of this contract, give the player ... ties and obligations hereunder, in which event the liabilities and obligations ... expiration of said one day. The player, at the expiration of said one day ... service to the club. If such notice be given to the player while "abroad" ... ses to the city of

... for no other party, during the period of this contract (unless with the written ... bition of the game of hockey as may be required of him by said club, at such ... for the National Hockey League season for the year 1941/42 beginning on ... of November 1941, and ending on or ... day of April, 1942, unless sooner terminated in accordance with other pro...

... ying season, or before the commencement or after the close thereof, participate ... lacrosse or football games or boxing or wrestling matches unless the written

... enter into a contract for the succeeding season upon all the terms and conditions ... and the salary to be paid the player in event of such renewal shall be the same as ... Clause One hereof unless it be increased or decreased by mutual agreement.

... of the player to any other club without furnishing the player in writing all of the ... showing what team has claim to his services, and what that claim is.

... paid by the Club to the Player as in this contract provided, the player hereby irrevo... any other persons, firms or corporations to make such use as it or such other persons, ... hs or of any reproduction of his likeness or of his signature for purposes of advertis... ing or publicity.

13. The player agrees and covenants that during the life of this contract he will not tamper with or enter into negotiations with any other player under contract or reservation to any club, member of this League, for, or regarding, his future or present services without written consent of the club of which the player negotiated with is a member, under penalty of a fine.

14. The "NOTICE" printed in red ink at the head of this contract is hereby made a part hereof.

15. If, because of any condition arising from a state of war, it shall be deemed advisable by the National Hockey League or by the Club to suspend or curtail operations, then in the event of suspension of operations this contract shall become void and at an end and in the event of curtailment but not suspension of operations the conditions set forth in Clause One hereof shall be automatically cancelled and shall be replaced by others to be mutually agreed upon between the Club and the Player.

In Testimony Whereof, the parties hereunto have executed this contract, this 14th. day of October A.D. 1941

MADISON SQUARE GARDEN CORP (NEW YORK RANGERS PROFESSIONAL HOCKEY CLUB)
By Lester Patrick Vice-President.
Lynn Patrick Player.
(SEAL)

WITNESSES:
Frank Boucher
Frank Boucher

Frank Boucher Returns to the Front

Lester Patrick consults with
coach Frank Boucher.

National Hockey League talent was a little sparse during the Second World War, as many players were away in action or serving war-time jobs. Frank Boucher, coach of the New York Rangers, looked around at his 1943 roster and put himself on the list, donning a jersey for the first time since the 1937–38 season. (He had previously served in the military with the 4th Princess Louise Dragoon Guards, Non-Permanent Active Militia.) Already the all-time leader in assists, there was no question that he could help the club—but his initial linemates upon his return, Bill Gooden and Jack McDonald, were war-time replacement players and were a far cry from his famous "Bread Line" colleagues, Bill and Bun Cook, whom Boucher had played with for 12 years. "A fellow doesn't want to make a fool of himself," Boucher told a luncheon meeting with the New York Hockey Writers Association. "But I have worked hard since the start of the training season, and I believe I can help the young fellows. Lester must believe I have a chance as he has not discouraged me in the decision." His general manager, Lester Patrick, had his back: "Naturally we don't expect Frank to backcheck," Patrick said. "His job will be to make the offensive plays, laying the puck on the sticks of his wingmen in attacks." Boucher played just 15 games, managing four goals and 10 assists. He did sign a contract for the following season, for $1,000, but never suited up. A few years later, he reminisced about his time with the two Cook brothers, and all three of them are in the Hockey Hall of Fame. "That's what I always used to be with them—not in the centre but right in the middle keeping all of us out of trouble."

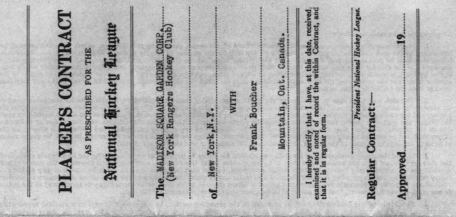

PLAYER'S CONTRACT

AS PRESCRIBED FOR THE

National Hockey League

The MADISON SQUARE GARDEN CORP.,
(New York Rangers Hockey Club)

of New York, N.Y.

WITH

Frank Boucher

Mountain, Ont. Canada.

I hereby certify that I have, at this date, received,
examined and noted of record the within Contract, and
that it is in regular form.

President National Hockey League

Regular Contract:—

Approved................................19

☛ IMPORTANT NOTICE TO PLAYERS AND CLUB PRESIDENTS ☚

Every player before signing a contract should carefully scrutinize the same to ascertain whether all of the conditions agreed upon between the Player and Club President have been incorporated therein, and if any have been omitted, the player should insist upon having all the terms, conditions, promises and agreements inserted in the contract before he signs the same.

NATIONAL HOCKEY LEAGUE

PLAYER'S CONTRACT (REGULAR)

Articles of Agreement between the Madison Square Garden

Corporation (New York Rangers Hockey Club)

of the City of New York, in the State/Province of New York

a club member of a League known as the "National Hockey League," party of the first part, hereinafter called the Club and

Frank Boucher

of the City of Mountain, in the State/Province of Ontario, Canada.

party of the second part, hereinafter called the Player.

Witnesseth:

That in consideration of the mutual obligations herein and hereby assumed, the parties to this contract severally agree as follows:

1. The club agrees to pay the player for the season of 19 1943/44, beginning on or about the First

day of November 19 xx1943, and ending on or about the Fifteenth

day of April 19 xx1944, a salary at the rate of $ 900.00 (Nine Hundred Dollars)

....for such season; and an additional sum at the rate of

$ 100.00 (One Hundred Dollars)

for such season said additional sum being in consideration of the option herein reserved to the club in Clause 10 hereof; said additional

sum to be paid whether said option is exercised or not, making the total compensation to the player for the season herein contracted

for $ 1,000.00 (One Thousand Dollars)

Attendance Woes Weaken Howell's New Deal

Talk about arriving at the wrong time. Harry Howell graduated from the Guelph Biltmores of the OHA to the New York Rangers in the 1952–53 season, and the squad proceeded to finish with a 17-37-16 record, good for last place. Fans stayed away too, as average attendance at Madison Square Garden dropped from 10,761 patrons in 1951–52, to 8,727, second worst in the league, ahead of the Bruins by a couple hundred fans. When Howell went to negotiate his 1953–54 contract, Rangers GM Frank Boucher offered him a $500 raise and a surprisingly honest reason why. "Had our gate receipts not fallen off so badly last season, I would have gladly given you a better increase," wrote Boucher in a letter dated July 25, 1953. Howell's response on August 4, 1953, having returned the contract unsigned, was professional and polite, hallmarks for the future Hall of Famer. The defensive stalwart was an anchor for the Rangers for 16 more seasons. In the Canadian Senate in March 2009, Senator Frank Mahovlich paid tribute to Howell: "Harry Howell will go down in the record books as the first Ranger to play 1,000 games. . . . He is a consummate gentleman, with a smile always on his face, and he always has time for his fans." Howell's subsequent contracts with the Rangers offered bonuses for the Rangers record—$500 for fourth place or better, meaning a playoff berth in the pre-expansion era—and rewards for being named an All-Star. Howell was elected to the Hockey Hall of Fame as an Honoured Member in 1979.

Harry Howell blocks the shot for his goaltender, Marcel Paille, as Billy Harris, Bill Gadsby, and Frank Mahovlich buzz around.

July 25th, 1953.

1952/53 - 6500.
1953/54 - 7000

Mr. Harry Howell
85 Dromore Crescent
Hamilton, Ont., Canada

Dear Harry:

    Enclosed please find your 1953/54 contract.

    You will note that I have increased your salary $500.00

    Had our gate receipts not fallen off so badly last season, I would have gladly given you a better increase.

    Please sign all copies (4) on the player's line, and return promptly.

    As soon as I have a response from you to this letter, you will then be advised of the details re date and place of reporting for the Rangers Training Camp this fall.

    Trsuting that you have had a pleasant summer, and expecting to hear from you at an early date, I remain,

                    Sincerely yours,

            MADISON SQUARE GARDEN CORPORATION

                    FRANK BOUCHER, Manager
                    New York Rangers Hockey Club

FB:pd
encls - as above.

---

85 Dromore Crescent,
Hamilton, Ontario.
August 4, 1953.

Dear Mr. Boucher,
        When I signed my Ranger contract last year we made an agreement. That agreement was that if I stuck with the Rangers and had a good season a substantial raise in salary could be expected. I do not think that the increase on my new contract is sufficient.
        My idea of a fair salary is eight thousand dollars. That would be the same amount I received last year including, of course, the bonus I received for turning professional.

                    Sincerely yours
                    Harry Howell.

Frank - Howell returned the contract unsigned - I have held onto it here along with the others.
                                    Pat

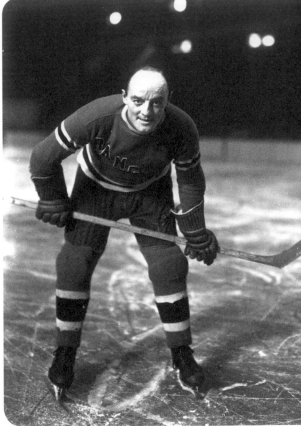

Still Smiling Through a Broken Jaw

In a 1964 *Hockey Illustrated* article, King Clancy listed the bruising 210-pound Ivan Wilfred "Ching" Johnson of the Rangers among the greatest defenceman of all time. "He looked menacing because he was bald, but he always had a smile on his face," said Clancy. "Ching smiled when you hit him hard. And when he hit you, he smiled too . . . maybe a little more." But Johnson couldn't smile after an incident in February 1930, where Dit Clapper of the Bruins sent him to the sidelines. "The result of which head-on collision was that Ching went to the hospital with his inferior maxillary—in the vulgar, his jawbone—fractured in four places," penned John Kieran in *The New York Times*. Johnson, a native of Winnipeg who didn't make the NHL until he was 30, was determined to help in the playoffs that year: "My ankles and shoulders are all right, and they're the important things in hockey. Your jaw doesn't count. What if I can't open my teeth? You're not allowed to bite in this game." On March 16, he did return to the ice for the Rangers' series against the original Ottawa Senators, wearing an aluminium and leather protector to hold the mending jaw in place. "The cheers accorded the returning Ranger served to speed the pace of the teams," reported the *Times*, as Johnson counted an assist, and the Rangers won in overtime on Bill Cook's goal. Johnson played another decade, and then he coached and refereed in the minors. He was elected to the Hockey Hall of Fame as an Honoured Member in 1958.

Ivan "Ching" Johnson was a star with the New York Rangers, and in 1958, NHL president Clarence Campbell welcomed Johnson to the Hockey Hall of Fame as an Honoured Member.

6436 Kansas Lane, Apt. # 22
Takoma Park, Maryland 20012
January 16, 1968

Dear Joe:

Referring to your question , in your letter of the 12th, as
to whether I returned to the game in the third period after breaking
my jaw, the answer is "No".

Here is the story on that accident. It was in the second
period of a Boston-Ranger game in Madison Square Garden. I was all
set to deliver a body check to an oncoming forward when he raised
his hockey stick to protect himself and the end of the handle struck
me in the jaw. The blow did not knock me down but when I reached up,
I found that a section of my jaw on the right side was loose, and I
realized that my jaw was fractured in two places. I set it as best I
could, skated to the bench and told Dr. Claus what had happened. His
only comment was, "After all your injuries, you should know". I returned to the dressing room, took a shower, got dressed and left the
Garden by an exit on 50th Street, and crossed the street to Polyclinic
Hospital. I was there for several weeks and returned to the game just
before the play-offs.

As to refereeing a match between Beezie Thomas and Long Sing
Que, I suggest that you get in touch with Joe Simpson and set up the
deal. Same rates- that will take some consideration- what you think?

I am planning to be with the old gang on February 11th when
the Rangers play in old Garden for the last time, and I plan to be in
the new Garden when it opens at night on the same date. See you then!

Best regards to you from Mrs. Johnson and myself.

Ching

As the captain, Mario Lemieux led the Laval Voisins to the QMJHL championships.

Scouting Mario

An amateur scout's job is a thankless one; they spend hours on the road, drinking stale coffee, and eating arena hot dogs to make it through yet another game. Then all that work watching a specific player can go for naught, when your team does not—or cannot—draft your chosen prospect. Consider Dan Summers, the New York Rangers' director of scouting, and his assessment of Mario Lemieux, then in his final year with the QMJHL's Laval Voisins. The Rangers finished eighth overall in the 1983–84 season, a solid 55 points ahead of the bottom-dwelling Pittsburgh Penguins, who selected *Mario le Magnifique* first overall and saved a floundering team. Pens GM Eddie Johnston once said: "The thing I'll remember most was making the decision to keep Mario. He was the one that got people back in the stands. That, I thought, was the turning point for our franchise." Summers nailed Lemieux pretty well: he would star in the NHL "with right supporting cast," because of his "golden touch" and "deceiving" skating. As for the negatives, Lemieux's "lack of consistent fire and drive" was a complaint that never left him, and it's tough to argue with a great line about Mario's desire bouncing "up and down like the proverbial toilet seat." One of Summers's biggest worries—"Hopefully he doesn't turn out to be a prima donna"—proved unfounded. The Hockey Hall of Fame inducted Lemieux as an Honoured Member in 1997, after his first retirement.

NEW YORK RANGERS

PLAYERS

GAME RATING _Average_ AMATEUR ☑ PRO ☐   DATE _Jan 4/84._

NAME _Mario Lemieux_ (_C_) POS. (_R_) S. HEIGHT _6.4_ WEIGHT _200_ YOB _Oct 5/65_

Laval TEAM (_8_) SCORE VS. _Drummondville_ OPPONENT (_6_) SCORE AT _Laval, Que._ LEAGUE _Q.M.J.H.L_

CHECK "✓" RATING

DEFENSE FORWARD	Desire Toughness	Skating	Puck Ct. Playmaking	Shot Scoring	Checking	GOAL TENDER	Concentration	Angles	Stand Up	Reflexes Recovery	Shot Blocking
Exceptional			✓✓	✓		Exceptional					
Very Good	✓ D.	✓			✓	Very Good					
Good	✓ To	To				Good					
Average		✓			To	Average					
Fair	✓ D.				✓	Fair					
Poor						Poor					

(Goaltender notes column, handwritten:) Jan 4 - Tied Pat Lafontaine's consecutive 43 game point record with an assist. Broke record Jan 6 with an assist - then thrown out of game with misconduct. These great offensive pluses feel will overshadow his lack of consistent fire & drive - Hopefully he doesn't turn out to be a prima donna + forsake his god given talents - This lack of effort be a bust.

POTENTIAL

	N.H.L.	MINOR	I.H.L.	NO PROSPECT
NOW –	✓ N.H.L.	☐ "	☐ "	☐ "
FUTURE –	✓ "	☐ "	☐ "	☐ "

COMMENTS: Initial 83/84 Report   *Much more so - than in past.

For Mario this was just an average game - Played with quite a bit of cautiousness, more physicalness, with a don't touch me type of attitude - Teammates seem to defend him also treat like Edmonton team protect Gretzky. This has lost the speed & size, toughness doesn't need this. The league's no challenge to him and he shows it, unfortunately - Can turn a game around by himself if & when he puts his mind to it. He's been here too long. He's a deceiving type on skates with his long stride - doesn't appear to be going that fast, most of the time is not - At his best, his speed is good - His swiftness & dekes class abo. good. He got the golden touch with the puck + a quick, heavy accurate shot - V. good offensive skills & know to put him well above ave. since first came into Jr. Unfortunately he has his goods - I feel he is a Frank Mahovlich type in this respect - Desire bounces up & down like the proverbial toilet seat - Can check (forecheck) would he wants - Bodychecking wanting. Has the offensive skills & tools to star at N.H.L. level with a right supporting cast and most importantly a rejuvinated intensity level - What this feel Poss N/a.

PLEASE PRINT   SCOUT _Dan Summers_ ✗ Present Manses-Coach

(page number: 3)

Bitter, Old Art Coulter

The negativity that Art Coulter showed towards the contemporary game was hardly confined to personal letters. When the New York Rangers were challenging for Lord Stanley's Cup in 1994, naturally the media sought out the captain of the last Rangers' Cup winners. Crusty and cantankerous, Coulter cracked, "Now they just shoot the puck in and chase it around like headless chickens. Christ, it's idiocy." Asked to compare Mark Messier and Brian Leetch to players from his era, Coulter was venomous. The Bread Line, Frank Boucher (who also coached the 1940 team) centring brothers Bill and Bun Cook, were the greatest ever, he said. "All of 'em are in the Hall of Fame," Coulter said in *The New York Times*. "They had brains, stickhandling, passing. They played the game like it should be played. Our old team that won the Stanley Cup could skate backwards blindfolded and whup the Rangers they've got today." Still Coulter's contributions were revered. Neil Smith, upon being named Rangers general manager in 1989, commissioned Stanley Cup rings for the seven living Rangers from that 1940 team and hung a battered jersey of Coulter's in his office. After hockey, Coulter lived in Miami, where his family had a hardware and importing business. Coulter was elected to the Hockey Hall of Fame as an Honoured Member in 1974 and died in October 2000 in Mobile, Alabama, at age 91.

Art Coulter in his heyday.

ARTHUR E. COULTER
10600 SW 128 ST.
MIAMI, FLA. 33176

Feb 11/84

Dear Mr. Roberts:

Have been out of pics for some time — there may be a new batch in the near future. I won't forget.

Raised in Winnipeg, Manitoba our family headed south for Dad's health. Older brother was working in Pittsburgh at the time. Stopped for a visit — stayed 9 years! Money was to good to leave — finally made it to Miami. Dad's health improved and he lived another 20 years. In Penna Coal shovels was one of his lines — he sold to Pgh Coal Co until

— OVER —

Andy Mellon found out — He was manufacturing his own steel goods —! traveled some with my Dad. Sure I have been through Barnesboro many times. Brothers wife born in Williamsport. Actor Jimmy Stewarts Dad had a mens & mill supply in maybe Indiana. Dad and Mr. Stewart were good friends. Poppa Stewart didn't like Jimmy going into the movie business. Sameway my family warn't thrilled to see me go into Pro Hockey. No skill or science in todays game. Olympic hockey quite as bad as N.H.L. But, still popular. Hope your Coal business is thriving. I'll be in touch.

Sincerely Art Coulter

EXPANSION

Bud Poile Begins to Build the Flyers

By the time he was tapped to lead the expansion Philadelphia Flyers into the National Hockey League, Norman "Bud" Poile had already been a hockey coach and executive for 27 years, and he knew exactly what he wanted: a good farm system. The general manager set about it in a couple of ways. The established NHL teams stacked the deck in their own favour, making the selection of players less than exciting in the 1967 expansion draft (protecting a goalie and 11 skaters from their main rosters), but ceding more access to amateurs (each team could protect only 15 amateurs). "We'll get a good shot at the amateurs, who are the secret of our success. I wasn't too excited about the draft of the pros," Poile said in January 1967 when the rules were established. Besides fishing for off-the-radar prospects, like Mike Doran (whose correspondence is reproduced here), who was at Cornell University and never played professional hockey, Poile and the Flyers bought the Quebec Aces of the AHL. Poile said it gave them "a little bit of flexibility. We have 16 pros to start with, some pretty good guys." The Flyers also signed a working agreement with the Seattle Totems of the Western Hockey League (where Flyers coach Keith Allen had been). While Poile was not around to bask in the Stanley Cup triumphs of the Broad Street Bullies—he was out in December 1969 and hired to set up the expansion Vancouver Canucks—his imprint was there through the names he got to the Flyers, like Bernie Parent, Ed Van Impe, Joe Watson, and Gary Dornhoefer, and draft picks such as Bobby Clarke, Dave Schultz, and Don Saleski.

Bud Poile made an impact as a hockey executive.

Find out what his status is.

PHILADELPHIA FLYERS
230 S. 15th ST., PHILA., PA., 19102 TEL. PE-5-9662-9663

April 4, 1967

Mr. George "Punch" Imlach
General Manager & Coach
Toronto Maple Leafs Hockey Club
Maple Leaf Gardens
60 Carlton Street
Toronto, Ontario, Canada

Dear Punch:

Just a note to wish you well in the upcoming Playoffs and to inquire about a player who is on your Inactive List.

Mr. Bill Putnam, our President, took in one of the college games and thought that a player by the name of Mike Doran could play minor league hockey. Would you be interested in trying to work out a deal where we may be able to purchase him and, if so, what price would you expect.

I would appreciate hearing from you on this, Punch, at your earliest convenience.

Again, best wishes in the Playoffs.

Yours sincerely,

N. R. "BUD" POILE

NRP/cjw

WILLIAM R. PUTNAM PRESIDENT • N. R. "BUD" POILE VICE PRESIDENT • JEROME S. SCHIFF SECRETARY-TREASURER • KEITH ALLEN COACH

August 9th, 1967

Mr. Mike Doran
c/o Hanshaws
346 Warren Road
Ithaca, New York
U. S. A.

Dear Mike:

Since you have graduated from an American College, we were wondering what your plans were concerning your hockey future.

Having talked to your Mother and finding that you have been accepted to go to school at Osgoode which would mean, more or less, your plans for professional hockey are worn out.

We are having a senior team in Maple Leaf Gardens and I was wondering if you would be interested in playing for them.

If you happen to be in Toronto before I leave for training camp in Peterboro which begins September 6th, I would appreciate hearing from you.

Yours truly,

R. E. Davidson
Chief Scout

RED:pd

Sittler's Days in Philadelphia

The February 1982 trade where Darryl Sittler left Toronto is often considered one of the worst trades in Leafs history. Philadelphia sent Toronto Rich Costello, a promising college prospect who played centre, and winger Ken Strong, who'd have most of his success in Austria. According to reports at the time, the Minnesota North Stars thought they had a deal in place for Sittler, but long-time Flyers GM, Keith "The Thief" Allen, prevailed, convincing Leafs owner Harold Ballard that prospects would be better than rumoured names like Behn Wilson, Rick St. Croix, and Brian Propp. "We certainly improved our hockey team," Allen said at the time. "I don't know how much closer to the Stanley Cup we are, but [Sittler is] similar to [Bobby] Clarke in dedication. We're very happy." Flyers coach Pat Quinn (who was replaced by Bob McCammon not long after the trade) positively gushed over Sittler. "He's been a dominant force in Toronto for years," Quinn said. "He is skilled mechanically in a number of ways. Whatever skills have diminished physically, he has compensated by his mental drive. He provides leadership, character, and a winning attitude. You can't have enough winners like that." All told, Sittler played 191 regular season games for the Flyers, but only 10 in the playoffs over three seasons.

It's a definite moment in time. Darryl Sittler with the Flyers, wearing Cooperalls, which the team wore only during the 1981–82 season.

IMPORTANT NOTICE TO PLAYER

Before signing this contract you should carefully examine it to be sure that all terms and conditions agreed upon have been incorporated herein, and if any has been omitted, you should insist upon having it inserted in the contract before you sign.

NATIONAL HOCKEY LEAGUE
STANDARD PLAYER'S CONTRACT
(1977 FORM)

Sittler to Phila

BETWEEN : **THE PHILADELPHIA HOCKEY CLUB, INC.**
hereinafter called the "Club"
a member of the National Hockey League, hereinafter called the "League"

– AND – **DARRYL SITTLER**
hereinafter called the "Player"

of Voorhees in Province / State of New Jersey

In consideration of the respective obligations herein and hereby assumed, the parties to this contract severally agree as follows:—

1. The Club hereby employs the Player as a skilled Hockey Player for the term of 3 + 1 year(s) commencing Jan. 20, 19 82 and agrees, subject to the terms and conditions hereof, to pay the Player a salary of Dollars ($).

1981/82 - $110,520.00 (payable $36,840 on March 15th, 1982
$36,840 on March 30th, 1982
$36,840 on April 15th, 1982)

1982/83 - $250,000.00
1983/84 - $250,000.00
1984/85 - $250,000.00 (option year)

Payment of such salary shall be in consecutive semi-monthly installments following the commencement of the regular League Championship Schedule of games or following the dates of reporting, whichever is later; provided, however, that if the Player is not in the employ of the Club for the whole period of the Club's games in the National Hockey League Championship Schedule, then he shall receive only part of the salary in the ratio of the number of days of actual employment to the number of days of the League Championship Schedule of Games.

And it is further mutually agreed that if the Contract and rights to the services of the Player are assigned, exchanged, loaned or otherwise transferred to a Club in another League, the Player shall only be paid at an annual salary rate of

Same salary as indicated above will be .... Dollars in the .... League.
paid in full in the Minor Leagues for the .... Dollars in the .... League.
or duration of the said contract. .... Dollars in the .... League.

2. The Player agrees to give his services and to play hockey in all League Championship, All Star, International, Exhibition, Play-Off and Stanley Cup games to the best of his ability under the direction and control of the Club in accordance with the provisions hereof.

The Player further agrees,

(a) to report to the Club training camp at the time and place fixed by the Club, in good physical condition,

(b) to keep himself in good physical condition at all times during the season,

(c) to give his best services to the Club and to play hockey only for the Club unless his contract is released, assigned, exchanged or loaned by the Club,

(d) to co-operate with the Club and participate in any and all reasonable promotional activities of the Club which will in the opinion of the Club promote the welfare of the Club and to cooperate in the promotion of the League and professional hockey generally,

(e) to conduct himself on and off the rink according to the highest standards of honesty, morality, fair play and sportsmanship, and to refrain from conduct detrimental to the best interest of the Club, the League or professional hockey generally.

The Club agrees that in exhibition games played after the start of the regular schedule (except where the proceeds are to go to charity, or where the player has agreed otherwise) the player shall receive his pro rata share of the gate receipts after deduction of legitimate expenses of such game. This provision re exhibition games is applicable in the National Hockey League only.

3. In order that the Player shall be fit in proper condition for the performance of his duties as required by this contract, the Player agrees to report for practice at such time and place as the Club may reasonably designate and participate in such exhibition games as may be arranged by the Club.

---

20. The parties agree that the rights provided in Section 18 and in any Addendum hereto and the promise of the Player to play hockey only with the Club, or such other club as provided in Sections 2, 11 and 12, and the Club's right to take pictures of and to televise the Player as provided in Section 8 have all been taken into consideration in determining the salary payable to the Player under Section 1 hereof.

21. It is severally and mutually agreed that the only contracts recognized by the President of the League are the Standard Player's Contracts, Player's Termination Contracts, and Player's Option Contracts which have been duly executed and filed in the League's office and approved by him (or his designated representative), and that this Agreement contains the entire agreement between the Parties and there are no oral or written inducements, promises or agreements except as provided herein.

In Witness Whereof, the parties have signed this 21st day of A.D. 19 82

WITNESSES:

The Philadelphia Hockey Club, Inc.
The Spectrum, Pattison Place
Philadelphia, Pa. 19148 *Club*
Address of Club

By .... *President*

Darryl Sittler *Player*
36 Holly Oak Drive
Voorhees, New Jersey 03043
Address of Player

I hereby certify that I have, at this date, received, examined and noted of record the within Contract, and that it is in regular form.

Dated JUN 8 1982 19

.... for the National Hockey League

Les parties ont par les présentes exprimé leur volonté expresse que ce contrat soit rédigé en anglais.
Parties hereby state their expressed wish that this contract be drafted in English language.

PHILADELPHIA FLYERS

THE SPECTRUM • PHILADELPHIA, PA. 19148 • 215-465-4500

KEITH ALLEN
EXECUTIVE VICE PRESIDENT
GENERAL MANAGER

April 5, 1982

Mr. Darryl Sittler
36 Holly Oak Drive West
Voorhees, New Jersey 08043

Dear Darryl:

This will confirm our agreement with respect to your contract, a copy of which contract is attached herein.

In addition to the specifics outlined in the contract, this will confirm that the Philadelphia Flyers fully undertake to pay the obligations outstanding in the option year in the event of an injury to you caused during the course of your employment. This is a variance from the Collective Bargaining Agreement and in fact guarantees you your entire salary for the full period through the 1984/85 option year season.

This will further confirm that on or before June 1, 1984 the Philadelphia Flyers have the right to extend the contract for an additional year which would then make the option year of the contract the 1985/86 season.

This will further confirm that you cannot be traded by the Philadelphia Flyers to a Canadian team during the contract, including the option year, without your written consent.

This will further confirm that you will be moving to Philadelphia in at least two stages within the next nine months and that all reasonable moving expenses will be paid by our Club.

We wish you every success in your career with the Flyers and trust you will be with us for many years after your playing days are over.

Sincerely yours,

THE PHILADELPHIA HOCKEY CLUB, INC.

Per:

SPORTS MANAGEMENT LIMITED

July 6, 1982

Mr. Darryl Sittler
36 Holly Oak Drive
Voorhees, New Jersey   08043
U.S.A.

Dear Darryl:

I enclose herewith a copy of your contract with the Philadelphia Hockey Club, Inc., which has been approved by the National Hockey League for your records. I have also sent a copy to Graeme Clark for his file.

This will confirm our agreement with respect to your contract that our fee for services rendered is in the amount of 8%. You and Graeme can agree on the payment dates with respect to the contract. The 8% figure will apply to the total as described in the contract from the 1981/82 season to the 1984/85 season.

I have also attached a copy of the letter dated April 5, 1982 which indicates that there is a possibility of an additional year at $250,000.00 for the 1985/86 season and it is understood that the 8% figure will apply to that as well.

Nancy and I are very happy you are enjoying Philadelphia so much. It is a great town and I am sure that with your contribution it will be a better town in the ensuing years. I would like to thank you and Wendy for your recent hospitality.

Sincerely yours,

Alan/p

R. Alan Eagleson, Q.C.

RAE:pw

80 RICHMOND ST. WEST, SUITE 2000, TORONTO, ONT. M5H 2C6 - TELEPHONE (416) 863-0372

Hutchison Says No to a Negotiating Bully

Dave Hutchison has plenty of stories from his NHL days, and some of the most colourful involve George Maguire, who was a scout and then general manager for the Los Angeles Kings. After four seasons with the Kings, Hutchison's name is signed to a 1978 contract extension. The salary sounds about right, but Hutchison swears nothing ever came of the deal; he'd already made arrangements on his own to go to the Toronto Maple Leafs. "I played out my four years, because that was the contract that I signed, and July 1st, when I became a free agent, the Leafs already kind of had me wrapped up. It's called collusion, but they had guys that had gotten to me, including my old teammates [Darryl] Sittler and Dan Maloney." Maguire and Hutchison got off on the wrong foot in 1972, when Hutchison was claimed from the London Knights of the OHL by the Kings (36th overall) and the WHA's Miami franchise. Still a scout, Maguire flew up to London, Ontario, to meet with the Hutchison family, where Maguire made a bad first impression. "Maguire comes to my house with this attitude and he says, 'And here's what you're going to get paid: $12,000 a year, $7,000 in the minors, because you're not going to make the team'—he tells me that right off the bat," recalled Hutchison. In the WHA, he had been offered $25,000 a year—over two years, plus a $50,000 signing bonus—and the bruising defenceman told Maguire he'd go to the WHA's Blazers. Maguire left the house in a huff, and Kings GM Jake Milford called to make amends. "You sent the wrong guy," Hutchison told him. After two seasons with the Blazers franchise in Philadelphia and Vancouver, Hutchison finally signed with the Kings. He never forgot Maguire's attitude, though, and when Maguire replaced Milford as GM in May 1977, Hutchison announced he wanted out. In June 1978, Maguire traded Hutch to Toronto, where he played two seasons, followed by a couple more seasons in Chicago, a year with the Devils during their first in New Jersey, and a last hurrah with the Leafs, hanging up his skates after the 1983–84 campaign.

Dave Hutchison goes hard around the net.

LOS ANGELES KINGS NHL THE FORUM BOX 10 INGLEWOOD CAL 90306 (213) 674-6000

July 25 1974

Mr David Hutchison
147 Emerson Avenue
London Ontario
Canada

Dear Dave

In addition to your National Hockey League Standard Player's
Contract and the Addendum attached thereto dated May 10, 1974,
the Los Angeles Kings agree to pay you the following bonuses
for each year of your three year contract, providing they are
earned:

    1)   Club will match any bonuses Player
           receives for League honors such as:

           N.H.L. All Star Selection
           M.V.P., etc.

In the event Player plays in "Minors" then
bonuses earned will be one-half of N.H.L.
bonuses.

        Very truly yours

        Los Angeles Kings Inc

        J. C. Milford

        John C Milford
        General Manager

Agreed to and Accepted:

Dave Hutchison

David Hutchison

JCM:f

NATIONAL HOCKEY LEA[GUE]

PLAYER'S OPTION CONTRACT

**LOS ANGELES KINGS HOCKEY CLUB
and/or CALIFORNIA SPORTS INCORPORATED**

.... DAVID HUTCHISON .... ("the Player"

respective obligations herein assumed, hereby agree and contract as follows

    The Club agrees to employ the Player as a skilled Hockey Player
so employed by the Club, on the same terms and conditions as are contain[ed]
League Standard Player's Contract between the Club and the Player dated
with the following exceptions only :

    1. The period of the Player's employment by the Club shall c[ommence]
current calendar year and terminate June 1 of the following calendar year
be a free agent, without any further obligation to provide services under this con[tract]
have the right, as provided by Section 9A of the National Hockey League By-Laws, a copy of which
Section is attached to said Standard Player's Contract, to negotiate and contract with any club in the
National Hockey League or with any other Club.

    2. The Player's salary for said period shall be the same as his entire salary for the final year
of said Standard Player's Contract. **Forty-Five Thousand Dollars — ($45,000.00).**

    3. The terms and conditions of Section 17 of said Standard Player's Contract shall not be a
part of this contract.

**LOS ANGELES KINGS HOCKEY CLUB
and/or CALIFORNIA SPORTS INCORPORATED**   *Dave Hutchison* Player
        Club   Dave Hutchison

By: *George Maguire*   147 Emerson Avenue Address of Player
    George Maguire   London Ontario Canada

    6 March 1978   6 March 1978
        Date   Date

                  [APR 1 7 1978

T.V.S.-1-74   NATIONAL HOCKEY LEAGUE

Portnoy/Hockey Hall of Fame

The bulk of Jimmy Rutherford's netminding career took place as a Red Wing.

Rutherford: 'The Goalie Understands the Game'

Jimmy Rutherford's path from goaltender to management began in the confusing days of 1980–81. Detroit dealt Rutherford to the Leafs in December 1980, after he had spent 10 years with the Red Wings and Penguins. The future general manager of the Hartford Whalers/Carolina Hurricanes and Pittsburgh Penguins only suited up for 18 games between the pipes for the Leafs, as he clashed with Leafs coach Joe Crozier, who didn't always keep his goalies informed. At the trade deadline in March 1981, the Leafs snagged Michel "Bunny" Larocque from the Canadiens, making Rutherford expendable, and he was on the road again—this time to Los Angeles. Rutherford was understandably confused when he talked to the media. "I'm not certain just what the Kings have in mind for me or how much they want me to play," Rutherford told the *Toronto Star*'s Frank Orr. "But maybe it's a good thing, because the situation here [in Toronto] hasn't been that good for me." In L.A., Rutherford backed up Mario Lessard, playing a handful of games as a King over two seasons. He had a brief hurrah back in Detroit before calling it quits. That Motown connection led him to running the Compuware Sports Corporation, which included the OHL's Windsor Spitfires and then the Plymouth Whalers. Rutherford feels that his time in net prepared him well for management. "Certainly the goalie understands the game. Maybe goalies are more long-term planners than day-to-day planners that coaches have to be," he said. When asked the secret to his success, including a 2006 Hurricanes Stanley Cup as general manager, Rutherford explained that it was more than one thing. "Patience is important. A plan is important. Having the right people around you is important. Relationships are important. The relationship you have with your owner, your boss, I think is very important as to how you communicate and work together with your boss to move forward. Those are probably the key areas."

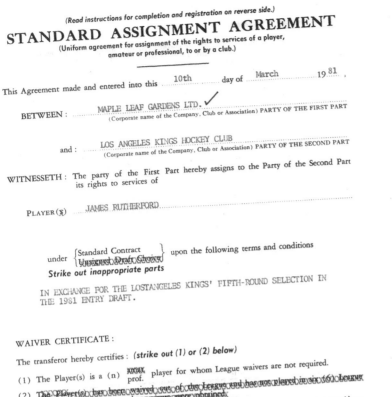

(Read instructions for completion and registration on reverse side.)

STANDARD ASSIGNMENT AGREEMENT
(Uniform agreement for assignment of the rights to services of a player, amateur or professional, to or by a club.)

This Agreement made and entered into this 10th day of March 19 81 ,

BETWEEN : MAPLE LEAF GARDENS LTD. ✓
(Corporate name of the Company, Club or Association) PARTY OF THE FIRST PART

and : LOS ANGELES KINGS HOCKEY CLUB
(Corporate name of the Company, Club or Association) PARTY OF THE SECOND PART

WITNESSETH : The party of the First Part hereby assigns to the Party of the Second Part its rights to services of

PLAYER (S) JAMES RUTHERFORD

under { Standard Contract / Unsigned Draft Choice } upon the following terms and conditions
Strike out inappropriate parts

IN EXCHANGE FOR THE LOSTANGELES KINGS' FIFTH-ROUND SELECTION IN THE 1981 ENTRY DRAFT.

WAIVER CERTIFICATE :

The transferor hereby certifies : *(strike out (1) or (2) below)*

(1) The Player(s) is a (n) ~~amat.~~ prof. player for whom League waivers are not required.

(2) ~~The Player(s) has been waived out of the League and has not played in six (6) League or Play-off games since the waivers were obtained.~~

IN WITNESS WHEREOF the parties hereto have subscribed through our respective Presidents or authorized agents, witnessed on the date set out above.

MAPLE LEAF GARDENS LTD.
CLUB

Gordon Stellick   By _____
WITNESS   (Party of the First Part)

LOS ANGELES KINGS HOCKEY CLUB
CLUB

Marcia Galloway   By _George Maguire_
WITNESS   (Party of the Second Part)

[stamp: CENTRAL REGISTRY REC'D / SEEN MAR 26 09 21 '81]
[stamp: ACTION Bull. 1789]

Instructions for Completion

(1) Fill in the **correct** date and the **correct** corporate names of the parties to the Agreement, as well as the correct **full** names of the players involved. Except in cases of trades, separate assignments should be prepared for **each** player.

(2) Strike out the inapplicable kinds of agreement and the inapplicable clause of the waiver certificate at the bottom.

(3) Have Agreements signed by authorized officers and each signature should be witnessed.

Instructions for Registration

(1) Write to Central Registry, 920 Sun Life Building, Montreal, Canada H3B 2W2; advising of the transaction and enclosing all copies of the Agreement, with instructions for registration. Send a copy of **this letter** for each league affected by the transaction except the National Hockey League and for each Club affected.

(2) Central Registry must be advised immediately by TWX of this transaction by both Clubs concerned. Copies of this agreement should be initiated by the Club transferring the player and forwarded to the Club receiving the player for completion and subsequent filing with Central Registry as described in (1) above.

(3) Sufficient copies of the Agreement should be prepared and sent to the Central Registry for the following purposes :

(a) Central Registry
One copy (signed) for **each** player involved.

(b) Each affected League
One copy.

(c) Each club involved
One copy (signed).

Send **all** copies of the Agreement to the Central Registry.

(4) Central Registry will report transaction in the first regular Bulletin after notice is received, which will serve as acknowledgment of receipt of the notice.

(5) Central Registry will record, time-stamp and distribute by mail, copies of Agreement received to the Leagues and Clubs affected, which will serve as acknowledgment of receipt of documents,—no other acknowledgment will be sent.

LOS ANGELES KINGS NHL THE FORUM BOX 10 INGLEWOOD CAL 90306 (213) 674-6000

March 18 1981

Mr George Imlach
Toronto Maple Leafs
Maple Leaf Gardens
60 Carlton Street
Toronto Ontario Canada
M5B 1L1

Dear George

I have completed the Standard Assignment forms for Jim Rutherford and forwarded them to NHL Central Registry.

Thank you for Rutherford's contract and the letter with respect to Branada Sports Management Lmtd.

Kind personal regards

George Maguire

George Maguire
General Manager

GM:mg

Bill Plager No Fan of Wren Blair

Bill Plager is a little puzzled by the nice note that he sent to general manager Wren Blair back in May 1968, after his rookie year with the Minnesota North Stars. "I'm not a Mr. Blair fan, I'll tell you that right now," he said when the letter was read to him. "You had to be polite in those days. General managers could make you or ruin you. They could send you down and bury you in the minors. So you had to bite your tongue a lot of times." In Plager's case, he had two big brothers already in the NHL, the notoriously tough Barclay and Bob Plager. Bill was Montreal property in junior, where he skated for the Peterborough Petes. Traded to Minnesota before the expansion era began, Bill Plager didn't feel he got a fair shake from Blair. "He pulled some shady stuff when I was there. I was the youngest defenceman that they had in the league that year, and I have to say that I had a very good playoff—it was against the Los Angeles Kings, and then we played St. Louis. I had a real good one going, and then he never played me the last game. I just sat on the bench. Everybody was telling me how good I was playing . . . then he traded me the next year." Over the next nine seasons, Plager played for a dizzying number of teams in the NHL (Blues, Flames, back to the North Stars), and he also had a series of minor-league stops in the CHL, AHL, and NAHL. He called it quits in 1977. "It was time to look in the mirror and say, 'I'd better find a job!'" he laughed. After the tough decision, Plager settled in Peterborough and was a supervisor at Quaker Oats for 32 years. He died of cancer in January 2016.

Bill Plager played in St. Louis, Minnesota, and Atlanta during his NHL career.

568 Simmons Ave.
Peterborough Ont.
May 11, 1968

Dear Wren
    Just a note to thank you for a good season. Hope to see you during the summer if we are ever up in Haliburton.

                    Yours truly,
                    Bill Plager

$142.81

May 31, 1968

Mr. William Plager
568 Simmons Avenue
Peterborough, Ontario,
Canada

Dear Bill:

Kindly find enclosed our check in the amount of
$184.00, representing your $250.00 bonus less
taxes for winning the first round of the playoffs in accordance with the terms of your contract.
Money for travel home will be forwarded to you by
separate check in the not too distant future, but
I wanted to get this out to you now.

League awards and an amount of $300.00 paid by me
personally will follow some time late in June or
early July.

Trust you are spending some enjoyable and relaxing
days, and I will be in touch with you shortly
regarding next season.

Kindest personal regards.

                                        Yours very truly,

                                        Wren A. Blair
                                        General Manager-Coach

WAB:mv

Plager Brothers Meet Up in St. Louis

For parts of four seasons, from 1968 to 1972, the St. Louis Blues could boast three Plager brothers in their lineup. The trio from Kirkland Lake in northern Ontario—Barclay, Bob, and Bill— were all tough-as-nails defenceman. Consider a Peterborough versus Guelph junior game from early 1963 where Bob and Bill started duking it out, the fight spilling from the ice to the penalty box and then underneath the stands. When their father was told of the brawl, he simply asked: "Did either one go down?" As special as it was to play with his siblings, Bill Plager relished his time away from them. "I enjoyed playing against them more than with them," he confessed. "More bragging rights if you won." The competitiveness was a big part of growing up, with a little more than four years separating them. "We all wanted the same thing. We wanted to be better than each other," said Bill. "You always tell people you lived a dream. You're a little kid from Kirkland Lake, Ontario, a little mining town, and you get to play in the biggest arenas in the world. And I've got to say, your two brothers are there competing for the Stanley Cup—even though we didn't win it—it's quite the feeling."

Bob, Bill, and Barclay Plager all suited up for the Blues.

June 28, 1973

Mr. Wren Blair
General Manager
Minnesota North Stars
Metropolitan Sports Center
Bloomington, Minnesota 55420

Dear Wren:

Enclosed please find standard assignment agreement forms in
favor of Bill Plager duly signed and witnessed by our organization.
I would appreciate if you would complete the documents and forward
them directly to Central Registry.

Yours truly,

CLIFF FLETCHER
General Manager

CF:t
Enclosures

(Read instructions for completion and registration on reverse side.)

STANDARD ASSIGNMENT AGREEMENT

(Uniform agreement for assignment of the rights to services of a player,
amateur or professional, to or by a club.)

This Agreement made and entered into this **28th** day of **June** 1973,

BETWEEN: **ATLANTA HOCKEY, INC.**
(Corporate name of the Company, Club or Association) PARTY OF THE FIRST PART

and: **NORTHSTAR FINANCIAL CORPORATION**
(Corporate name of the Company, Club or Association) PARTY OF THE SECOND PART

WITNESSETH: The party of the First Part hereby assigns to the Party of the Second Part
its rights to services of

PLAYER(S) **BILL PLAGER**

under { Standard Contract ~~Option "B"~~ } upon the following terms and conditions
{ ~~Try-Out "A" Option "C"~~ }
Strike out inappropriate parts

Claimed under bi-law 16A5B

WAIVER CERTIFICATE:

The transferor hereby certifies : *(strike out (1) or (2) below)*

(1) The Player(s) is a (a) ~~xxxx~~ prof. player for whom League waivers are not required.

(2) ~~The Player(s) has been waived out of the League and has not played in six (6) League
or Play-off games since the waivers were obtained.~~

IN WITNESS WHEREOF the parties hereto have subscribed through our respective Presidents
or authorized agents, witnessed on the date set out above.

ATLANTA HOCKEY, INC.
CLUB

Jenna Adams
WITNESS

BY _____
(Party of the First Part)

NORTHSTAR FINANCIAL CORPORATION
CLUB

Marilyn A. Vaughan
WITNESS

BY _____
(Party of the Second Part)

Instructions for Completion

(1) Fill in the **correct** date and the **correct** corporate names of the parties to the Agreement, as well as the correct **full** names of the players involved. Except in cases of trades, separate assignments should be prepared for **each** player.

(2) Strike out the inapplicable kinds of agreement and the inapplicable clause of the waiver certificate at the bottom.

(3) Have Agreements signed by authorized officers and each signature should be witnessed.

Instructions for Registration

(1) Write to Central Registry, 922 Sun Life Building, Montreal, Canada, advising of the transaction and enclosing all copies of the Agreement, with instructions for registration. Send a copy of **this letter** for each league affected by the transaction except the National Hockey League and for each Club affected.

(2) If the transaction affects an active professional player during the playing season, **wire** to the Central Registry advising of the transaction and send a copy of the wire by mail for each league affected by it, except the National Hockey League.

(3) Sufficient copies of the Agreement should be prepared and sent to the Central Registry for the following purposes :

    (a) Central Registry
        One copy (signed) for **each** player involved.

    (b) Each affected League
        One copy.

    (c) Each club involved
        One copy (signed).

Send **all** copies of the Agreement to the Central Registry.

(4) Central Registry will report transaction in the first regular Bulletin after notice is received, which will serve as acknowledgment of receipt of the notice.

(5) Central Registry will record, time-stamp and distribute by mail, copies of Agreement received to the Leagues and Clubs affected, which will serve as acknowledgment of receipt of documents,—no other acknowledgment will be sent.

The Injury-Prone Career of Fred Barrett

Unlike a lot of his peers, defenceman Fred Barrett knew that many of his old documents from the Minnesota North Stars had entered the market-place and were up for auction. He contacted the auction house, which agreed to remove his medical records from the auction—and Barrett, with his mind-boggling number of injuries during a career that lasted from 1970 to 1984, had a *lot* of medical records. "People go, 'What the hell did you do to yourself back then?'" Barrett explained. While still a junior, he split his kneecap and then suffered through a bone chip in his ankle, followed by a broken hand. Then with the North Stars, he experienced a fractured femur, separated shoulder, broken jaw, another broken hand, and more ankle issues. But there was always a spot for him on the Minnesota blue line, though he had to work for it. "When we merged with Cleveland, I went to camp and we had 12 defencemen. I don't mind going to training camp and winning my job. I'd go out and play the same game every night, get eight or 10 hits a night and be a plus-player, so at the end of training camp, they have to say, 'We've got to keep this guy.'" He was a big part of a team post hockey too, as a firefighter for the City of Ottawa. "You get used to that rush, that exhilaration, the challenge of things. That's kind of what firefighting is. You get out the door heading to that call, and you're pumped." For Barrett, it was just like hockey, but with fewer injuries.

Fred Barrett in 1975.

June 24, 1970

Mr. Fred Barrett
P.O. Box 103 - R.R. #6
Ottawa, Ontario, Canada

Dear Fred:

I would like to take this opportunity to officially welcome you to the Minnesota organization. We were very pleased to acquire you in the recent Amateur Draft and look forward to seeing you at training camp. Your letter of invitation to training camp, which will be held at Winnipeg, Manitoba, will be sent some time in mid-August.

I am told by our scouts that you play both the left and right side and I would like to point out to you that we are badly in need of a defense-man on the major league club on the right side this season (probably to team up with Ted Harris). It is our intention to give you a good look at camp in this position in the hope that you might possibly be able to make the major league team, although this is a very big step for you from Junior "A" hockey. If you are not quite ready for the major league, we are sure you can make our American League club at Cleveland and, hope-fully, the major league club in the not too distant future.

Trust you are preparing yourself, both mentally and physically, over the summer to give an all-out effort at training camp, and I will look forward to seeing you at that time.

If you have any questions or if there is anything I can help you with, please do not hesitate to write me and I will be in touch with you.

Kindest personal regards.

Yours very truly,

Wren A. Blair
General Manager

Airliner MOTOR HOTEL

TELEX 035267 ★ PHONE 775-7131 ★ 1740 ELLICE AT MADISON ★ WINNIPEG 21, MANITOBA

Fred Barrett

6 - to Sign
2 - More to stay or eventually made
/8   Minimum 40 games.

$ 12500. in majors
  7500. in Minors

Latest Demand by Barrett Sept. 23/70

$ 10000 to Sign
  15000 N.H.L. Contract
  10000 Minor League Contract.

          Or
$ 10000 to Sign
  12000 N.H.L. & Minor League Contract.

H. Cotton.

COURTESY CAR ★ 120 AIR-CONDITIONED UNITS ★ COLORED TELEVISION ★ HEATED SWIMMING POOL ★ 5 MINUTES TO AIRPORT ★ 5 MINUTES FROM DOWNTOWN

GM Nanne Okays Defenceman Nanne's Retirement

In 1978, defenceman Lou Nanne signed his own retirement papers—
"That's never been done before or since," he said—so that he could take
over as coach and general manager of the Minnesota North Stars. He has
a remarkable recollection of the decision. "We were playing in New York
on a Wednesday night. We got beat 5–0 and I went back to my hotel room,
and that was February 8th, and one of the owners called me: 'When you get
in tomorrow, we want you to come over to our office.'" Nanne heard their
pitch for the new roles. Knowing he was going to retire at the end of the
season, he agreed and went before the full board the next morning. "They
asked me a lot of questions, things I thought I could do with the team, what
they wanted, what to expect, blah, blah, blah, and they made me coach and
general manager February 10th." For the next decade, Nanne was North
Stars hockey, and to this day, he's still called upon to talk pucks on radio
and TV. He coached only until the end of that 1977–78 season. "I liked the
business end more than the repetition of coaching day-to-day," said Nanne,
who got an education while playing at the University of Minnesota. What
he did not like was the stress, and he battled obsessive-compulsive disorder
as the team had its ups—like the 1981 run to the Stanley Cup Finals—and
downs. He sought help for his issues. "After eight years, I went to the Mayo
Clinic to try to stop some of the stupid-ass stuff that I used to do, like go
around a chair four times one way and four times another way—just crazy-
ass stuff." Choosing his health over hockey, Nanne moved seamlessly into
the business world, and he is now senior managing director and national
sales manager for RBC Global Asset Management, Inc.

Lou Nanne moved right from the ice to
management with the North Stars.

APPLICATION TO BE PLACED ON
VOLUNTARILY RETIRED LIST

—————

April 9, 1979 .... 19........

TO THE PRESIDENT,

DEAR SIR:

    I desire to retire from professional hockey and I request that my name be placed on the Voluntarily Retired List under the provisions of the League By-Laws.

....
WITNESS   SIGNATURE OF PLAYER

5801 Hidden Lane
Edina, Minnesota 55436
....
HOME ADDRESS OF PLAYER

TO THE LEAGUE PRESIDENT:

    Approval is granted for placing this player's name on the Voluntarily Retired List.

Northstar Hockey Partnership (Minnesota
.... North Stars)
HOCKEY CLUB

PER ....
Mr. Lou Nanne, General Manager

CENTRAL REGISTRY

| REC'D | SEEN |

Apr 19   09   '79

| ACTION |

1M-T.V.B.-9-67

Frank Prazak/Hockey Hall of Fame   O-Pee-Chee/Hockey Hall of Fame

Dean Prentice ended his career
as a Minnesota North Star.

Dean Prentice Loses His Touch

After 21 years in the NHL, Dean Prentice knew it was time to call it quits. A native of Schumacher, Ontario, he played on three Original Six teams (Rangers, Bruins, Red Wings) starting in 1953, and then he spent two seasons in Pittsburgh and three in Minnesota. During the 1973–74 season, he wrote to North Stars GM Wren Blair, explaining that he was finished. "I was 41 years of age, so that's old enough. I was getting near the end. What happened was my legs were good but my timing was getting a little bit off, the sharpness in handling the puck and getting the shot off right away," said Prentice. "I could tell." During December 1973, Prentice sat out nine straight games and had trouble with his confidence. Blair initially called Prentice a "quitter" in the media. But Prentice came to terms with the situation. "I would never have made it without the help of the Lord," Prentice told the *Minneapolis Star* after retiring. "I was feeling useless. I wasn't part of the team. I wanted to help." Prentice, a left winger by trade, ended up with 391 goals and 469 assists in 1,378 NHL games. His nephew, Jim Prentice, the former premier of Alberta, called Uncle Dean the "best player from that era never to make the Hall of Fame." Post hockey, Dean Prentice tried coaching in the AHL for a season, but he found a lot more fulfillment working for Hockey Ministries International.

APPLICATION TO BE PLACED ON VOLUNTARILY RETIRED LIST

January 5,   1974

TO THE PRESIDENT.

DEAR SIR:

I desire to retire from professional hockey and I request that my name be placed on the Voluntarily Retired List under the provisions of the League By-Laws.

WITNESS   x   SIGNATURE OF PLAYER

4200 Parklawn Avenue, Apt. 104, Edina, MN 55435
HOME ADDRESS OF PLAYER

TO THE LEAGUE PRESIDENT:

Approval is granted for placing this player's name on the Voluntarily Retired List.

NORTHSTAR FINANCIAL CORPORATION
HOCKEY CLUB

PER

N MINNESOTA NORTH ST★RS Metropolitan Sports Center, Bloomington, Minnesota 55420

March 21, 1973

WREN BLAIR, General Manager

M E M O

TO: Dean S. Prentice

FROM: Wren A. Blair,
        General Manager

As agreed in our discussion today upon signing your 1973-74 contract, the conditions for 1974-75 would be that if you are not protected in the Expansion Draft of 1974 and are claimed by another club, you would receive a cash bonus of $5,000.00 on the basis that you negotiate a contract with the club that claims you and play for that club the following season.

However, if you are not claimed or if we fill with you and you, therefore, remain with the Minnesota organization, your contract for the next season would be at $57,000.00, plus similar bonuses to those you now have in your contract, to play in the 1974-75 season with the Minnesota organization.

Also, it was agreed that you and I would discuss at the completion of the 1973-74 season your thoughts on whether or not you will play in the 1974-75 season.

WAB:mv

NATIONAL HOCKEY LEAGUE

4200 Parklawn Avenue,
Edina, Minnesota 55435

January 5th., 1974.

Mr. Wren Blair,
General Manager,
Minnesota Northstars Hockey Club,
Metropolitan Sports Centre,
Bloomington, Minnesota.

Dear Wren:

As a result of our conversation on January 3rd., and after much thought and finally facing reality that my career has come to an end, I would like you to accept my retirement.

I sincerely hope Wren that you will not take this as a hasty or bitter decision, as I truthfully thank you for keeping your promise to me. That being, you would let me know when I could no longer do my job.

I thank you for bringing me here to this organization as I have enjoyed my tenure here.

As you know, I would like to go into the coaching field and if possible would you let it be known around the leagues that this is my desire.

Respectfully yours,

Dean

Dean Prentice

Lou Angotti's Brief Turn as Blues GM

The resumé of Lou Angotti is pretty impressive. After graduating from St. Michael's College in Toronto, he continued his education—and his hockey—with the Michigan Tech Huskies. The team lost in the 1960 NCAA finals, but they won in 1962, when Angotti, primarily a centre, was named tournament MVP. He then played over 700 NHL games, including playoffs. Highlights include assisting on Bobby Hull's 500th NHL goal and being the first captain of the Philadelphia Flyers. While playing with the St. Louis Blues, he was chosen to finish the 1973–74 season as coach, replacing Jean-Guy Talbot; he later coached the Pittsburgh Penguins in 1983–84, and then moved on to coach in the AHL. What gets left out of his career summaries, though, is his brief stint as Blues general manager, which lasted "maybe a couple of months," said Angotti. "I was coaching at the time, then they added the title of general manager on to my coaching duties." Angotti was in charge of the team as the 1973–74 campaign ran down and through the summer. (GM Chuck Catto had left the Blues for the WHA's Indianapolis Racers.) "I negotiated some contracts. I remember going to the NHL Draft, the meetings; I went to the general managers' meetings," said Angotti. He didn't want to go into specifics, but he didn't totally see eye-to-eye with the Salomon family, who owned the team. "It didn't have anything to do with the actual title, it had to do with some of the responsibilities and some of the things that they expected me to do," he said. Angotti left the executive office (Gerry Ehman took over as Blues GM) and returned to play on the ice for a final season in 1974–75, coaxed by his buddy Pat Stapleton to join the Chicago Cougars in the WHA. "I spent a month or so getting in shape with them," said Angotti. "I played that one year and I went to training camp, but I knew I couldn't keep up with everybody else. Even in the WHA I couldn't keep up."

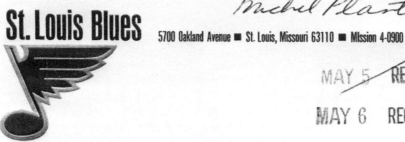

St. Louis Blues 5700 Oakland Avenue ■ St. Louis, Missouri 63110 ■ MIssion 4-0900

Michel Plante

From the
Office of
LOU ANGOTTI
Coach and
General Manager

AIR MAIL

April 23, 1974

Mr. Jim Gregory,
General Manager
Toronto Maple Leafs Hockey Club
60 Carlton Street
Toronto 200, Ontario, Canada

Dear Jim:

Per your conversation with Sid III, here is the agreement relative to the sale of Michel Plante to the St. Louis Blues.

The following is in effect only if the player is a member of the St. Louis Blues Organization:

1. If player plays in 25 games in minor pro, St. Louis will pay Toronto $5,000.00.

2. If player is protected in the Intra-League draft, St. Louis will pay Toronto $20,000.00. If player is drafted in the Intra-League draft, St. Louis will pay Toronto $15,000.00.

We are enclosing Standard Assignment Agreement papers in triplicate. Please execute these documents on behalf of your club and return along with executed acknowledgement copy of this letter to me at your earliest convenience.

Sincerely,

Lou Angotti

LA/mh

AGREED TO AND ACCEPTED BY: AGREED TO AND ACCEPTED BY:

Member
National
Hockey
League

_____   _____
Jim Gregory   Lou Angotti,
General Manager   General Manager/Coach
Toronto Maple Leafs   St. Louis Blues

Fergie Jenkins a Steal for $1

Most know Ferguson Jenkins as the first Canadian member of the National Baseball Hall of Fame, but few are aware of his contract with the NHL's St. Louis Blues. Signed on January 30, 1975, it was a publicity stunt (that didn't get much press) suggested by Jenkins's lawyer, who also represented a couple of NHL players. His NHL contract was for $1, a little less than what Jenkins was seeking in his contract dispute with the Chicago Cubs. "I worked out with the team for about an hour, hour and a half, skating, until they did some two-on-twos, three-on-threes. But I skated, shot the puck against some of the goalies, had some fun," recalled Jenkins. Interestingly, the deal is signed directly with Blues owner Sid Salomon III, but it may not have ever been filed with the league—the Clarence Campbell signature on the contract was signed by someone other than Campbell himself. Growing up in Chatham, Ontario, Jenkins always enjoyed getting out on the ice. "I was a hockey player, as high as Junior B. I enjoyed it in the time I had in Chatham, but my best sport was baseball." He obviously made the right decision. Jenkins won 284 games during his 19-year baseball career, playing for the Cubs, Rangers, and Red Sox. He won the National League Cy Young Award in 1971, had his number 31 retired by the Cubs, and was enshrined in Cooperstown in 1991. Though Oklahoma is home now, he is often back in Canada for events run by his Fergie Jenkins Foundation, which raises millions of dollars for charities across North America.

Fergie Jenkins used the Blues as a distraction during his contract negotiations with the Chicago Cubs. Jenkins has always liked hockey, whether suiting up for a game at home in Chatham or posing with Bobby Orr at a Hockey Hall of Fame function.

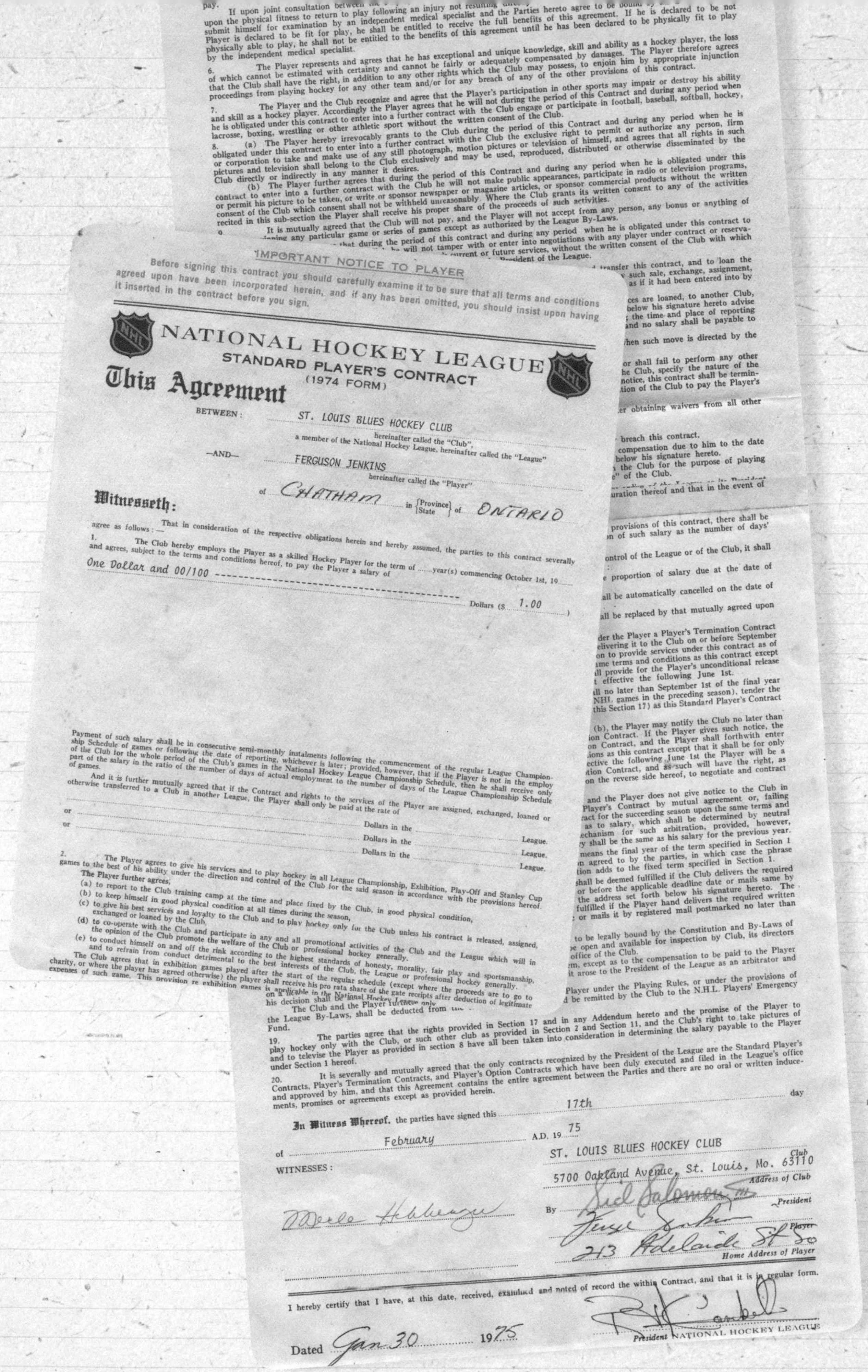

If upon consultation between ... [faded]
upon the physical fitness to return to play following an injury not resulting ... the Parties hereto agree to be bound by ...
submit himself for examination by an independent medical specialist and the Parties hereto agree to be bound by this agreement. If he is declared to be not
Player is declared to be fit for play, he shall be entitled to receive the full benefits of this agreement until he has been declared to be physically fit to play
physically able to play, he shall not be entitled to the benefits of this agreement.
by the independent medical specialist.

6. The Player represents and agrees that he has exceptional and unique knowledge, skill and ability as a hockey player, the loss
of which cannot be estimated with certainty and cannot be fairly or adequately compensated by damages. The Player therefore agrees
that the Club shall have the right, in addition to any other rights which the Club may possess, to enjoin him by appropriate injunction
proceedings from playing hockey for any other team and/or for any other breach of any of the other provisions of this contract.

7. The Player and the Club recognize and agree that the Player's participation in other sports may impair or destroy his ability
and skill as a hockey player. Accordingly the Player agrees that he will not during the period of this Contract and during any period when
he is obligated under this contract to enter into a further contract with the Club engage or participate in football, baseball, softball, hockey,
lacrosse, boxing, wrestling or other athletic sport without the written consent of the Club.

8. (a) The Player hereby irrevocably grants to the Club during the period of this Contract and during any period when he is
obligated under this contract to enter into a further contract with the Club the exclusive right to permit or authorize any person, firm
or corporation to take and make use of any still photograph, motion pictures or television of himself, and agrees that all rights in such
pictures and television shall belong to the Club exclusively and may be used, reproduced, distributed or otherwise disseminated by the
Club directly or indirectly in any manner it desires.
(b) The Player further agrees that during the period of this Contract and during any period when he is obligated under this
contract to enter into a further contract with the Club he will not make public appearances, participate in radio or television programs,
or permit his picture to be taken, or write or sponsor newspaper or magazine articles, or sponsor commercial products without the written
consent of the Club which consent shall not be withheld unreasonably. Where the Club grants its written consent to any of the activities
recited in this sub-section the Player shall receive his proper share of the proceeds of such activities.

9. It is mutually agreed that the Club will not pay, and the Player will not accept from any person, any bonus or anything of
[faded] any particular game or series of games except as authorized by the League By-Laws.
[faded] that during the period of this contract and during any period when he is obligated under this contract or reserva-
[faded] will not tamper with or enter into negotiations with any player under contract or reserva-
[faded] current or future services, without the written consent of the Club with which
[faded] ident of the League.

NATIONAL HOCKEY LEAGUE
STANDARD PLAYER'S CONTRACT
(1974 FORM)

This Agreement

BETWEEN:

ST. LOUIS BLUES HOCKEY CLUB

a member of the National Hockey League, hereinafter called the "Club",
and of the National Hockey League, hereinafter called the "League"

—AND—

FERGUSON JENKINS

hereinafter called the "Player"

of CHATHAM in {Province} {State} of ONTARIO

Witnesseth:

That in consideration of the respective obligations herein and hereby assumed, the parties to this contract severally
agree as follows:—

1. The Club hereby employs the Player as a skilled Hockey Player for the term of ...... year(s) commencing October 1st, 19......
and agrees, subject to the terms and conditions hereof, to pay the Player a salary of

One Dollar and 00/100 ——————————————————————————

Dollars ($ 1.00)

Payment of such salary shall be in consecutive semi-monthly instalments following the commencement of the regular League Championship Schedule of games or following the date of reporting, whichever is later; provided, however, that if the Player is not in the employ
of the Club for the whole period of the Club's games in the National Hockey League Championship Schedule, then he shall receive only
part of the salary in the ratio of the number of days of actual employment to the number of days of the League Championship Schedule
of games.

And it is further mutually agreed that if the Contract and rights to the services of the Player are assigned, exchanged, loaned or
otherwise transferred to a Club in another League, the Player shall only be paid at the rate of

or .... Dollars in the .... League.

or .... Dollars in the .... League.

.... Dollars in the .... League.

2. The Player agrees to give his services and to play hockey in all League Championship, Exhibition, Play-Off and Stanley Cup
games to the best of his ability under the direction and control of the Club for the said season in accordance with the provisions hereof.
The Player further agrees,
(a) to report to the Club training camp at the time and place fixed by the Club, in good physical condition,
(b) to keep himself in good physical condition at all times during the season,
(c) to give his best services and loyalty to the Club and to play hockey only for the Club unless his contract is released, assigned,
exchanged or loaned by the Club,
(d) to co-operate with the Club and participate in any and all promotional activities of the Club and the League which will in
the opinion of the Club promote the welfare of the Club or professional hockey generally,
(e) to conduct himself on and off the rink according to the highest standards of honesty, morality, fair play and sportsmanship,
and to refrain from conduct detrimental to the best interests of the Club, the League or professional hockey generally.
The Club agrees that in exhibition games played after the start of the regular schedule (except where the proceeds are to go to
charity, or where the player has agreed otherwise) the player shall receive his pro rata share of the gate receipts after deduction of legitimate
expenses of such game. This provision re exhibition games is applicable to the National Hockey League only.
his decision shall be ....
The Club and the Player further ......
the League By-Laws, shall be deducted from the ......
Fund.

19. The parties agree that the rights provided in Section 17 and in any Addendum hereto and the promise of the Player to
play hockey only with the Club, or such other club as provided in Section 2 and Section 11, and the Club's right to take pictures of
and to televise the Player as provided in section 8 have all been taken into consideration in determining the salary payable to the Player
under Section 1 hereof.

20. It is severally and mutually agreed that the only contracts recognized by the President of the League are the Standard Player's
Contracts, Player's Termination Contracts, and Player's Option Contracts which have been duly executed and filed in the League's office
and approved by him, and that this Agreement contains the entire agreement between the Parties and there are no oral or written inducements, promises or agreements except as provided herein.

In Witness Whereof, the parties have signed this ..... 17th ..... day

of February ..... A.D. 19 75

WITNESSES :

ST. LOUIS BLUES HOCKEY CLUB

5700 Oakland Avenue, St. Louis, Mo. 63110
Address of Club

By .... *President*

213 Adelaide St. So.
Home Address of Player

I hereby certify that I have, at this date, received, examined and noted of record the within Contract, and that it is in regular form.

Dated Jan 30 1975

President NATIONAL HOCKEY LEAGUE

When Baz Bastien's career in net ended, he went into management. Here, he's poring over notes with King Clancy.

Pittsburgh's Mr. Hockey

When Baz Bastien was struck in the right eye during the Maple Leafs training camp in Welland, Ontario, in October 1949, he took a brave stand and predicted his future quite accurately, knowing his on-ice career was over. "I guess I've had it as far as goaltending is concerned, but I'm certainly not through with the game," Bastien told *The Hockey News.* "I like hockey too much to drop it now, and although I don't know exactly what I can do to stay with it, I think I'll find something." Bastien only ever played five NHL games for the Leafs, stuck behind Turk Broda in the depth chart, but he was the starter for the AHL's Pittsburgh Hornets for four seasons, until his injury. After adjusting to his new circumstances, Bastien moved into the Hornets front office, and he coached the team for the 1953–54 season. He later put himself behind the bench after turfing coaches in 1962 and 1963, coaching the two Calder Cup–winning Pittsburgh squads just before the NHL expanded. Along with two Calder Cups from his time as business manager with the Hershey Bears, and an earlier one with the Hornets, Bastien could lay claim to five AHL titles. The AHL's top goaltender each year is now presented with a trophy bearing Bastien's name. Starting in 1967, Bastien was assistant GM to Sid Abel of the Detroit Red Wings, which had been the parent club of the Hornets. Bastien had a similar, short-lived role with the expansion Kansas City Scouts before returning to his true home—after all, he's known as "Pittsburgh's Mr. Hockey." Bastien was the GM of the Penguins from December 1976 until his death on March 15, 1983, when his car collided with a motorcycle while on his way home from a dinner sponsored by the Pittsburgh chapter of the Professional Hockey Writers Association.

PITTSBURGH
Penguins

Civic Arena
Pittsburgh, Pennsylvania 15219
(412) 434-8911

November 20, 1980

Mr. George Imlach
General Manager
Toronto Maple Leafs
Maple Leaf Garden
Toronto, Ontario
Canada M5B 1L1

Dear Punch:

Enclosed please find contracts for Paul Marshall and Kim Davis.
Would appreciate receiving the contracts of Dave Burrows and
Paul Gardner.

Kindest and best.

Sincerely,

Aldege "Baz" Bastien
General Manager

ABB:pjd

Enclosures

Sheppard Confronts Sinden on the Golf Course

There's a lasting beef that Gregg Sheppard has with former Boston Bruins general manager Harry Sinden. It turns out that Sinden never called Sheppard, who'd played centre for the Bruins from 1972 to 1978, to let him know that he'd been traded to the Atlanta Flames on September 6, 1978, during training camp. (He was then flipped to the Pittsburgh Penguins.) Sheppard's lawyer had been negotiating a new deal with Sinden. "We skated in the morning and then we went golfing in the afternoon. When I got home, my wife says to me, 'I think we got traded,'" recalled Sheppard from his Saskatchewan home. Because he didn't have a signed deal, Sheppard didn't report immediately to Pittsburgh, and he attended a Bruins golf tournament run by defenceman Brad Park a few days later. There, he confronted Sinden as he came over the hill in a foursome with other Bruins executives. "Over on the side of the green, he says, 'Gregg, I'm sorry I didn't call you. Pittsburgh wanted to break the story right away. That's why they were calling you.' I just said, 'Harry, where have you been the last five days? I've just been home. You never called me once.'" With the Pens, Sheppard was a solid contributor for four years, but then he hurt his knee in practice late in the 1981–82 season and never played again. "I hit Randy Carlyle behind the net and tore my right knee up. Actually, my stick got stuck in the boards and we both fell over, and he fell on top of my leg," he lamented. Recovering in Pittsburgh for a year, Sheppard took a real estate course and, when his knee didn't hold up when he skated a year later, moved into a new line of work.

The last four seasons of Gregg Sheppard's NHL career were in Pittsburgh.

NATIONAL HOCKEY LEAGUE
STANDARD PLAYER'S CONTRACT
(1977 FORM)

BETWEEN : **PITTSBURGH PENGUINS, INC.**
hereinafter called the "Club"
a member of the National Hockey League, hereinafter called the "League"

AND — **GREGORY SHEPPARD**
hereinafter called the "Player"

of **PITTSBURGH** in Province of **PENNSYLVANIA**
State
/Plus Option Year

In consideration of the respective obligations herein and hereby assumed, the parties to this contract severally agree as follows:

1.   The Club hereby employs the Player as a skilled Hockey Player for the term of .. **3 YRS.** ../year(s) commencing October
1st, 19 **79** .... and agrees, subject to the terms and condition hereof, to pay the Player a salary of
————No/100 Dollars ($**160,000.00**.).

1979-80 – ONE HUNDRED & SIXTY THOUSAND AND ————————No/100 $160,000.00
1980-81 – ONE HUNDRED & SIXTY THOUSAND AND ————————No/100 $160,000.00
1981-82 – ONE HUNDRED & SIXTY THOUSAND AND ————————No/100 $160,000.00
OPTION YR 1982-83 – ONE HUNDRED & SIXTY THOUSAND AND ————No/100

SEE ADDENDUM "A" ATTACHED.

Payment of such salary shall be in consecutive semi-monthly installments following the commencement of the regular League Championship Schedule of games or following the dates of reporting, whichever is later; provided, however, that if the Player is not in the employ of the Club for the whole period of the Club's games in the National Hockey League Championship Schedule, then he shall receive only part of the salary in the ratio of the number of days of actual employment to the number of days of the League Championship Schedule of Games.

And it is further mutually agreed that if the Contract and rights to the services of the Player are assigned, exchanged, loaned or otherwise transferred to a Club in another League, the Player shall only be paid at an annual salary rate of

.... Dollars in the .... League.

.... Dollars in the .... League.

or

.... Dollars in the .... League.

or

2.   The Player agrees to give his services and to play hockey in all League Championship, All Star, International, Exhibition, Play-Off and Stanley Cup games to the best of his ability under the direction and control of the Club in accordance with the provisions hereof.

The Player further agrees,

(a) to report to the Club training camp at the time and place fixed by the Club, in good physical condition,
(b) to keep himself in good physical condition at all times during the season,
(c) to give his best services to the Club and to play hockey only for the Club unless his contract is released, assigned, exchanged or loaned by the Club,
(d) to co-operate with the Club and participate in any and all reasonable promotional activities of the Club which will in the opinion of the Club promote the welfare of the Club and to cooperate in the promotion of the Club and professional hockey generally,
(e) to conduct himself on and off the rink according to the highest standards of honesty, morality, fair play and sportsmanship, and to refrain from conduct detrimental to the best interest of the Club, the League or professional hockey generally.

The Club agrees that in exhibition games played after the start of the regular schedule (except where the proceeds are to go to charity, or where the player has agreed otherwise) the player shall receive his pro rata share of the gate receipts after deduction of legitimate expenses of such game. This provision re exhibition games is applicable in the National Hockey League only.

In order that the Player shall be fit in proper condition for the performance of his duties as required by this contract, the Player agrees to report for practice at such time and place as the Club may reasonably designate and participate in such exhibition

...

In Witness Whereof, the parties have signed this .... **12th** ....day
of .... **July** .... A.D. 19 **79**

WITNESSES:

PITTSBURGH PENGUINS, INC. Club
CIVIC ARENA – GATE 7
PITTSBURGH, PA. 15219   Address of Club

By .... President

.... Player
Gregory Sheppard
Pittsburgh, Pennsylvania   Home Address of Player

I hereby certify that I have, at this date, received, examined and noted of record the within Contract, and that it is in regular form.

.... for the National Hockey League

Dated .... **NOV. 05 1979** . 19 ....

Schutt Caught in Penguins Power Struggle

Rod Schutt was in Pittsburgh during a time of transition. General manager Baz Bastien had died in a car accident in March 1983, leaving a power vacuum. Into the void stepped Eddie Johnston, the former goalie-turned-coach. "I didn't get along with him, to put it quite bluntly. It was a bit of a conflict, because Baz Bastien had brought a bunch of us guys in, me being one of them. [Johnston] and Bastien didn't get along, and with that in mind, anybody that Bastien brought in, Johnston wanted to get rid of," said Schutt. He offered up the example of how a coach goes from an ally to a foe. When Johnston first stepped behind the bench, Schutt was on the first or second line as a left winger. After a contract dispute sent both parties to arbitration, it was a different story. "It was like I couldn't even make the minor-league team," said the native of Bancroft, Ontario, drafted from the OHL's Sudbury Wolves by the Montreal Canadiens in 1976. "When we got out of the arbitration, one of the things [Johnston] said to me was, 'You'll pay for this.' Not sure what all that meant, but he certainly lived up to his word." Schutt found himself in the AHL, lining up for the Baltimore Skipjacks for a couple of years. After the 1984–85 season with the IHL's Muskegon Lumberjacks, the bottom-dwelling Toronto Maple Leafs signed Schutt to a free-agent deal. He played only six games for the big club and was mainly used with the AHL's St. Catharines Saints. Schutt feels he didn't really get a fair shake with the Leafs, but there were other circumstances at work. "I had back problems, so I knew I couldn't compete at the same level I did prior to that," Schutt said. "I remember thinking, 'If I can't stick there, I guess it's about time to hang 'em up.' And that's what I did." The Detroit Red Wings called for the next year, but he said no. Post hockey, Schutt deals in office furniture and oversees a general contracting business.

Rod Schutt readies for a game.

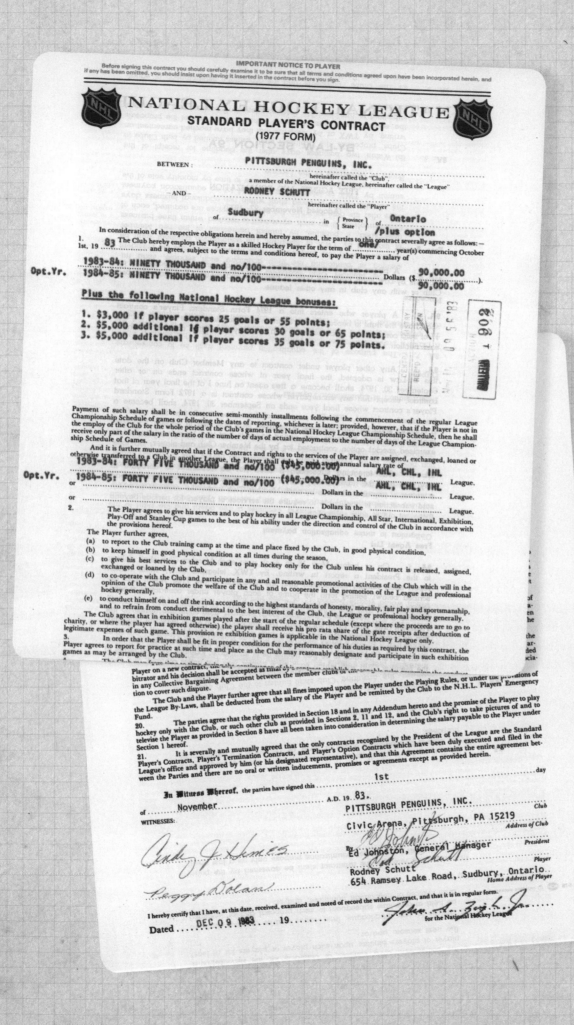

NATIONAL HOCKEY LEAGUE
STANDARD PLAYER'S CONTRACT
(1977 FORM)

BETWEEN: **PITTSBURGH PENGUINS, INC.**

hereinafter called the "Club",

a member of the National Hockey League, hereinafter called the "League"

—AND—   **RODNEY SCHUTT**

hereinafter called the "Player"

of   **Sudbury**   in { Province / State } of   **Ontario**

/plus option

In consideration of the respective obligations herein and hereby assumed, the parties to this contract severally agree as follows: —

1. The Club hereby employs the Player as a skilled Hockey Player for the term of **one.** year(s) commencing October 1st, 19 **83** and agrees, subject to the terms and conditions hereof, to pay the Player a salary of

Opt.Yr.   **1983-84: NINETY THOUSAND and no/100------------------------   90,000.00**

1984-85: NINETY THOUSAND and no/100------------------------   Dollars ($ 90,000.00   ).

Plus the following National Hockey League bonuses:

1. $3,000 if player scores 25 goals or 55 points;
2. $5,000 additional if player scores 30 goals or 65 points;
3. $5,000 additional if player scores 35 goals or 75 points.

Payment of such salary shall be in consecutive semi-monthly installments following the commencement of the regular League Championship Schedule of games or following the dates of reporting, whichever is later; provided, however, that if the Player is not in the employ of the Club for the whole period of the Club's games in the National Hockey League Championship Schedule, then he shall receive only part of the salary in the ratio of the number of days of actual employment to the number of days of the League Championship Schedule of Games.

And it is further mutually agreed that if the Contract and rights to the services of the Player are assigned, exchanged, loaned or otherwise transferred to a Club in another League, the Player shall receive a mid-annual salary rate of

Opt.Yr.   **1983-84: FORTY FIVE THOUSAND and no/100 ($45,000.00)**   **AHL, CHL, IHL**

or   **1984-85: FORTY FIVE THOUSAND and no/100 ($45,000.00)**   Dollars in the   **AHL, CHL, IHL**   League.

or   .... Dollars in the .... League.

or   .... Dollars in the .... League.

2. The Player agrees to give his services and to play hockey in all League Championship, Play-Off and Stanley Cup, All Star, International, Exhibition games to the best of his ability under the direction and control of the Club in accordance with the provisions hereof.

The Player further agrees,

(a) to report to the Club training camp at the time and place fixed by the Club, in good physical condition,

(b) to keep himself in good physical condition at all times during the season,

(c) to give his best services to the Club and to play hockey only for the Club unless his contract is released, assigned, exchanged or loaned by the Club,

(d) to co-operate with the Club and participate in any and all reasonable promotional activities of the Club which will in the opinion of the Club promote the welfare of the Club and to cooperate in the promotion of the League and professional hockey generally,

(e) to conduct himself on and off the rink according to the highest standards of honesty, morality, fair play and sportsmanship, and to refrain from conduct detrimental to the best interest of the Club, the League or professional hockey generally.

The Club agrees that in exhibition games played after the start of the regular schedule (except where the proceeds are to go to charity, or where the player has agreed otherwise) the player shall receive his pro rata share of the gate receipts after deduction of legitimate expenses of such game. This provision re exhibition games is applicable in the National Hockey League only.

3. In order that the Player shall be fit in proper condition for the performance of his duties as required by this contract, the Player agrees to report for practice at such time and place as the Club may reasonably designate and participate in such exhibition games as may be arranged by the Club.

bitrator and his decision shall be accepted as final by the continuation of this contract and all reasonable rules governing the conduct of the Player on a new contract, under the ....

in any Collective Bargaining Agreement between the member clubs or under the Playing Rules, or under the provisions of tion to cover such dispute.

The Club and the Player further agree that all fines imposed upon the Player under the By-Laws of the League By-Laws, shall be deducted from the salary of the Player and be remitted by the Club to the N.H.L. Players' Emergency Fund.

20. The parties agree that the rights provided in Section 18 and in any Addendum hereto and the promise of the Player to play hockey only with the Club, or such other club as provided in Sections 2, 11 and 12, and the Club's right to take pictures of and to televise the Player as provided in Section 8 have all been taken into consideration in determining the salary payable to the Player under Section 1 hereof.

21. It is severally and mutually agreed that the only contracts recognized by the President of the League are the Standard Player's Contracts, Player's Termination Contracts, and Player's Option Contracts which have been duly executed and filed in the League's office and approved by him (or his designated representative), and that this Agreement contains the entire agreement between the Parties and there are no oral or written inducements, promises or agreements except as provided herein.

In Witness Whereof, the parties have signed this .... **1st** .... day

of .... **November** ....   A.D. 19 **83.**   **PITTSBURGH PENGUINS, INC.**   Club

WITNESSES: Civic Arena, Pittsburgh, PA 15219   Address of Club

.... President

By Ed Johnston, General Manager

Rodney Schutt   Player

Rodney Schutt   654 Ramsey Lake Road, Sudbury, Ontario   Home Address of Player

I hereby certify that I have, at this date, received, examined and noted of record the within Contract, and that it is in regular form.

Dated .... **DEC 09 1983** .... 19 .... for the National Hockey League

Three Teams, Never Traded

There are only a handful of players who can lay claim to being a part of the unique history of the California Seals moving to Cleveland to become the Barons, and then merging with the Minnesota North Stars. Defenceman Greg Smith was one of them, getting in right at the wire. After three years studying business administration at Colorado College and playing hockey, Smith recognized that the time was perfect for a jump to the pros. He started in the Seals organization with the Salt Lake Golden Eagles. "I got called up for the last game that was played in Oakland. I think we were in Tucson, and I got a call at five in the morning: 'Greg, you've got to get up and play in Oakland tonight.' Frank Spring and I flew from Tucson to Oakland and played that night. That summer the team moved to Cleveland." Life with the Barons was chaotic, including a missed payday. "Still, you're young, you're excited, and that's what it was all about," he said. "I learned a lot in two years!" One thing Smith learned was to not always trust the general manager. After the 1977–78 season, before he bought a house in Cleveland, Smith sought assurance from GM Bill McCreary that the Barons would stay in town. "We just moved our stuff from our apartment into [the house] and went back home to Canada for the summer. Two weeks later, I get a call from a real estate agent: 'Do you want to sell your house?' 'What? Sell the house?' 'Well, the team is moving.' That's how I found out." Life with the North Stars was far better, and the run to the 1981 Stanley Cup Finals is a career highlight. "That was an exciting time. We had a lot of young kids. Some of the Olympians that played in the '80 Olympics were on that team."

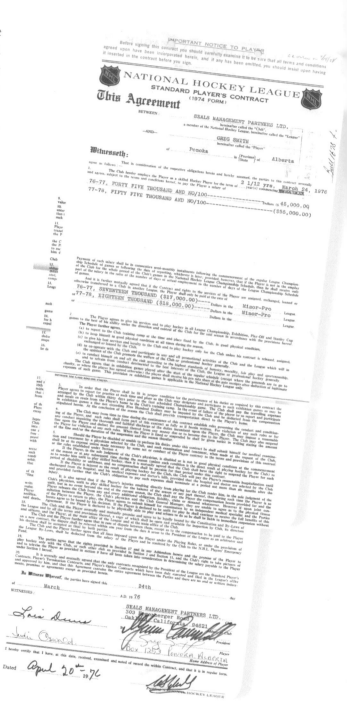

Portnoy/Hockey Hall of Fame

Greg Smith was one of 49 players who suited up as a Cleveland Baron.

April 2, 1976

Mr. Greg Smith
Salt Lake Golden Eagles
100 S. W. Temple
Salt Lake City, Utah 84101

Dear Greg:

Welcome to the California Seals!

Although this contract and addendum has not been
negotiated in person and in your presence, it has
been done through your agent, Art Kaminsky, who and
has had it proof-read to him over the phone and
is in complete agreement with the figures.

Please sign the four copies of the contract and
addendum where indicated and return to my attention
at this office as soon as possible.

Best wishes and good luck, not only for the balance
of this season, but for many years to come. Look
forward to seeing you in Salt Lake City during the
playoffs.

Sincerely,

Bill McCreary
General Manager

BMcC:ld

Enc.

NATIONAL HOCKEY LEAGUE

PLAYER'S OPTION CONTRACT

NORTHSTAR HOCKEY PARTNERSHIP (Minnesota North Stars)
.... ("the Club") and

GREG SMITH
.... ("the Player"), in consideration of the
respective obligations herein assumed, hereby agree and contract as follows :

The Club agrees to employ the Player as a skilled Hockey Player, and the Player agrees to be
so employed by the Club, on the same terms and conditions as are contained in the National Hockey
League Standard Player's Contract between the Club and the Player dated **March 24, 1976**,
with the following exceptions only :

1. The period of the Player's employment by the Club shall commence October 1 of the
current calendar year and terminate June 1 of the following calendar year, whereupon the Player will
be a free agent, without any further obligation to provide services under this contract, and as such will
have the right, as provided by Section 9A of the National Hockey League By-Laws, a copy of which
Section is attached to said Standard Player's Contract, to negotiate and contract with any club in the
National Hockey League or with any other Club.

2. The Player's salary for said period shall be the same as his entire salary for the final year
of said Standard Player's Contract.

3. The terms and conditions of Section 17 of said Standard Player's Contract shall not be a
part of this contract.

Northstar Hockey Partnership

By : ....Lou Nanne.................................... Club
.....Mr. Lou Nanne, General Manager....

.......8-22-78........
Date

Greg Smith ....Greg Smith......... Player
Box 1253,
Ponoka, Alberta
Canada TOC 2HO

....
Address of Player

.......8-28-78.......
Date

T.V.B.-1-74 NATIONAL HOCKEY LEAGUE

Harry Howell's Many Franchise Nightmares

Harry Howell has the distinction, er, indignity, of being a part of two of the biggest fashion crimes in hockey history. After 17 storied seasons with the New York Rangers—at the time, he was the youngest captain in NHL history at age 22, though he didn't keep the "C" for too many years—Howell was sold to the Oakland Seals in June 1969. The defenceman's back had been an issue, and he played only 55 games for the Seals that first year. Over the summer, Charlie Finley assumed ownership of the team, and he decided that white skates would make his Seals better. "We opened up in Detroit," Howell told the *Hamilton Spectator* in 2009. "They turned out the lights and put on the spotlight and who comes out first? Me. Talk about whistles. It was like the Ice Capades." Howell plugged away for the Seals, then the Los Angeles Kings, before moving to the WHA in the fall of 1973. His patience as a hockey man was further tested by the New York Golden Blades, for whom Howell was a player-coach. The team also wore white skates—with gold-tinted blades, naturally. But the Blades couldn't afford the rent at their home away from home, Madison Square Garden, so the team moved to Cherry Hill, New Jersey, and became the Jersey Knights. Howell played and coached for two more years in the WHA. "Hockey has been my life and I'd like to stay in the game in some capacity," said Howell upon his retirement after 23 years, in September 1975. He did stay involved in hockey, but his poor franchise-luck continued, as he was the general manager for the Cleveland Barons in 1978 when the team merged with the Minnesota North Stars. Howell was inducted to the Hockey Hall of Fame as an Honoured Member in 1979.

Harry Howell went from the ice to the boardroom.

STANDARD PLAYER'S CONTRACT
NATIONAL HOCKEY LEAGUE

The CALIFORNIA SPORTS, INC.

of LOS ANGELES, CALIFORNIA

WITH

HARRY V. HOWELL

AMENDED FORM
MARCH 1972

IMPORTANT NOTICE TO PLAYER

Before signing this contract you should carefully examine it to be sure that all terms and conditions agreed upon have been incorporated herein, and if any has been omitted, you should insist upon having it inserted in the contract before you sign.

NATIONAL HOCKEY LEAGUE
STANDARD PLAYER'S CONTRACT

This Agreement

BETWEEN: CALIFORNIA SPORTS, INC.
hereinafter called the "Club",
a member of the National Hockey League, hereinafter called the "League"

—AND— HARRY V. HOWELL
hereinafter called the "Player"

of Hamilton in {Province} of Ontario

Witnesseth:

That in consideration of the respective obligations herein and hereby assumed, the parties to this contract severally agree as follows:—

1. The Club hereby employs the Player as a skilled Hockey Player for the term of one year commencing October 1st, 1972 and agrees, subject to the terms and conditions hereof, to pay the Player a salary of

FIFTY THOUSAND and No/100 —————————————————— Dollars ($ 50,000.00)

NO MINOR LEAGUE CLAUSE

Payment of such salary shall be in consecutive semi-monthly instalments following the commencement of the regular League Championship Schedule of games or following the date of reporting, whichever is later; provided, however, that if the Player is not in the employ of the Club for the whole period of the Club's games in the National Hockey League Championship Schedule, then he shall receive only part of the salary in the ratio of the number of days of actual employment to the number of days of the League Championship Schedule of games.

And it is further mutually agreed that if the Contract and rights to the services of the Player are assigned, exchanged, loaned or otherwise transferred to a Club in another League, the Player shall only be paid at the rate of

_____ Dollars in the _____ League.

or _____ Dollars in the _____ League.

or _____ Dollars in the _____ League.

2. The Player agrees to give his services and to play hockey in all League Championship, Exhibition, Play-Off and Stanley Cup games to the best of his ability under the direction and control of the Club for the said season in accordance with the provisions hereof.

The Player further agrees,

(a) to report to the Club training camp at the time and place fixed by the Club, in good physical condition,

(b) to keep himself in good physical condition at all times during the season,

(c) to give his best services and loyalty to the Club and to play hockey only for the Club unless his contract is released, assigned, exchanged or loaned by the Club,

(d) to co-operate with the Club and participate in any and all promotional activities of the Club and the League which will in the opinion of the Club promote the welfare of the Club or professional hockey generally.

(e) to conduct himself on and off the rink according to the highest standards of honesty, morality, fair play and sportsmanship, and to refrain from conduct detrimental to the best interests of the Club, the League or professional hockey generally.

The Club agrees that in exhibition games played after the start of the regular schedule (except where the proceeds are to go to charity, or where the player has agreed otherwise) the player shall receive his pro rata share of the gate receipts after deduction of legitimate expenses of such game. This provision re exhibition games is applicable in the National Hockey League only.

3. In order that the Player shall be fit in proper condition for the performance of his duties as required by this contract the Player agrees to report for practice at such time and place as the Club may designate and participate in such exhibition game. The Club shall pay the travelling expenses arranged by the Club within thirty days prior to the first scheduled Championship game. In the event of failure of the player to report and participate and meals en route from the Player's home to the Club's training camp. In the event of failure of the player to report and participate in exhibition games a fine not exceeding Five Hundred Dollars may be imposed by the Club and be deducted from the compensation stipulated herein. At the conclusion of the season the Club shall provide transportation direct to the Player's home.

4. The Club may from time to time during the continuance of this contract establish rules governing the conduct and condition- ing of the Player, and such rules shall form part of this contract as fully as if herein written. For violation of any such rules or for any conduct impairing the thorough and faithful discharge of the duties incumbent upon the Player, the Club may impose a reasonable fine upon the Player and deduct the amount thereof from any money due or to become due to the Player. The Club may also suspend the Player for violation of any such rule. When the Player is fined or suspended he shall be given notice in writing stating the amount of the fine and/or the duration of the suspension and the reason therefor.

---

20. It is severally and mutually agreed that the only contracts recognized by the President of the League are the Standard Player's Contracts which have been duly executed and filed in the League's office and approved by him, and that this Agreement contains the entire agreement between the Parties and there are no oral or written inducements, promises or agreements except as contained herein.

In Witness Whereof, the parties have signed this _____ First (1st) _____ day

of _____ May _____ A.D. 19 72

WITNESSES:

California Sports, Inc.
_____   By _____ Club
                                        Larry Regan, General Manager
_____   _____ Player
                                        Harry Howell
                                        Hamilton, Ontario, Canada   Home Address of Player

T.V.R. © NATIONAL HOCKEY LEAGUE

Glenn Anderson's Very Brief Vancouver Homecoming

Glenn Anderson did two tours of duty with the Edmonton Oilers.

Knowing that he was nearing the end of his career, Glenn Anderson decided he wanted to play with the Vancouver Canucks. He'd grown up in nearby Burnaby, B.C., and after a Hall of Fame career at right wing with the Oilers, Leafs, Rangers, and Blues, as well as internationally representing Canada and playing in leagues in Germany, Switzerland, and Finland, he felt the call of home. "I wanted Mom and Dad to see me play the last little bit of my career, and I wanted to end it in Vancouver. Whenever you play in front of your family, there's always a little more incentive," said Anderson. As a free agent playing in Europe, he made a deal with Canucks assistant GM George McPhee for the remainder of the 1995–96 season, roughly 30 games. According to Anderson, McPhee didn't listen to his advice. "I had done a contract like this before, so I knew that I had to clear waivers," said Anderson, who suggested the contract be front-loaded to detract suitors. "So he goes, 'There's no frickin' way anybody's going to pick you up for the amount of money that we're paying you,'" recalled Anderson. He went to one single practice as a Canuck—at the rink he grew up playing at in Burnaby—before his old boss in Edmonton, Glen Sather, made it known that he wanted the last of the veteran, "I get a phone call from Sather saying, 'I'm picking you up off of waivers and you're coming to Edmonton if you still want to play hockey.' I go, 'Don't pick me up, because I don't want to go there.' It was like 40 below up there in Edmonton. Sure enough, he picks me up." Anderson played 17 games for the Oilers that year. He was inducted to the Hockey Hall of Fame as an Honoured Member in 2008.

CRR737
96/01/25
12:00:46

A W A R D E D   W A I V E R S

TO: EDMONTON OILERS   USER: NANCY

FROM: Central Registry   TIME: 12:00:00

DATE: JANUARY 25, 1996

SUBJECT: Waivers - GLENN ANDERSON

You have been awarded player GLENN ANDERSON, placed on
waivers at $ 3,750. Please forward $ 3,750 to the
VANCOUVER CANUCKS. Player's name will be transferred to
your reserve list immediately.

Edmonton Oilers
MEMBER OF THE NATIONAL HOCKEY LEAGUE

To: Mike Keenan - St. Louis Blues

From: Glen Sather - Edmonton Oilers

Date: March 12, 1996

Re: Glenn Anderson

Under Article 13.18(b), the Edmonton Oilers hereby offer player Glenn Anderson to
the St. Louis Blues for the waiver price of $3,750. Failure to respond by 11:45 am
Wednesday March 13, 1996 will be interpreted as a lack of interest on your part
towards this player.

Please sign below if you accept the transfer of Glenn Anderson on the above condition.

Michael E. Keenan
Mike Keenan

cc: Garry Lovegrove - NHL MTL
      David Zimmerman - NHL NY

800 Griffiths Way
Vancouver, B.C.
Canada V6B 6G1

Tel ● 899.7400
Fax 604/899.7401

Member of
National
Hockey League

SPECIAL ADDENDUM NO. ONE: RE: NATIONAL HOCKEY LEAGUE STANDARD PLAYER'S CONTRACT (1995 FORM) ("CONTRACT") BETWEEN THE **VANCOUVER HOCKEY CLUB LTD.** AND **GLENN ANDERSON** ("PLAYER") DATED JANUARY 22, 1996

1. **TERM:**

This Agreement shall cover the 1995/96 season.

2. **SALARY:**

Player shall receive the following salary:

Season	**NHL**
1995/96	$400,000.00 US

3. **PLAYOFF BONUS**

In the event:

i)   the Club advances to engage in post season NHL playoff play; and

ii)   the Player has played in at least 25 regular season games of the Club;

the sum of $25,000.00 US shall be paid by the Club to the Player not later than 15 days following the first playoff game played by the Club.

4. **PLAYOFF SERIES WON BONUS**

In the event:

NHL CENTRAL REGISTRY

JAN 23 '96 PM 3:51

i)   the Club is the winner of any playoff series; and

ii)   the Player has played in at least 50% of the games in the series (and where the number of games in the series is an odd number, the Player has played in the majority of games in the series);

the sum of $10,000.00 US shall be paid by the Club in respect of the first round won and the sum of $15,000.00 US shall be paid by the Club in respect of each of the second, third and fourth round wins not later than 15 days following the last game of each respective series.

5.   **GOALS SCORED BONUS**

In the event that Player scores 8 goals in the regular season Player shall receive the sum of $10,000.00 US payable at the end of the regular season.

6.   **WITHHOLDING:**

It is agreed and understood that all payments made hereunder shall be less all amounts required to be withheld by Federal, Provincial and all other applicable income tax laws, regulations and rulings, and shall be made pursuant to normal Club payroll practices.

AGREED TO BETWEEN: **VANCOUVER HOCKEY CLUB LTD.**

_____   _____
Witness   J.B. PATRICK QUINN

_____   _____
Witness   GLENN ANDERSON

NHL CENTRAL REGISTRY
JAN 23 '96 PM 3:51

Graig Abel/Hockey Hall of Fame

The Playoff Bonuses of Glenn Anderson

When Glenn Anderson ended up back in Edmonton in January 1996, claimed off waivers from the Vancouver Canucks—for whom he never played—he hunkered down with Oilers GM Glen Sather to renegotiate his deal. Anderson wanted to be in the playoffs, and he told Sather, "You guys don't look like you're going to make it. Re-do the contract and give me bonuses if we do make the playoffs. Or if you trade me, the team that I get traded to has to pay my bonuses if we make the playoffs." Anderson and Sather hashed out details without an agent. "[Sather] couldn't believe that we sat there for three hours and argued and just talked about hockey, the world, and the whole nine yards," chuckled Anderson. Because Anderson had only just arrived back in the NHL after playing in Europe during the fall, he saw the postseason bonuses as an extra payday; a standard NHL contract only pays out during the regular schedule. "You don't get paid in the playoffs, you get paid by the league," he said. "So I wasn't getting paid, so I tried to get the same amount of money if we were to be successful in the playoffs." The winger's stay in Edmonton wasn't long in his second go-around, and the playoff-bound St. Louis Blues picked him up on waivers on March 12, 1996. Mike Keenan, the coach and GM with the Blues, didn't like the addendum to the contract. "He said that he wasn't going to carry those bonuses with him because he didn't write them," said Anderson. "We got into a huge fight over it." Anderson delivered an ultimatum: "I'm not going to play if you're not going to honour the bonuses," and he sat out the first two games of the playoffs. "We have a meeting again and he says, 'Okay, you can have your bonuses.' Then, I go, 'Not only that, but you'd better add another one, if I score a game-winning goal, because you're being such a prick about it.'" The Blues knocked off Toronto in the first round—and Anderson got one winner—but St. Louis fell to Detroit in seven games in the second round.

Glenn Anderson played for four different NHL teams—Oilers, Maple Leafs, Rangers, and Blues—and signed with the Canucks, but he never got to play for them. He also played in Finland, Germany, Italy, France, and for Team Canada. Here, he suits up for the 2008 Hockey Hall of Fame Legends Classic.

In addition to the NHL Standard Player's Contract and the special addendum from the Vancouver Canuck's, the Edmonton Oilers agree to pay the player, Glenn Anderson the following bonuses;

If the player is a plus player he receives $25,000 U.S. ✓

For making the playoffs, receives $100,000 U.S. ✓

Winning first round of the playoffs, receives $100,000 U.S. ✓

Winning second round of the playoffs, receives $100,000 U.S. ✓

Winning third round of the playoffs, receives $100,000 U.S. ✓

Winning Stanley Cup, receives $100,000 U.S. ✓

$1200.00 A MONTH RENT $100,000 Can-

25,000 making playoffs - 25 games.

10,000   1st rd
15   2nd } 50% of games.
15   3rd
15   4th.
15

64,000   350
    65   410   420

25,000 -
10,000
15,000   25,000
50,000
15,000   100,000

125,000
10,000
25,000
50,000
100,000

525 x .36%
189
$714,000

O-Pee-Chee/Hockey Hall of Fame

Ridley Goes into Hiding to Escape Vancouver

Curt Ridley knew his days in Vancouver were numbered. He'd spent most of the 1978–79 season with the CHL's Dallas Black Hawks—where the team won the Jack Adams Trophy as the league champs—and the upcoming year didn't look any better. So the goaltender took matters into his own hands. "I flew back to Vancouver and basically hid out. They didn't know where I was," chuckled Ridley. Eventually Canucks GM Jake Milford found him, and Ridley begged Milford to let him make his own deal out of town. He called an old teammate who was running the Edmonton Oilers—Glen Sather. "We came to an agreement," said Ridley, knowing he'd be heading to the minors again. "They had great goaltenders, and I didn't have a problem." But word got around. "Milford got wind of this, and the next day, I got a phone call. 'You've been bought by Toronto.'" Growing up in Winnipeg, Ridley was a Maple Leafs fan, but he was walking into a crazy situation. "Goddamn, it was tough there," he admitted. In all, Ridley played only six games for the Leafs over two seasons—and over those two campaigns, Toronto used six other goalies (Mike Palmateer, Paul Harrison, Jiri Crha, Vincent Tremblay, Jim Rutherford, and Bunny Larocque). Ridley remembers his last deal with the Leafs distinctly, as there was a Canadian postal strike going on in the summer of 1981, and scout Dick Duff hand delivered the contract to his apartment. Ridley broke his hand, though, and never got back his form, even in the minors. He tried scouting for the team, but Punch Imlach's massive heart attack in the fall of 1981 meant the Leafs were in need of new management. "Basically they cleaned house, and that was it for me," said Ridley.

Curt Ridley played most of his NHL career with Vancouver.

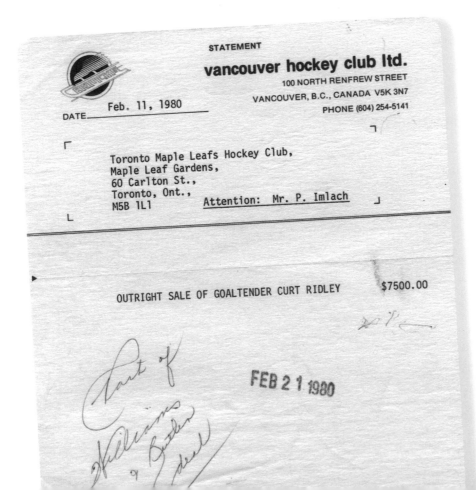

VANCOUVER CANUCKS

Member Of
National Hockey League

100 North Renfrew Street
Vancouver, British Columbia
Canada V5K 3N7
Telephone (604) 254-5141
TWX 610-292-2054

February 11, 1980.

Mr. George "Punch" Imlach,
General Manager,
Toronto Maple Leafs,
60 Carlton Street,
TORONTO, Ontario.
M5B 1L1

Dear Punch:

Enclosed is a copy of CURT RIDLEY's contract. Also enclosed are
three copies of Standard Assignment Agreement forms for you to sign
and forward on to Central Registry regarding the trade.

Yours truly,

J. C. Milford (signature)

J. C. Milford,
General Manager,
Vancouver Hockey Club Ltd.

JCM/dl
Encl.

FEB 15 1980

Portnoy/Hockey Hall of Fame

Tracy Pratt tries to slow down Garry Unger during a game in 1974.

Happy Birthday, Tracy Pratt

On March 8, 1977, Tracy Pratt got a very special birthday present—he was dealt by the Colorado Rockies to the Toronto Maple Leafs, the team that had been home to his Hall of Fame father, Babe Pratt, for so many years. The younger Pratt was near the end of his career, and immediately he became the oldest player on his new team. In all, the stay-at-home defenceman suited up for 11 games in the blue-and-white before retiring. The Leafs gave up Randy Pierce, a third-round draft pick, for Pratt. "We were desperate," Leafs owner Harold Ballard said at the time. "We tried pretty much all the other teams in the league to get a defenceman, but there aren't many around. We made the deal at 20 minutes to noon." The controversial Ballard also wistfully added, "Ah, his father was a wonderful hockey player." In 1985, Tracy Pratt talked about his father in the *Globe and Mail.* "Nobody paid money because of your name. You had to go out there and earn your paycheque. Babe and I were more like brothers than father and son. I made it more on brawn and he made it on finesse." Back in 1977, though, facing the Toronto media, Tracy was brutally honest about his talents: "I get paid for clearing my part of the ice. . . . My talents lie with the defensive. Offensively, I stink." In 580 NHL games, Pratt potted 17 goals and 97 assists, but had a solid 1,026 in penalty minutes. After his playing days ended, Pratt coached junior hockey in Abbotsford, B.C., and then took over as general manager of the New Westminster Bruins; he also ran a nightclub, T.R.'s Cabaret, before settling into property management.

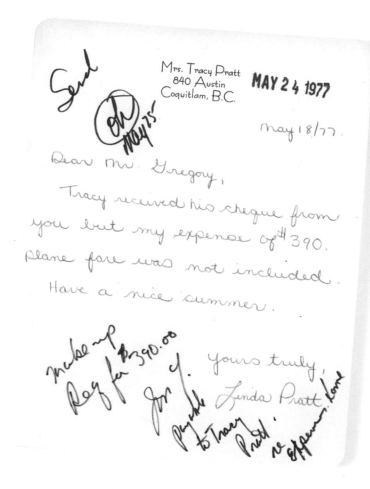

COLORADO ROCKIES

Copy to
Don Gump
Apr. 6/77

March 24, 1977

Mr. Jim Gregory
General Manager
Toronto Maple Leafs
Maple Leaf Gardens
60 Carlton Street
Toronto, Ontario M5B 1L1
CANADA

Dear Jim:

Please excuse the delay in sending you
the following information on Tracy Pratt, but I
have been out of town for some time now and just
returned to Denver this afternoon.

As you will see in the enclosed contract
and addendum, Pratt had many bonuses while with the
Vancouver Hockey Club. These bonuses were only
good while he was performing for that club. When
he reported here we talked about working out some
kind of an agreement on bonuses and finally worked
out a verbal agreement whereby he would receive
a bonus of $5,000.00 if our club made the play-
offs in the Smythe Division. The only other agreement that we made with Tracy was that we would pay
for his wife's expenses to travel to Denver to
visit with him during the season. She did come
and stayed for some time and recently handed me
her expenses on the night of March 16th when the
Leafs were playing here in Denver. This we will

McNichols Sports Arena,

Mr. Jim Gregory
Page Two
March 24, 1977

look after as per our agreement with the Pratts.

If there should be any further questions
regarding our dealings with Pratt, feel free to
contact me at any time.

With best wishes for a strong run at the
Stanley Cup,

Sincerely,

Ray Miron
General Manager

RM/mlw

Enclosures

Finn Learned to Lead with Nordiques

Now a motivational speaker and a sportscaster on TVA Sports in Quebec, Steven Finn is appreciative of the chances he got in pro hockey. "The average career in the NHL is four and a half years, and 50 percent of the players play less than 100 games. I was very fortunate to play 12 years," he said. Finn, a defenceman with the Laval Voisins, went 57th overall in the 1984 NHL Draft. "When you're 18 and you're ready to get drafted, your biggest wish is to get drafted by a team that will need you as soon as possible. That was the case with the Nordiques," said Finn. Finn was returned to junior after 17 NHL games and spent only a little time in the AHL the following season before finding a regular spot with the big club. Mario Marois was a mentor. "[Marois] would push me a lot. This guy was a true leader. He was a very vocal guy in the dressing room and he was a warrior on the ice." Later, Finn was called upon to be a leader. In March 1990, the Nords dealt captain Peter Stastny to the Devils, opening up the captain's role. The team voted, and the result was a tie between Finn and Joe Sakic. "I was captain on the road and Joe at home. I think I was 24 then, and Joe was even younger." Finn retired after playing in the IHL for the 1997–98 season; after that, he moved seamlessly into working in sales in Quebec's pharmaceutical industry. Part of the reason Finn found success in sales was that he paid attention to his contracts during his playing days. "My agent would always start the discussion with the team, and once they got closer, I would join the negotiations in person," Finn said. "Your number one role as an athlete is to perform on the ice, but there's a business side to the game that it's nice to get a taste of. It always helps when you retire and you want to do something else in life."

ADDENDUM

This addendum shall be part of the attached contract between LE CLUB DE HOCKEY LES NORDIQUES (1979) SOCIETE EN COMMANDITE, and Player, Steven Finn.

1– SALARY *

	MAJOR LEAGUE	MINOR LEAGUE
1988–89	$ 135,000.	$ 50,000.
1989–90	$ 150,000.	$ 50,000.
1990–91 (option)	$ 160,000.	$ 50,000.

* After the Player shall have actually played in 30 NHL games, the salary specified under "minor league" shall be deleted and the Contract shall thereafter be a "one-way" contract for the balance of its terms, including the option year.

2– NHL BONUSES:

If Club finishes first in its Division:	$ 10,000.
If Club finishes first overall in the NHL:	$ 25,000.
If Club participate to the Play-Offs:	$ 5,000.
If Club wins the first round of Play-Offs:	$ 5,000.
If Club wins its Division Championship:	$ 10,000.
If Club wins its Conference Championship:	$ 10,000.
If Club wins the Stanley Cup:	$ 25,000.

3– NHL AWARD BONUS:

If Player wins one individual trophy in the NHL: $ 10,000.

Signed this ....24.......... day of ...August.......... 1988

BY: LE CLUB DE HOCKEY LES   PLAYER
      NORDIQUES (1979) INC.

Martin Madden   _Steven Finn_
Martin Madden   Steven Finn
General Manager   1319 Choisy Leroi
                                  Cap Rouge, Québec
                                  G1Y 3L6

AUG 26 10   4 8 '88

ACTION

Paul Bereswill/Hockey Hall of Fame

Steven Finn spent a decade as a Nordique.

IMPORTANT NOTICE TO PLAYER

Before signing this contract you should carefully examine it to be sure that all terms and conditions agreed upon have been incorporated herein, and if any has been omitted, you should insist upon having it inserted in the contract before you sign.

NATIONAL HOCKEY LEAGUE

STANDARD PLAYER'S CONTRACT

(1986 FORM; REVISED 1987)

BETWEEN   Le Club de Hockey les Nordiques (1979) Société en Commandite

hereinafter called the "Club,"

a member of the National Hockey League, hereinafter called the "League."

AND   Steven Finn

hereinafter called the "Player"

of   in   Province / State   of

In consideration of the respective obligations herein and hereby assumed, the parties to this contract severally agree as follows:—

1.   The Club hereby employs the Player as a skilled Hockey Player for the term of ...2 + 1... year(s) commencing October 1st. 19 88   and agrees, subject to the terms and conditions hereof, to pay the Player a salary of

SEE ATTACHED ADDENDUM

.... Dollars ($..................).

Payment of such salary shall be in consecutive semi-monthly installments following the commencement of the regular League Championship Schedule of games or following the dates of reporting, whichever is later; provided, however, that if the Player is not in the employ of the Club for the whole period of the Club's games in the National Hockey League Championship Schedule, then he shall receive only part of the salary in the ratio of the number of days of actual employment to the number of days of the League Championship Schedule of Games.

And it is further mutually agreed that if this Contract and rights to the services of the Player are assigned, exchanged, loaned or otherwise transferred to a Club in another League, the Player shall only be paid at an annual salary rate of

SEE ATTACHED ADDENDUM

or .... Dollars in the .... League.

or .... Dollars in the .... League.

2.   .... Dollars in the .... League.

The Player agrees to give his services and to play hockey in all League Championship, All Star, International, Exhibition, Play-Off and Stanley Cup games to the best of his ability under the direction and control of the Club in accordance with the provisions hereof.

The Player further agrees,

(a)   to report to the Club training camp at the time and place fixed by the Club, in good physical condition,

(b)   to keep himself in good physical condition at all times during the season,

(c)   to give his best services to the Club and to play hockey only for the Club unless his contract is released, assigned, exchanged or loaned by the Club,

(d)   to co-operate with the Club and participate in any and all reasonable promotional activities of the Club which will in the opinion of the Club promote the welfare of the Club and to cooperate in the promotion of the League and professional hockey generally,

(e)   to conduct himself on and off the rink according to the highest standards of honesty, morality, fair play and sportsmanship, and to refrain from conduct detrimental to the best interest of the Club, the League or professional hockey generally.

The Club agrees that in exhibition games played after the start of the regular schedule (except where the proceeds are to go to charity, or where the player has agreed otherwise) the player shall receive his pro rata share of the gate receipts after deduction of legitimate expenses of such game. This provision re exhibition games is applicable in the National Hockey League only.

3.   In order that the Player shall be fit in proper condition for the performance of his duties as required by this contract, the Player agrees to report for practice at such time and place as the Club may reasonably designate and participate in such exhibition games as may be arranged by the Club.

4.   The Club may from time to time during the continuance of this contract establish reasonable rules governing the conduct and conditioning of the Player, and such reasonable rules shall form part of this contract as fully as if herein written. For violation of any such rules or for any conduct impairing the thorough and ...

... shall be deducted from the salary of the Player and be ...

20.   The parties agree that the rights provided in Section 18 and in any Addendum hereto and the promise of the Player to play hockey only with the Club, or such other club as provided in Sections 2, 11 and 12, and the Club's right to take pictures of and to televise the Player as provided in Section 8 have all been taken into consideration in determining the salary payable to the Player under Section 1 hereof.

21.   It is severally and mutually agreed that the only contracts recognized by the President of the League are the Standard Player's Contracts, Player's Termination Contracts, Player's Option Contracts, Post-Option Year Termination Contracts, Standard Contracts (Corporate), Standard Termination Contracts (Corporate), Standard Option Contracts (Corporate) and Post-Option Year Termination Contracts (Corporate) which have been duly executed and filed in the League's office and there are no oral or written inducements, promises or agreements except as provided herein.

In Witness Whereof, the parties have signed this ...24th... day of ...August... A.D. 19 88

WITNESSES:

Liza Boivin

Les Nordiques de Québec (1979) Inc.   Club

2205, ave du Colisée - Québec, Qc   G1L 4W7   Address of Club

By Martin Madden   President

Martin Madden, General Manager

1319 Choisy Leroi - Cap Rouge, Qc   G1Y 3L6   Home Address of Player   Player

I hereby certify that I have, at this date, received, examined and noted of record the within Contract, and that it is in regular form.

Dated ...SEP 26 1988... 19......   for the National Hockey League

Coffey Gets Hot in Edmonton

When the Sault Ste. Marie Greyhounds of the Ontario Major Junior Hockey League drafted defenceman Paul Coffey from the North York Rangers in June 1978, it was expected that he'd suit up with an old teammate—Wayne Gretzky. "Coff" and "Gretz" had played together on the Seneca Nationals of Toronto's Metro Junior B league in the 1976–77 season. Instead, the reunion on the ice had to wait until Coffey made the NHL, as The Great One jumped to the WHA as a 17-year-old. As for Coffey, he spent a year and a half in the Soo, before being traded to the Kitchener Rangers. The Edmonton Oilers took 19-year-old Coffey in the first round, sixth overall, in the 1980 NHL Entry Draft. Coffey's agent, Gus Badali, clashed initially with Oilers GM Glen Sather: "I guess he figures because Paul is underage he doesn't deserve as much as draft-age players. Our talks haven't gone too well," Badali said in July 1980, just two weeks before Edmonton announced the signing of three players: Coffey, left winger Jari Kurri (drafted in the third round), and veteran Pat Price. It is Coffey's rookie contract with the Oilers that is reproduced here. Armed with developing stars like Gretzky and Mark Messier, Sather knew he had a number of gems on the roster, and he even went on to say that the Oilers had "the best nucleus in the NHL of young, promising hockey players." After three Stanley Cups and two Norris Trophies as an Oiler, Coffey was dealt to Pittsburgh in November 1987, and his career continued there, and for seven more NHL teams. In September 2012, Coffey reminisced about his Oiler days: "One of my highlights early on was just walking into the Oilers dressing room," he told the *Saskatoon Star-Phoenix*. "I remember feeling a lot of pride when I saw the Oilers jersey sitting there." Coffey was inducted into the Hockey Hall of Fame as an Honoured Member in 2004.

ADDENDUM

THE PARTIES DO HEREBY ADOPT THIS ADDENDUM AND INCORPORATE SAME AS A PART OF THE ATTACHED NATIONAL HOCKEY LEAGUE STANDARD PLAYER'S CONTRACT.

PRE PERFORMANCE BONUSES

In addition to the salary shown in the Standard Player's Contract, the CLUB further agrees to pay the PLAYER the following pre-performance bonuses:

1. The sum of Fifty Thousand Dollars ($50,000.00) on September 1, 1980.

2. The sum of Fifteen Thousand Dollars ($15,000.00) on September 1, 1981.

3. The sum of Ten Thousand Dollars ($10,000.00) on September 1, 1982.

THE PARTIES ACKNOWLEDGE THAT THEY HAVE READ THIS ADDENDUM AND THAT, BY ADDING THEIR SIGNATURES BELOW, DESIRE TO MAKE IT PART OF THE ATTACHED NHL STANDARD PLAYER'S CONTRACT EFFECTIVE THIS *12* DAY OF *September* 1980.

EDMONTON WORLD HOCKEY ENTERPRISES LTD.

WITNESS OF SIGNATURE

BY: GLEN SATHER - GENERAL MANAGER

WITNESS OF SIGNATURE

BY: PAUL COFFEY - PLAYER

NOV 6 11 45 '80
ACTION

Bob Shaver/Hockey Hall of Fame

Paul Coffey in action in October 1980, his rookie season in the NHL.

NATIONAL HOCKEY LEAGUE
STANDARD PLAYER'S CONTRACT
(1977 FORM)

BETWEEN : EDMONTON WORLD HOCKEY ENTERPRISES LTD.
hereinafter called the "Club"
a member of the National Hockey League, hereinafter called the "League"

AND   PAUL COFFEY   hereinafter called the "Player"

of   Mississauga   in { Province / State } of   Ont.

In consideration of the respective obligations herein and hereby assumed, the parties to this contract severally agree as follows:—

1. The Club hereby employs the Player as a skilled Hockey Player for the term of   Three   year(s) commencing October
1st, 19 80   and agrees, subject to the terms and conditions hereof, to pay the Player a salary of

.... Dollars ($ 60,000.00.....).

		Dollars ($ 70,000.00)
1980-81 1st Season NHL	Sixty Thousand	
1981-82 2nd Season NHL	Seventy Thousand	
1982-83 3rd Season NHL	to be arbitrated	OPT. YR.
1983-84 4th Season NHL	to be arbitrated	

Payment of such salary shall be in consecutive semi-monthly installments following the commencement of the regular League Championship Schedule of games or following the dates of reporting, whichever is later; provided, however, that if the Player is not in the employ of the Club for the whole period of the Club's games in the National Hockey League Championship Schedule, then he shall receive only part of the salary in the ratio of the number of days of actual employment to the number of days of the League Championship Schedule of Games.

And it is further mutually agreed that if the Contract and rights to the services of the Player are assigned, exchanged, loaned or otherwise transferred to a Club in another League, the Player shall only be paid at an annual salary rate of

1980-81 1st Season	Thirty-Five Thousand	Dollars in the	any Minor	League.
1981-82 2nd Season	Thirty-Five Thousand	Dollars in the	any Minor	League.
1982-83 3rd Season	To be arbitrated	Dollars in the	any Minor	League. OPT. YR.
1983-84 4th Season	To be arbitrated			

2. The Player agrees to give his services and to play hockey in all League Championship, All Star, International, Exhibition, Play-Off and Stanley Cup games to the best of his ability under the direction and control of the Club in accordance with the provisions hereof.

The Player further agrees,

(a) to report to the Club training camp at the time and place fixed by the Club, in good physical condition,

(b) to keep himself in good physical condition at all times during the season,

(c) to give his best services to the Club and to play hockey only for the Club unless his contract is released, assigned, exchanged or loaned by the Club,

(d) to co-operate with the Club and participate in any and all reasonable promotional activities of the Club which will in the opinion of the Club promote the welfare of the Club and to cooperate in the promotion of the League and professional hockey generally,

(e) to conduct himself on and off the rink according to the highest standards of honesty, morality, fair play and sportsmanship, and to refrain from conduct detrimental to the best interest of the Club, the League or professional hockey.

The Club agrees that in exhibition games played after the season the player shall receive his pro rata share of the gate receipts after deduction of legitimate expenses of such game. This provision re exhibition games is applicable in the National Hockey League only.

3. In order that the Player shall be fit in proper condition for the performance of his duties as required by this contract, the Player agrees to report for practice at such time and place as the Club may reasonably designate and participate in such exhibition games as may be arranged by the Club.

4. The Club may from time to time during the continuance of this contract establish reasonable rules governing the conduct and conditioning of the Player, and such reasonable rules shall form part of this contract as fully as if herein written. For violation of any such rules or for any conduct impairing the thorough and faithful discharge of the duties incumbent upon the Player, the Club may impose a reasonable fine upon the Player and deduct the amount thereof from any money due or to become due to the Player. The Club may also suspend the Player for violation of any such rules. When the Player is fined or suspended, he shall be given notice in writing stating the amount of the fine and/or the duration of the suspension and the reason therefor. Copies of the rules referred to herein shall be filed at the main offices of the League and the National Hockey League Players' Association.

5. (a) Should the Player be disabled or unable to perform his duties under this contract he shall submit himself for medical examination and treatment by a physician selected by the Club, and such examination and treatment, when made at the request of the Club, shall be at its expense unless made necessary by some act or conduct of the Player contrary to the terms and provisions of this contract or the rules established under Section 4.

(b) If the Player, in the judgment of the Club's physician, is disabled or is not in good physical condition at the commencement of the season or at any subsequent time during the season (unless such condition is the direct result of any injury sustained during the course of his employment as a hockey player with the Club, including travel with his team or on business requested by the Club) so as to render him unfit to play skilled hockey, then it is mutually agreed that for that period under this contract. If upon joint consultation between the Player, the Club's physician and the Club General Manager, they are unable to agree upon the Player's disability for such period of disability or unfitness, and no compensation shall be payable for that period under this contract. The Player's disability or physical condition, the Player agrees to submit himself for examination by an independent medical specialist and the Parties hereto agree to be bound by his decision.

(c) If the Player is injured during the course of his employment as a hockey player with the Club, including travel with his team or on business requested by the Club, the Club will pay the Player's reasonable hospitalization until discharged from the hospital, and his medical expenses and doctor's bills, provided that the hospital and doctor are approved by the Club. This approval will not be unreasonably withheld.

(d) It is also agreed that if the Player, in the sole judgment of the Club's physician, is disabled and unable to perform his duties as a hockey player by reason of an injury sustained during the course of his employment as a hockey player, including travel with his team or on business requested by the Club, he shall be entitled to receive his remaining salary due in accordance with the terms of this contract for the remaining stated term of this contract as long as the said disability and inability to perform continue but in no event beyond the expiration date of the fixed term of this contract, which fixed term shall in no event be deemed to include any option period related to a playing season after the playing season in which the injury occurred and the Player releases the Club from any and every additional obligation, claim or demand whatsoever. Any disagreement as to disability or inability to perform shall be determined conclusively by doctors of the Club and of the Player and, in the event said doctors are unable to agree, by an independent doctor selected by said doctors. If the Player is declared to be unfit for play, he shall continue to receive the full benefits of this Agreement. If the Player is declared to be physically able to play and refuses to do so, he shall be liable to immediate suspension without pay.

(e) In connection with a disability which is not caused by an injury sustained during the course of his employment as a hockey player, including travel with his team or on business requested by his Club, if upon joint consultation between the Player, the Club's physician and the Club General Manager, they are unable to agree upon the Player's physical fitness to return to play, the Player agrees to submit himself for examination by an independent medical specialist and shall be entitled to receive the full benefits of this Agreement until he has been declared to be fit for play by the independent medical specialist. If the Player is declared to be not physically able to play, he shall not perform his duties hereunder and shall be entitled to receive the full benefits of this Agreement until he has been declared to be physically fit to play by the independent medical specialist.

6. The Player represents and agrees that he has exceptional and unique knowledge, skill and ability as a hockey player, the loss of which cannot be estimated with certainty and cannot be fairly or adequately compensated by damages. The Player therefore agrees that the Club shall have the right, in addition to any other rights which the Club may possess, to enjoin him from playing hockey for any other team and/or for any breach of any of the other provisions of this contract.

7. The Player and the Club recognize and agree that the Player's participation in other sports may impair or destroy his ability and skill as a hockey player. Accordingly the Player agrees that he will not during the period of this Contract or during any period when he is obligated under this contract to enter into a further contract with the Club engage or participate in football, baseball, softball, hockey, lacrosse, boxing, wrestling or other athletic sport without the written consent of the Club, which consent will not be unreasonably withheld.

8. (a) The Player hereby irrevocably grants to the Club during the period of this Contract and during any period when he is obligated under this contract to enter into a further contract with the Club the exclusive right to permit or authorize any person, firm or corporation to take and make use of any still photograph, motion pictures or television of himself, and agrees that all rights in such pictures and television shall belong to the Club exclusively and may be used, reproduced, distributed or otherwise disseminated by the Club directly or indirectly in any manner it desires.

It is severally and mutually agreed that the only contracts recognized by the President of the League are the Standard Player's Contracts, Player's Termination Contracts, and Player's Option Contracts which have been duly executed and filed in the League's office and approved by him (or his designated representative), and that this Agreement contains the entire agreement between the Parties and there are no oral or written inducements, promises or agreements except as provided herein.

In Witness Whereof, the parties have signed this   12th
of   September   A.D. 19 80   day

WITNESSES:

Edmonton World Hockey Enterprises Ltd.
.... Club

Northlands Coliseum
Edmonton, Alberta
.... Address of Club

By ....
.... President

P. Coffey
.... Player

3341 Etude Drive, Mississauga, Ont.
.... Home Address of Player

I hereby certify that I have, at this date, received, examined and noted of record the within Contract, and that it is in regular form.

Dated   MAR 12 1981   19......

.... for the National Hockey League

Muni's Knee Woes Started Early

Craig Muni waits for a pass in
a game against the Islanders.

While Craig Muni would go on to play 819 NHL games over 17 seasons and win three
Stanley Cups with the mighty Edmonton Oilers, in May 1981, he was just a kid who
wanted to be in the lineup. He'd been selected by the Toronto Maple Leafs 25th overall
in the 1980 NHL Entry Draft, a hard-working defenceman from the OHL's Windsor
Spitfires. "You ask any 18-, 19-, 20-year-old kid that, and they always think they're ready.
I was no different," recalled Muni. After his junior season ended, he was assigned to the
AHL's New Brunswick Hawks, a team that Toronto split with Chicago. "I remember
when I got there, I wasn't allowed to play because of roster sizes and freezes. In order to
play, somebody had to get hurt—someone did, but I can't remember who it was." Muni
played two games in those playoffs, the Hawks going out in the Calder Cup semifinals.
At Leafs training camp the next fall, Muni blew out a knee. He spent six weeks in a leg
cast and was returned to junior after recovery. The knee remained an issue as he played
with seven different NHL teams. "I ended up playing my whole career with two knee
braces. I always played with that one knee brace, where I did hurt my knee. Later in my
career in Edmonton, I hurt my other knee and I had to have surgery, and I put a knee
brace on that one," he said. "It just becomes part of the equipment, and helps stabilize
it for any side blows or guys falling into your knee."

branada
BSM LTD.
sports management

William W. Watters
PRESIDENT

66 charles st. east, toronto, ontario m4y 1t1 • (416) 968-2974

May 25th, 1981.

Mr. Punch Imlach, General Manager,
Toronto Maple Leaf Hockey Club,
60 Carlton Street,
Toronto, Ontario.
M5B 1L1

Dear Punch :

Re : Craig Muni

According to Craig Muni's arrangement with Gerry
MacNamara, he was to receive $100.00 per game or half
a playoff share, whichever was greater.

According to the details I have from Craig, he received
$550.00 from Moncton. According to my information, a
full playoff share was approximately $1,700.00. There-
fore, Craig's half share would be $850.00.

Would you please draw a cheque for the difference in
Craig's name and forward it to my office.

Your anticipated co-operation is greatly appreciated.

Sincerely,

Bill

W.W. Watters,
President.

WWW:sms

The Wooing of Vladimír Růžička

Vladimír Růžička was on the Maple Leafs' radar for a long time. He was Toronto's fifth choice, 73rd overall, in the 1982 Entry Draft, the year they took four Czechoslovakians: Růžička, brothers Peter and Miroslav Ihnačák, and Eduard Uvíra. A 1986 scouting report from the World Championships says that Růžička is "a player worth waiting for." But by 1989, the Leafs had given up, trading his rights to the Edmonton Oilers. The Oilers brain trust, GM Glen Sather and top scout Barry Fraser, set out to woo the 26-year-old Růžička. The duo brought 200 Oilers caps to give away while in Czechoslovakia in late 1989. "We were building goodwill," Sather said at the time. It took some behind-the-scenes manoeuvrings, with Růžička's club team, Litvinov, saying no to him leaving after the country's hockey federation had said yes. On December 14, 1989, it was announced that Růžička had signed a four-year contract with the Oilers. In January, he arrived in Edmonton with his wife and two children, met at the airport by fans and media. "Hockey is quite popular in Czechoslovakia, but, obviously, not as popular as here," Růžička said. "I can't imagine such crowds meeting a player back home." Růžička's stay was short in Edmonton, though, and he was knocked for his defensive liabilities. When the Bruins traded for the 6-foot-3 centre in October 1990, they gave him a little more freedom and he became a fan-favourite goal scorer. But he never picked up the defensive side of the sport, and after a few games with the expansion Ottawa Senators, he returned home where he helped the Czech Republic win the 1998 Olympic gold medal.

Vladimír Růžička became a fan favourite in Boston.

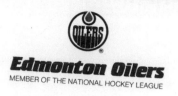

Edmonton Oilers

MEMBER OF THE NATIONAL HOCKEY LEAGUE

July 4, 1989

Mr. Gord Stellick
General Manager
Toronto Maple Leafs
Maple Leaf Gardens
60 Carlton Street
Toronto, ON
M5B 1L1

Dear Gord:

RE: Vladimir Ruzicka

Further to our recent telephone conversation, please advise us
via mail or FAX as to the compensation you are requesting should
we be successfull in acquiring this player.

Yours sincerely,

EDMONTON OILERS HOCKEY LEAGUE

Barry Fraser
Director of Player Personnel

BF:lw

cc: Glen Sather

FAX (403) 471-2171

ESS
European Sport Services Oy

May, 1986

WORLD CHAMPIONSHIPS, MOSCOW 1986
****

REPORT TO TORONTO

Vladimir Ruzicka was the best center in the Moscow-tournament,
even if his team was struggling in the tournament. Ruzicka
played very well together with Rosol and Hrdina and saved
the Czechoslovakian team from dissaster. Ruzickas line scored
5o% of Czechoslovakian goals. Ruzicka tried hard in all games,
very good attitude, excellent passer and play-maker. Fine shot.
Good team-player. Gets a lot of advice from club coach Ivan
Hlinka. Ruzicka is one of the player who should get an official
relise from Czechoslovakia when he turns 28.
A "profile" on and off ice, a player worth waiting for.

Peter Slanina was not even close to Ruzickas standard.Had a
poor start and played only 5 games. Dissapointment for the
team. Difficult to see him as a NHL-prospect in the future.

WORLD HOCKEY ASSOCIATION

Wren Blair Takes Proactive Approach to Fighting WHA

The initial World Hockey Association draft, held in Anaheim, California, in February 1972, was designed to stock the proposed 12 teams. Players on one-year NHL contracts and free agents were draftable, though by the final rounds, anything went; the WHA Dayton team—which never played a game and moved to Houston—took Phil Esposito and Bobby Orr, for example. To protect talent, some NHL teams elected to ink players to longer-term contracts. Wren Blair was proactive. "Minnesota general manager Wren Blair executed a coup of sorts during the end of last season when he signed virtually all his athletes to lengthy and wealthy contracts, thus averting defections to the World Hockey Association," reported the *Chicago Tribune*. The last player to sign was team captain Ted Harris, who had been wooed by the Winnipeg Jets. Leafs GM Jim Gregory was a great pal of Blair's—they ran a hockey camp together for a while—and said that "The Bird" Blair was on the ball, ready to outwit the executives of other teams. "Wren really believed [the WHA] was going to go [ahead]. He had no qualms to talk to anybody to say, 'Don't take this as a ho-hum, it's not going to happen' kind of thing." Remarkably, Blair did a lot of his work from his hospital bed and while recuperating at home, as evidenced by the letter reproduced here urging his players not to defect to the WHA—sent to most (if not all) of the North Stars. Blair had part of his right lung removed, necessitated by a bout of pneumonia as a youth. Jack Gordon, coach of the North Stars, sympathized with the woes of the hard-hit NHL clubs. "I can understand the problems of teams like Boston and New York," Gordon told the *Boston Globe*. "They were involved in the Stanley Cup Finals and signing players was difficult at that stage. We had a little more time."

Wren Blair was in hockey management for decades.

December 15, 1971

Mr. Murray Oliver
10901 Abbott Avenue South
Bloomington, Minnesota 55431

Dear Murray:

First, I would like to indicate to you that I am dictating this letter to Marilyn from my hospital bed to let you know that my progress following surgery has been excellent. I expect to be released from hospital tomorrow. All of my doctors have expressed positive results with respect to the surgery on my right lung and, accordingly, my health should be greatly improved in the not-too-distant future.

I would also like to take this opportunity to thank you and your family, and indeed all members of the team, for your beautiful flowers, your nice card, and your many thoughts on my behalf, particularly during the day and time of the surgery. All members of my family also wish to express thanks to you. When I return home, I will have a convalescent period, probably until shortly after New Year's when I will return to the office to resume my normal duties as General Manager of the club.

In the meantime, there is one very important subject I would like to discuss with you privately and that has to do with the rumors, newspaper conversations, etc. surrounding the proposed new World Hockey Association. Naturally, many reporters will treat this kind of advent as a field day and will try to draw many of us into conversations which in the final analysis can only be harmful to us. As General Manager of the organization, I would like to convey to you the thought that as a productive player we certainly have plans for you in our organization. I like to feel that I personally brought each player to the North Stars and, as such, I have more than a special interest in your career. I, therefore, want to let you know that I will be meeting with you individually and personally immediately upon my return to my duties after New Year's. I realize that the possibility of another league has to be advantageous to a player from an economic point of view. I also realize that you only have one career and it is more than natural for you to want to derive

-2-   December 15, 1971

Mr. Murray Oliver

as much from that career as possible. In recognizing these items, I want to see that you derive as much from your talents as possible and I am firmly of the opinion that over the long haul these can be most derived from the National Hockey League in general and from the Minnesota North Stars in particular. After all, loose talk is cheap and there is much being said about the WHA that is not factual.

In any event, I want to assure you that you have a good future with our organization and it is my plan to discuss it with you in detail early in January. In the meantime, I think that the interests of you as an individual and all of us as an organization can best be served by refraining from comments in the press, and by indicating to the public at large that your loyalties at this time are with the North Stars and with the people who are supporting us so strongly at the box office.

May I also at this time congratulate each of you on the tremendous showing the club has made to date in the 1971-72 season. It augurs well for an attractive bonus for you at the halfway point and a very exhilerating feeling to be fighting for top spot in the National League race. May I also extend my very best wishes to you and your family for a joyous Christmas and a happy new year.

Kindest personal regards.

                                   Yours very truly,

                                   Wren A. Blair
                                   General Manager

WAB:mv

Leafs Watch Many Leave for WHA

The Maple Leafs, under the stubborn ownership of Harold Ballard, refused to renegotiate contracts before the end of the season, a long-standing policy, and suffered greatly when a chunk of the team jumped to the World Hockey Association for the 1972–73 season. Jim Gregory, the Leafs GM, admits that it was chaotic at the time. "We had lots of different kind of advice" on what to do about the WHA. "I had mixed feelings, because some of the people around us weren't sure if [the WHA] had enough money to go, but I think in the end, I thought they were going to go because there were too many players signing," said Gregory. From the 1971–72 squad, Toronto's obvious losses to the WHA were Bernie Parent, Jim Dorey, Jim Harrison, Brad Selwood, and Guy Trottier, but there were others too. Marcel Pronovost was the coach of the Toronto farm club in Tulsa and had just taken the team to the CHL finals; he had hoped to get a promotion, but instead he went to the WHA's Chicago Cougars. "Well, you can't hold a guy up when he gets a chance like this. There was no way we could match their offer, because Marcel already was one of the top-salaried guys in [the CHL]," said Ballard. "It's not hard to spend money and put yourself out of business, y'know. [The WHA] throws around thousands like you and I might throw hundreds." Philadelphia lawyer, Howard Casper, who was operating as Parent's agent, called the defections early: "Make no mistake about it," Casper told reporter Dick Beddoes in March 1972. "Because Toronto refuses to renegotiate contracts, Toronto will be the one NHL club hardest hit by the WHA."

Marcel Pronovost coached the WHA's Chicago Cougars for a single season, 1972-73. Notes on opposite page are handwritten by King Clancy.

July 5/72.

Talked to Marcel Pro.
he is going to a press
Conference in Chicago. I told
him he wasn't jeopardizing his
Chonaswick Trust accepting
a job in Chicago. Best of
Luck. he is going to get
15,000 00 a year.

[signature]

625-3617   Marcel Pronovost. July 5/72

Didn't ask Pro. because I
was closer to scene, and he didn't
know how long McPherson would be
away.

Always speaks to manager. ✓

Security for Family.

More involved in lovely Teens
both Toronto and Tulsa.

Chicago 2 year contract at $5000 00
per year.

Full obligated.   Stand in way

---

13 July, 1972.

Mr. Marcel Pronovost,
1400 Winding Trail,
#47,
MISSISSAUGA, Ontario.

Dear Marcel,

          I was extremely disappointed to hear that you had
left our Organization for work in the other League.   I felt that Maple
Leaf Gardens treated you extremely well and I did everything in my power
to make you feel that you were part of our Organization.

          I cannot wish you good luck because I hope you and
your league fall flat on your ass, but this certainly would not prevent
me from remaining on a friendly basis with you.

          Mr. Clancy told me of some of the things which
caused you concern and for them I am sorry and regret that they were not
worked out to your satisfaction, but in doing one's job you sometimes
offend people unknowingly.

          There are some matters which remain to be cleaned
up here at Maple Leaf Gardens and I would ask that you give them your
earliest consideration.

          Yours very truly,

JMG/sb   J.M. GREGORY,
                                          General Manager

Cheevers Bolts Bruins for Cleveland Crusaders

Gerry Cheevers's decision to jump to the World Hockey Association came a month after Bobby Hull had signed with the Winnipeg Jets, but it was almost as important. While Hull was a star scorer, Cheevers was *the* star goalie in the NHL at the time, having just backstopped the Boston Bruins to a second Stanley Cup in three years. At a July 1972 press conference to announce his reported six-year, $1-million contract with the Cleveland Crusaders, Cheevers addressed departing the team he loved. "I weighed a lot of things in the past three weeks," he said. "Don't forget I'm leaving the greatest team in hockey, but the security of my family comes first." Nick Mileti, owner of the Crusaders, called the deal "as fine a contract as any goalie ever received and probably one of the finest in sports." Cheevers made $45,000 in the 1971–72 season in Boston, and he was actually chosen by the New England Whalers in the WHA draft of 1972 before his rights were dealt to Cleveland for cash at the beginning of June. A fascinating clause exists on page two of addendum B of Cheevers's contract with the Crusaders, addressing the Canada-U.S.S.R. Summit Series. Cheevers's handlers anticipated the backlash that "Cheesy"—and Hull—would face, with the power brokers behind the games, NHL president Clarence Campbell and NHLPA president Alan Eagleson, insisting that anyone who had signed with the WHA be prohibited from suiting up for the games against Russia. It didn't end well for Cheevers in Cleveland though, with the goalie walking out on the team in January 1976 and, subsequently, being suspended by the team; he secured his release from the team and returned to the Bruins days later. Cheevers was inducted into the Hockey Hall of Fame as an Honoured Member in 1984.

Gerry Cheevers of the Cleveland Crusaders plays the puck behind the net, out of the reach of teammate Paul Shmyr and Wayne Carleton of the Toronto Toros.

IMPORTANT N

Before signing this agreement, you should c
agreed upon have been incorporated herein, and
it inserted in the contract before you sign.

World Hock

Uniform P

By this cor

CLEVELAND CR
(h

GERRY CH

(hereafter "Player"), to perform in or on behalf of

This Contract is based on the following facts:

1. The Club is a member and holds a franch
championship games sponsored by the League.

2. Player has the skill, or potential skill, and t

1. Compensation.

1.1 The Club agrees to pay the Player for t
of such salary shall be in twelve (12) equal s
playing season.

14.1 in the event of reduction of operations, the Player's salary shall be renegotiated;

14.2 in the event of suspension of operations, the Player shall be entitled only to the proportion of salary due at the date of suspension;

14.3 in the event of cessation of operations the Player's salary shall be automatically cancelled on the date of cessation.

15. Approval by League President.
This contract, if not inconsistent with the League's Certificate of Incorporation and by-laws shall be valid and binding upon the Club and the Player immediately upon its execution. The Club agrees to file this contract with the League President within ten (10) days after its execution.

Steve Arnold hereby approves contract
on behalf of League.

16. Player Negotiations.
16.1 If the Player and the Club fail to sign a new contract for the season following the termination of this contract before June 1, the arbitration procedure outlined in this Paragraph 16 shall automatically go into effect.

16.2 *Arbitration Procedure.*
16.2.1 On or before July 4 following the last playing season of this contract, in the event the Player and the Club fail to enter into a new contract, the Player and the Club shall each appoint one person to hear and determine the dispute preventing the signing of such new contract. If these persons are able to reach agreement on or before July 15 of the year of the dispute, no further proceedings are necessary. If they are unable to reach agreement on or before that date, then they shall immediately select a third impartial arbitrator whose decision shall be reached on or before July 31 of the year of the dispute.

16.2.2 Player and Club agree to arbitrate in good faith.

16.2.3 If the Player and Club agree that the decision of the impartial arbitrator is fair, a new contract will be executed embodying the terms of his decision.

16.2.4 If either the Player or the Club disagree with the decision of the impartial arbitrator, they may refuse to enter into a contract and the Player automatically enters into a special "secondary draft" pool on August 1 of the year of the dispute.

16.3 *Secondary Draft.*
16.3.1 Once a Player enters the secondary draft pool, he may not sign a contract with any other club until he is drafted.

16.3.2 The League will hold, in accordance with its normal draft procedure, a "secondary draft" on or about August 15 of each year. Teams will draft in the same order as in the normal yearly draft.

16.3.3 The Club with which the Player was under contract immediately prior to the secondary draft may not draft the Player in this manner.

16.4 *Subsequent Secondary Drafts.*
In the event the Player and the club that drafted him in the secondary draft are unable to reach an agreement by September 1, the Player will enter a pool for a new secondary draft, the date of which will be determined by the League President.

16.5 *Costs of Arbitration.*
The costs of the arbitration, including costs expended by the President and his staff if his services are required, will be borne equally by the Club and the Player, and the Player hereby authorizes his employing club to deduct his share of the expenses from the first payment due the Player under the next contract he signs.

17. Miscellaneous and Procedural Provisions.
17.1 Any notice required or permitted to be given under this agreement shall be sufficient if in writing, sent by certified mail, return receipt requested, to the Player's residence or to the Club's office.

17.2 This agreement contains the entire understanding between the parties and it cannot be terminated or changed orally.

17.3 This agreement shall be governed and construed according to the laws of the State of _____ Ohio _____
(Province of _____).

17.4 If any part, paragraph or provision of this agreement should be held or become invalid, then all remaining parts, paragraphs and provisions shall continue to be fully effective.

THE PARTIES ACKNOWLEDGE THAT THEY HAVE EACH READ THIS AGREEMENT AND THAT, BY ADDING THEIR SIGNATURES BELOW, DESIRE TO MAKE IT EFFECTIVE THIS 23rd DAY OF July, 1972.

_____
Witness to Signature

CLEVELAND CRUSADERS LTD.
(CLUB)

BY: _____

BY: _____
Nick J. Mileti, Personally

Lawrence D Godon
Witness to Signature

_____
(PLAYER)

_____
(PLAYER'S ADDRESS)

Gretchen Mileti, Personally

Witness to Signature

Norm Ullman Loves His Weetabix

Forty years later, Norm Ullman doesn't exactly remember how he became a spokesman for Weetabix breakfast cereal, but he's happy it happened. Not only did it help his finances a bit in the 1970s, but he and his wife became lifelong pals with Harold Connell, who ran the business. "They were a good company. We became really close friends," recalled the centre. Aside from appearing on ads for the whole-grain, palm-sized cereal, Ullman also sat on the board of directors. A veteran by the time he arrived in Toronto in March 1968, Ullman was a solid 20-plus goals-a-year man. He did three ads for Weetabix. He recalled the one reproduced here: "The family was involved. We did it at the house, even though you can't see too many people, they're all around the table." He also filmed an ad with Maple Leafs teammate Darryl Sittler, and another with Denis Dupere. When Ullman bolted for the WHA's Edmonton Oilers for the 1975–76 season, though, it created a problem for Weetabix. The company had already compensated the Leafs for use of the team logo and needed to work out a new deal now that their spokesman was in the competing league. They ended up amending the advertisement slightly. Ullman said that he was compensated with some product as well. "I used to eat it occasionally. I didn't eat it a lot," he admitted. And now? "I look on the shelves every once in a while, and they still do have it." Ullman was inducted into the Hockey Hall of Fame as an Honoured Member in 1982.

WEETABIX
The whole wheat cereal biscuit.
NORM ULLMAN "ON THE ROAD"
(LENGTH 30 SECONDS)

NORMAN ULLMAN: (VO) I'm Norm Ullman of the Maple Leafs. What do I have for breakfast when I'm on the road?

Same thing as when I'm home with my family . . .

I start the day off right with Weetabix.

Weetabix is whole wheat . . .

Full of wholesome food energy.

You can actually taste its goodness.

Start your day . . .

with whole wheat nourishment.

Join the Weetabix eaters!

WEETABIX LIMITED
WILLOWDALE, ONTARIO

PRINTED IN U.S.A. 10/12/73

Graphic Artists/Hockey Hall of Fame

Norm Ullman's defection to the Edmonton Oilers of the WHA caused an issue with his ad, which was filmed when he was with the Toronto Maple Leafs of the NHL.

D'Arcy-MacManus & Masius
Advertising

Harold you Comments please?

Regrets

September 19, 1975

Mr. James Gregory
Manager
Maple Leafs Sports Productions, Ltd.
111 Richmond Street, West
Toronto, Ontario
Canada

Dear Mr. Gregory:

We are the advertising agency for Weetabix of Canada, Ltd. and are responsible for the advertising for Weetabix Whole Wheat Cereal.

We have an agreement with Norman Ullman, which was effective February 15, 1974, for the use of his services in advertising Weetabix Whole Wheat Cereal. Further this agreement with Ullman includes arrangements which he made with the Maple Leafs, for his use of the Maple Leaf uniform and insignia. Our payment to you for this permission was $2,500.

As you undoubtedly are aware, Ullman recently arranged to join the Edmonton Oilers with a proviso in his agreement that if either party is not satisfied they can terminate it. Norm has said that he expects to reach a decision by the end of this calendar year. This works out well for both of us since under the terms of our agreement with him the current cycle expires February 14, 1976.

At the present time, we are using a 30 second TV Commercial entitled, "On the Road" a copy of which is enclosed marked "Original." You will note there is a reference to the Maple Leafs by Norm Ullman in Frame # 1. Further, Ullman appears in Frames #7 and #8 in a Maple Leaf Uniform.

We would like to continue to use this commercial between now and the end of the year, when Norm Ullman expects to reach a decision as to whether he will stay with the Edmonton Oilers, with the following change.

D'Arcy-MacManus & Masius, Inc., 437 Madison Avenue, New '
Bloomfield Hills (Detroit), Chicago, Cleveland, Los Angeles,
Adelaide, Amsterdam, Auckland, Brisbane, Brussels, Copenh
Mexico City, Milan, Oslo, Paris, Pretoria, Stockholm, Sydney,

---

Mr. James Gregory   -2-   September 19, 1975

We would re-record the sound track to eliminate the reference in Frame 1 to the Maple Leafs. Since we can not change the video in Frames 7 and 8, we would like to continue to use this film footage. The change is shown on the second storyboard which is enclosed and is marked "Revision."

We would like to have your permission to continue to use through February 14, 1976 the video portion of the commercial with the word changes as indicated on the storyboard marked "Revision."

Norm Ullman, Harold Connell of Weetabix of Canada and we at D'Arcy-MacManus & Masius would very much appreciate receiving your permission since it would help solve a problem for all of us.

Accordingly, will you please indicate your agreement by signing the enclosed duplicate copy of this letter and returning it to us.

Very truly yours,

A.J. Roby
Vice President

AJR:sjr

Enc.

cc: H.F. Connell - Weetabix of Canada, Ltd.
     N.V.A. Ullman

         *   *   *
We hereby grant to D'Arcy-MacManus & Masius, Inc. the right to use the Weetabix commercial "On the Road" marked "Revision" as described in the foregoing letter, through February 14, 1976.
     MAPLE LEAF GARDENS, LIMITED
     ~~MAPLE LEAF SPORTS PRODUCTIONS, LTD.~~

     By_____
            Title

Date

Wayne Gretzky of the Edmonton Oilers lines up against Mark Messier of the Cincinnati Stingers in WHA action.

The Early Days of Mark Messier

Given their success together, the careers of Wayne Gretzky and Mark Messier will be forever linked. But there's a tie-in well before their days together on the power-house Edmonton Oilers of the 1980s. On November 3, 1978, the *Edmonton Journal* announced Gretzky's arrival in town, fleeing the Indianapolis Racers of the WHA. In the same edition, there's a piece about a 17-year-old from the St. Albert Saints of Alberta's junior league who had signed with the same Racers and was about to debut. That was Mark Messier, who was noted as the son of Doug, a tough defenceman who had survived years of battles in the Western Hockey League. The Racers, already strapped of cash and forced to sell Gretzky to the Oilers, folded just five games into Messier's pro career. He then inked a deal with the Cincinnati Stingers. The Stingers contract reproduced here is signed by Mark and William DeWitt, Jr., the executive vice-president of the Stingers, and witnessed by Messier's mother, Mary Jean Messier, who was tasked with moving Mark, his brother, Paul, and sisters Jenny and Mary Kay, from Portland, Oregon, where they had settled after Doug's career and where Mark had skated briefly with the junior Winter Hawks, to Edmonton. "We did everything together, and when we were living in the basement and I was sharing a bedroom with Paul, that was great," Mark Messier told *The New York Times* in 1992. "It just brought us closer." Messier scored only a single goal in 47 games in that one season in the WHA before the league folded and he ended up property of the Oilers as a third-round pick—48th overall—in the 1979 NHL Entry Draft. "It's a good thing they don't judge you on one season," joked Messier years later. Messier was inducted into the Hockey Hall of Fame as an Honoured Member in 2007.

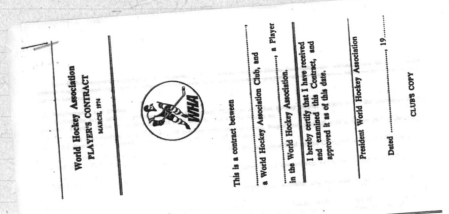

World Hockey Association

Player's Contract

By this contract,

CINCINNATI STINGERS COMPANY
(hereafter "Club") employs

MARK MESSIER

(hereafter "Player"), to perform in or on behalf of the Club's participation in the World Hockey Association (hereafter the "League").

This Contract is based on the following facts:

1. The Club is a member and holds a franchise in the League, and will participate in exhibitions, regularly scheduled and championship games sponsored by the League.

2. Player has the skill, or potential skill, and training to enable him to compete with other players in the League.

Agreement

1. Compensation.

1.1 The Club agrees to pay the Player for rendering the services described herein the following salary:

1978-79 Hockey Season - for services in the regular scheduled season, a salary of Twenty-Six Thousand Dollars ($26,000) payable as follows: Seven Thousand Dollars ($7,000) on or before December 31, 1978; and Nineteen Thousand Dollars ($19,000) in consecutive semi monthly installments of Two Thousand Three Hundred and Seventy Five Dollars ($2,375) commencing January 15, 1979 and terminating May 15, 1979.

1.2 If the Player is not on the Club's roster for the whole period of the Club's WHA League games, then he shall receive only part of the salary in the ratio of the number of games during which he is on the Club roster to the number of games in the League schedule. If the Player is assigned, exchanged or otherwise transferred to a club in a lower classification league, the Player shall only be paid at the rate of $ .... for that period in which he is on the roster of the lower classification league. However, if the Player is on the roster of the Club for at least twenty-five (25) regular WHA League and/or play-off games, he shall receive his full WHA salary as provided in Paragraph 1.1.

---

from a state of war or other similar cause beyond the control of the League or of the .... League or the Club to suspend or cease or reduce operations, then:

.... erations, the Player's salary shall be renegotiated;

.... erations, the Player shall be entitled only to the proportion of salary due at the date of

.... erations the Player's salary shall be automatically cancelled on the date of cessation.

.... the League's Certificate of Incorporation and by-laws shall be valid and binding upon .... execution. The Club agrees to file this contract with the League President within ten

.... ration or by-laws, the President disapproved this contract within ten (10) days after .... on, terminate and be of no further force or effect and the Club and the Player shall .... and liabilities hereunder.

.... g a new contract for the season following the termination of this contract before .... is Paragraph 16 shall automatically go into effect.

.... the last playing season of this contract, in the event the Player and the Club fail to .... Club shall each appoint one person to hear and determine the dispute preventing .... ersons are able to reach agreement on or before July 1st of the year of the dispute, ... are unable to reach agreement on or before that date, then they shall immediately .... on shall be reached on or before July 31 of the year of the dispute.

.... ate in good faith.

.... t the decision of the impartial mediator is fair, a new contract will be executed

.... agree with the decision of the impartial mediator, they may refuse to enter into .... o a special "secondary draft" pool on August 1 of the year of the dispute.

.... draft pool, he may not sign a contract with any other club until he is drafted. .... e with its normal draft procedure, a "secondary draft" on or about August 15 .... r as in the normal yearly draft.

.... was under contract immediately prior to the secondary draft may not draft

.... im in the secondary draft are unable to reach an agreement by September 1, ... the date of which will be determined by the League President.

.... d by the President and his staff if his services are required, will be borne .... hereby authorizes his employing club to deduct his share of the expenses .... contract he signs.

.... under this agreement shall be sufficient if in writing, sent by certified mail, ... the Club's office.

.... g between the parties and it cannot be terminated or changed orally.

.... according to the laws of the State of Ohio

.... agreement should be held or become invalid, then all remaining parts, ... ive.

.... THEY HAVE EACH READ THIS AGREEMENT AND THAT, BY ADDING .... BELOW, DESIRE TO MAKE IT EFFECTIVE THIS 24th DAY OF January, 19 79.

_____
Witness to Signature

_____
Witness to Signature

_____
Witness to Signature

Cincinnati Stingers Company
(CLUB)

BY: _____ Exec VP

BY: _____

_____
(PLAYER)

#1 Sunbird Place Mallard, Alta
(PLAYER'S ADDRESS)

Cincinnati Stingers

RIVERFRONT COLISEUM • CINCINNATI, OHIO 45202 • (513) 241-1818

February 20, 1979

Mr. Ron Ryan
WHA League Office
17th Floor
One Financial Plaza
Hartford, Connecticut 06103

Dear Ron:

Enclosed please find 3 copies of executed contracts
for Mark Messier.

Please approve these on behalf of the league and
return two copies to me.

Thanks and regards.

Sincerely yours,

William O. DeWitt, Jr.
Executive Vice President

WOD,JR/mr
Enclosure

2.26.79
Filed w/o approval pending
clarification on approval of
contracts for under-aged Jr.
by legal counsel.

Member: World Hoc

---

vices. All offers under this paragraph must be in writing, and
any club making said offer must prove that it has the ability
to meet all obligations of said offer.

14. If Club shall not exercise its option on or before
August 15, 1979, it is further agreed that Club shall in no way
prevent or attempt to prevent Player from returning to play junior
hockey.

IN WITNESS WHEREOF, the parties hereto have set their
hands this 24th day of January, 1979.

ATTEST: CINCINNATI STINGERS COMPANY

Martha L. Ryan   By: William O. DeWitt Exec.V.P.

Mary Jean Messier
                               MARK MESSIER

Acknowledgements

For so many years now, I've written about athletes, talking to them about their lives, their careers, and their injuries. Then on Father's Day weekend 2014, I went and wrecked my right knee playing soccer. (I was the goalie and *did* stop the shot, if you are wondering.) For this book, I felt far more like an athlete than ever before, able to sympathize with the likes of Craig Muni and his knee woes. Besides thanking my wonderful wife, Meredith, and son, Quinn, for their help as I limped around the house, I must say thanks to the staff at Toronto's St. Joseph's Hospital, and my arthroscopic surgeon, Dr. Carlos Lopez, for the top-notch care. Did it delay the book? Probably. For that, I need to thank the patience and support of the ECW Press crew, especially my editor/friend, Michael Holmes.

Fortunately, so much can be done with a computer now, whether I'm stuck on a couch with my leg immobilized and laptop running, or at a desk. I'm especially enamoured with the wealth of databases available with a click of a mouse. There were many tangents I went down upon finding something interesting; one day, those might be full-grown stories too.

My friends in the Society for International Hockey Research continue to be a great resource for everything from advice to entertainment, but most importantly contacts, suggestions, and statistics. Some of the great documents that Allan has unearthed allowed me to actually add to the SIHR database, primarily with the details of players who never made the NHL but may have had tryouts along the way. It's oddly fulfilling to be a contributor to a huge historical database, knowing that it's aiding hockey researchers for centuries to come.

The rest of the thank yous go to the folks at ADR Chambers and the Stitt Feld Handy Group, who tolerated my presence as I poured through documents and hogged the photocopier, with and without crutches, and the players and management I got to talk to, many of whom were set up through Ron Ellis—thanks Ron!

Finally, thanks to Allan Stitt himself, for his passion for this game and desire to share his treasures with the world.

Selected Bibliography

Béliveau, Jean with Chrys Goyens and Allan Turowetz. *My Life in Hockey*. Vancouver: Greystone Books, 2005.

Boucher, Frank with Trent Frayne. *When the Rangers Were Young*. New York: Dodd, Mead & Company, 1973.

Boyd, William T. *All Roads Lead to Hockey: Reports from Northern Canada to the Mexican Border*. Lincoln, Nebraska: Bison Books, 2006.

Brown, William. *Doug: The Doug Harvey Story*. Montreal: Vehicule Press, 2002.

Carpiniello, Rick. *Messier: Steel on Ice*. Toronto: Stoddart, 1999.

Imlach, Punch with Scott Young. *Hockey Is a Battle: Punch Imlach's Own Story*. Toronto: Macmillan Company of Canada, 1969.

Irvin, Dick. *The Habs: An Oral History of the Montreal Canadiens, 1940–1980*. Toronto: McClelland & Stewart, 1991.

Klein, Jeff Z. *Messier*. Toronto: Doubleday Canada, 2005.

Sandor, Steven. *The Battle of Alberta: A Century of Hockey's Greatest Rivalry*. Victoria, BC: Heritage House, 2005.

Strachan, Al assisted by Wayne Gretzky. *99: Gretzky: His Game, His Story*. Toronto: Fenn-M&S, 2013.

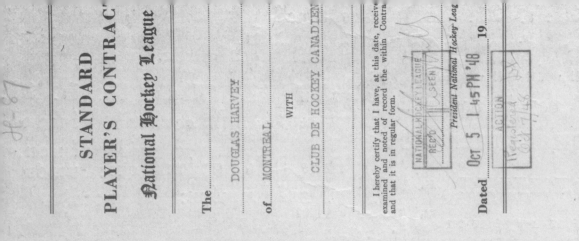

STANDARD PLAYER'S CONTRACT
National Hockey League

The DOUGLAS HARVEY of MONTREAL with CLUB DE HOCKEY CANADIEN

I hereby certify that I have, at this date, received the within Contract, examined and noted of record the within form, and that it is in regular form.

Dated Oct 5 1-45 PM '48 19

President National Hockey League

NATIONAL HOCKEY LEAGUE REC'D SEEN ACTION

IMPORTANT NOTICE TO PLAYER

Before signing this contract you should carefully examine it to be sure that all terms and conditions agreed upon have been incorporated herein, and if any has been omitted, you should insist upon having it inserted in the contract before you sign.

NATIONAL HOCKEY LEAGUE

STANDARD PLAYER'S CONTRACT

This Agreement

BETWEEN:　　　CLUB DE HOCKEY CANADIEN

hereinafter called the "Club",
a member of the National Hockey League, hereinafter called the "League".

— AND —　　　DOUGLAS HARVEY

hereinafter called the "Player".

of　Montreal　in (Province/State) of　Quebec

Witnesseth:

That in consideration of the respective obligations herein and hereby assumed, the parties to this contract severally agree as follows:—

1. The Club hereby employs the Player as a skilled Hockey Player and agrees to pay the Player for the season of 1948/49 ("season" meaning the period commencing the date on which the Player reports to the Club at its training camp or other place designated by the Club, and ending on the completion of the Club's games in the National Hockey League Championship Schedule, Play-off and Stanley Cup Series) a salary of

Seven thousand ....Dollars ($7,000.).

If Goalkeeper William Durnan wins the Vezina Trophy Douglas Harvey will receive a bonus of $500.

If Douglas Harvey is named on either "All Star" team he shall receive a bonus of $500.

Payment of such salary shall be in semi-monthly instalments following the commencement of the regular League Championship Schedule of Games or following the date of reporting, whichever is later. Provided, however, that if the player is not in the employ of the Club for this entire period, then he shall receive such proportion of the salary as the number of days of actual employment bears to the total number of days in the said period.

And it is further mutually agreed that if the contract and the rights to the services of the player are assigned, exchanged, loaned or otherwise transferred to a club in another league, the player shall only be paid at the rate of

................................Dollars for the season in the................................League;

or................................Dollars for the season in the................................League.

2. The Player agrees to give his services and to play hockey in all League Championship, Exhibition, Play-Off and Stanley Cup games to the best of his ability under the direction and control of the Club for the said season in accordance with the provisions hereof.

The Player further agrees:

(a) to report to the Club training camp at the time and place fixed by the Club, in good physical condition,

(b) to keep himself in good physical condition at all times during the season,

(c) to give his best services and loyalty to the Club and to play hockey only for the Club unless his contract is released, assigned, exchanged or loaned by the Club,

(d) to co-operate with the Club and participate in any and all promotional activities of the Club and the League which will in the opinion of the Club promote the welfare of the Club or professional hockey generally,

(e) to conduct himself on and off the rink according to the highest standards of honesty, morality, fair play and sportsmanship, and to refrain from conduct detrimental to the best interests of the Club, the League or professional hockey generally.

3. In order that the Player shall be fit and in proper condition for the performance of his duties as required by this contract the Player agrees to report for practice at such time and place as the Club may designate and participate in such exhibition games as may be arranged by the Club within thirty days prior to the first scheduled Championship game. The Club shall pay the travelling expenses and meals en route from the Player's home to the Club's training camp. In the event of failure of the player to so report and participate in exhibition games a fine not exceeding Five Hundred Dollars may be imposed by the Club and be deducted from the compensation stipulated herein.

4. The Club may from time to time during the continuance of this contract establish rules governing the conduct and condition-ing of the Player, and such rules shall form part of this contract as fully as if herein written. For violation of any of such rules or for any conduct impairing the thorough and faithful discharge of the duties incumbent upon the Player, the Club may impose a reasonable fine upon the Player and deduct the amount thereof from any money due or to become due to the Player. The Club may also suspend the Player for violation of any such rules. When the Player is fined or suspended he shall be given notice in writing stating the amount of the fine and/or the duration of the suspension and the reason therefor.

Dear Mr. Bou[...]

When I [...] contract last y[...] an agreement. [...] was that if I [...] Rangers and h[...] a substantial [...] could be expe[...] think that the [...] new contract is [...]

My idea o[...] is eight thous[...] That would be [...] amou[...] rec[...] incl[...] I re[...]

Su[...]

ADDE[...]

THE PARTIES DO HEREBY ADOPT THIS ADD[...]
THE ATTACHED NATIONAL HOCKEY LEAGUE [...]

PRE PERFORMANCE BONUSES

In addition to the salary shown in [...]
CLUB further agrees to pay the PLAYE[...]

1. The sum of Fifty Thousand Dollar[...]

2. The sum of Fifteen Thousand Doll[...]

3. The sum of Ten Thousand Dollars [...]

THE PARTIES ACKNOWLEDGE THAT THEY HA[...]
THEIR SIGNATURES BELOW, DESIRE TO MA[...]
PLAYER'S CONTRACT EFFECTIVE THIS [...]

WITNESS OF SIGNATURE